Bernard Lonergan's Third Way of the Heart and Mind

Bridging Some Buddhist-Christian-Muslim-Secularist Misunderstandings with a Global Secularity Ethics

John Raymaker

Hamilton Books

An Imprint of
Rowman & Littlefield
Lanham • Boulder • New York • Toronto • Plymouth, UK

Copyright © 2016 by Hamilton Books
4501 Forbes Boulevard, Suite 200, Lanham, Maryland 20706
Hamilton Books Acquisitions Department (301) 459-3366

Unit A, Whitacre Mews, 26-34 Stannary Street,
London SE11 4AB, United Kingdom

All rights reserved
Printed in the United States of America
British Library Cataloguing in Publication Information Available

Library of Congress Control Number: 2016947610
ISBN: 978-0-7618-6832-3 (cloth : alk. paper)
ISBN: 978-0-7618-6848-4 (pbk : alk. paper)
ISBN: 978-0-7618-6833-0 (electronic)

∞™ The paper used in this publication meets the minimum requirements of American National Standard for Information Sciences Permanence of Paper for Printed Library Materials, ANSI/NISO Z39.48-1992.

Contents

Introduction: In Which We Lay Out This Book's Principles and
    Mode of Procedure   v

**I: Introducing the Heart-Mind Interdisciplinary Issues
    Explored in This Book**   1

**II: Sketching a GEM-FS Bridge's MEDIATING PHASE as
    Outlined in *MiT*'s First Four Specialties : Probing into
    Buddhist-Christian-Muslim Teachings so as to Best Broach
    a Global Secularity Ethics**   37

1 First Functional Specialty: Researching Data on Christianity,
    Islam and an Ethical Secularity   39

2 Second Functional Specialty: Interpreting Religious Scriptures,
    Democracy, and Secularism so as to Avoid Misunderstandings
    or Resentment   43

3 Third Functional Specialty: GEM-FS Judgments of Value and
    Historical Perspectives   57

4 Fourth Functional Specialty: Dialectics Pointing to Where We
    Need to Go: GEM-FS' Apophatic-Kataphatic Ability Can Help
    Integrate Secularity with the World's Religions   63

**III: Sketching a GEM-FS Bridge's Mediated Phase as Outlined
    in *MiT*'s Last Four Specialties: Toward Enabling Needed
    Transformative Changes among the Religions and Secularity**   75

5 Fifth Functional Specialty: Foundations and Its Underlying
    Premises   77

6	Sixth Functional Specialty: Policies Based on a Logic of the Heart's Value Judgments	93
7	Seventh Functional Specialty: Adjusting, Transforming Systems	109
8	Eighth Functional Specialty: Communicating so as to Overcome Intolerance	113

Conclusion	117
Short Glossary of Islamic Terms in Relation to This Book's GEM-FS Process	119
Notes	121
Index	171

Introduction

*In Which We Lay Out This Book's Principles
and Mode of Procedure*

THE IMPORTANCE OF THE APOPHATIC
IN BRIDGING RELIGIOUS-SECULAR DIVIDES

The problem with Christianity said Chesterton is that it has never really been tried: even more so with Bernard Lonergan's breakthrough method that could help solve many vital issues facing humanity. This ambitious, wide-ranging book's proposals can only be viable from a long-term perspective.

We begin by noting that much of human communication is "phatic", non-verbal. Phatic communication seeks to establish relationships more than to convey ideas.[1] For example, "hello, how are you?" is phatic. The phatic function keeps open lines of communication among persons. Through it, two or more speakers reassure themselves that not only are they being heard but that they are also understood. One of the characteristics of autism (and its societal or cultural versions) leads to one's being isolated due to a deficit in phatic communication. This book uses Lonergan's method to probe the phatic in our lives and to explore what in spirituality and theology is called the difference between a*pophatic* (negating) and kata*phatic* theologies.[2] There are, for example, wordless apophatic forms of prayer as well as kataphatic ones which do use words. Both the apophatic and kataphatic should impact on our daily lives. Prayerful "union" with God can help one reach into one's deeper self as well as promote communication with others. This book explores Lonergan's method as a *Third Way* of the heart and mind. Each person should ideally have his/her own way of reflecting on self and of communicating with others. What makes Lonergan's method unique is that he explored both the apophatic and kataphatic aspects of our lives thereby enabling us to integrate the needs of our hearts with the realities of what our minds are about. Unless persons integrate heart and mind in their lives, they shall fail to communicate on religious, ethical, philosophic or societal issues. This book sketches ways we humans might communicate, e. g. in tackling urgent problems[3] in Europe, that is the failure of "multiculturalism" and the need to integrate Muslim immigrants. Our attempt to culturally integrate persons' minds and hearts touches on the issue of inculturating a religion's message and its comportment within a nation's political and social realities.

Lonergan refers to his transcendental method as a "third way" which differs from the methods of the natural and human sciences: it goes behind their procedures "to something both more general and more fundamental."[4] It studies our minds' basic pattern of operations employed in any cognitional enterprise. His method is relevant in formulating other, more special methods appropriate to other fields. This book uses this method to radically explore the *heart*[5] in ways that can help one experience the apophatic-ineffable, prayerful dimensions of life. When speaking of Lonergan's "generalized empirical method"[6] (GEM), we are referring to a person's "normative pattern of recurrent and related operations yielding cumulative and progressive results." In *Method in Theology* (*MiT*), Lonergan elaborates how GEM, a *Generalized* Empirical Method can be Functionally *Specialized*, yielding what we name "GEM-FS." As with the scientific method, GEM proceeds from data, hypotheses, verification. It is not a mere "set of rules" but is a "prior, normative pattern of operations from which the rules may be derived." (p. 6). Focusing on this pattern and its logical and meta-logical aspects helps us go beyond both Aristotle's interest in "the necessary and immutable" and Hegel's dialectic--"a movement enclosed within a complete system." (Ibid). Lonergan's Third Way of the mind and heart helps us explore the reach of our logical and non-logical operations which are foundational to any type of endeavor. Through an operation, a conscious subject becomes aware of an object involving both psychological and intentional dimensions. Still, the quality of the awareness can change. (8). *MiT* can help us link our heartfelt operations with the mind.

If secularists, too, cannot but appeal to the heart, how might a "mystical apophatic" help reinforce phatic and kataphatic communication? We answer by stressing *both* heart *and* mind. This might be illustrated by noting childhood experiences of John Raymaker, this book's principal author.[7] John grew up (1936-1947) in a French-speaking suburb of Brussels within two miles from where the March 2016 ISIS-led attacks occurred. As a child during World War II, he experienced apophatic-ineffable realities; he realized that there are *ineffable* aspects of life that cannot be communicated with mere words. Through second-hand information about St. Thomas Aquinas and upon hearing a sermon on Damien the Leper, John was early sensitized to a logic of the heart—a topic he eventually wrote about in his *A Buddhist-Christian Logic of the Heart*. Secularity, the state of being devoted to the affairs of the world, and a logic of the heart, dedicated to "apophatic mystery", both play vital roles in this text's attempt to build caring kataphatic, interdisciplinary, religious bridges informed by a viable global ethics. A recurrent theme in our text is that many mystics have sought to verbalize ineffable experiences. Our bridge of mind and heart realizes that major problems occur when, for example, fundamentalist Christians or Erdogan's brand of Islam prevent access to the ineffable links between political realities and merciful hearts--an access also denied by radical secularists. We seek ways to help restore better access to the ineffable.[8]

I

Introducing the Heart-Mind Interdisciplinary Issues Explored in This Book

LONERGAN'S GEM-FS, A *"GENERALIZED* EMPIRICAL METHOD—FUNCTIONALLY *SPECIALIZED,"*[1] IS UNIQUE

The kataphatic (cataphatic) deals with what can be positively asserted about ultimate reality or God. In the history of Christian theology, beginning with the neo-Platonists, "God" became increasingly abstract and less personal. An apophatic theology which asserts *"what God is not"* arose early in the Church's history. Commentators on the apophatic have assumed that God's perfection is beyond human language or understanding. In this book, "apophatic" includes such mystical approaches as a *via negativa* (the negative way), Nicholas of Cusa's *doctrina ignorantia* (acquired ignorance),[2] *and* a link between God's mercy (misecordia) with the promptings of generous hearts in our demanding societies. Misecordia meaning "pain of the heart," implies that, like God, we, too, should show mercy--be compassionate.[3]

In Islam, a similar distinction between the kataphatic and the apophatic emerged. Allah can be known as he has manifested[4] Himself. Kataphatic theology describes God positively according to what Allah has revealed of Himself to humanity in Scripture and nature. The kataphatic can be defined in terms of *tashbih* ("similarity") - i.e. God is 'closer to you than your jugular vein' (Quran 50:16). It inclines towards Beauty and Mercy rather than Majesty and Justice, towards diversity rather than singularity. Apophatic theology could be defined in terms of Arabic *tanzi*h ('incomparability')—'utterly remote is God, in His limitless glory, from anything to which men may ascribe a share in His divinity!'" (Quran 59:23). In Jewish and Christian Scriptures also, many passages indicate a very profound meaning for "mercy". For example, *hesed* refers to a mutual dependable love between God and humans, or among humans in general; *hen/hanan* points to an aesthetic sense of "grace"; Luke uses *eleos* in the sense of *hesed*. If one wants to link the apophatic-kataphatic notions of mercy, the Hebrew *rahamin*, referring to "womb love", implies a very deeply *felt* apophatic compassion resulting in action: womb-love "leads to forgiveness."[5]

This book distinguishes between faith and beliefs; faith is rooted in the apophatic side of religion; beliefs touch on the kataphatic. Since secularists tend to ignore this distinction,[6] our text speaks to the human heart as a way to bridge what separates spiritually-oriented persons--grounded in a faith apophatic--from secular-oriented persons' beliefs. Having recourse to Buddhist-Christian-Islamic traditions, we argue that Lonergan's method can help bridge current divides. We interpret his method as "*GEM-FS*," a *generalized-empirical-method-functionally-specialized*, due to the vast bridging potential it opens up.

We seek to help bridge differences between moderate religious views and secularist reservations as to religion. We merely *sketch* what GEM-FS[7] might contribute to address our world's complex problems. "Christianity", "Islam" and "secularism" are labels for complex historical movements now interacting with one another. This can lead to confusion, even conflicts, if proper recourse to ethics and to a sense of the apophatic is not had. Lonergan's expertise in both the kataphatic and apophatic can help here. We invoke his expertise in arguing that 1) secularity can help correct secularism; 2) Christian and Muslim fundamentalisms need hearts steeped in faith so as to erect ethical-secularity bridges between opposed religious-secular mentalities. A *global secularity ethics* avoids both a false dichotomy between a *secular humanism* (seeking to ground ethics independently from religion)[8] and a self-referent religious ethics. GEM-FS helps ground an ethical secularity that is *spiritual* before it is *religious* (based on beliefs). Secular humanism is embraced by nonbelievers but feared by religious conservatives. An ethical secularity embodies the intellectual, moral tradition going back to Socrates' challenge to religious authority. The apophatic--open to such benevolent attitudes as generosity and mercy—implicitly reinforces secular humanism[9] for it helps ground effective transformations that go beyond mere theories or doctrines.

1. PRELIMINARY ISSUES IN FOSTERING BUDDHIST-CHRISTIAN-MUSLIM-SECULARIST COOPERATION: HUMANITY'S RELIGIOUS-SECULAR DIVIDES AND THE PIVOTAL ROLES THAT AN ETHICAL SECULARITY CAN PLAY

Many communities in the West today fail to adequately alert young persons of their intellectual and moral potential. Such failures call for reevaluations of both religious and secular education. Secularists and believers are alienated from one another to the extent that secularists are cut off from religious traditions' deep insights. We provisionally define secularism as an "ism" little concerned with religion. Secularization has led to the declining influence of religious values both in the Western world and in socialist-communist spheres of influence such as in China. Secular humanism and socialism-communism imply a belief in human self-sufficiency. The result has led to many confrontations throughout the globe.

In Europe, for example, jobless young Muslims often feel marginalized in the frantic world of money and power. Resenting their being ostracized, some resort to violence. Sectarian fundamentalists who oppose ("atheist") secularism feel "justified" to try to silence their opponents in many parts of the world. To engage in a dialogue about secularity and religion is to swim in very muddied waters. Over time, there have accrued layers of different meanings for both religion and secularism. This book seeks to address these issues by focusing on a global secularity ethics that "uplifts" secularism. An ethical, globally-open secularity does imply a retreat of religion from public life: belief in God becomes just *one option* among others,[10] but it avoids the negative implications of an anti-religious secularism. Religion includes the basic faith, beliefs, values and practices of human communities throughout history. We shall try to relate these various elements to one another. Not all cultural beliefs, values and practices are religious, but many of them do affect everyday life peculiar to a civilization. "Everyday life" is important for those oriented either toward religion or secular values. The basic religious or secular orientations operate at many levels including such values as the ethical,[11] emotional and artistic. Most people are only implicitly aware of the foundational role of religion and spirituality in their lives. To help foster cooperative dialogue among Christians, Muslims, and secular mentalities, this book seeks strategic answers to such questions as

1. In an increasingly secularized world committed to modern culture[12] (a process violently opposed by e. g. ISIS) how can the world's religious leaders cooperate so as to jointly address pressing global problems?
2. How can viable bridges be established to facilitate exchanges between Christian-Muslim-secular(ity) claims in the face of rising indifference to religion among many citizens in secular Western societies?

3. How can scholars, philosophers and theologians best address the complex, underlying issues?[13]

Bridging Three Vastly Different Notions of "Radical" through "Transvaluations"[14] of Values

As we try to bridge the divides separating Christians, Muslims and secularists, we study the issues that led, for example, to the terrorist attack on Charlie-Hebdo in Paris in January, 2015. As with the violent protests provoked by the Muhammad caricatures,[15] many Muslims have felt provoked by insensitive caricaturists--some of whom boast of their atheism. The "Islamic State", ISIS, now accused of genocide, further complicates possibilities of bridging Buddhist-Christian-secularist-Islamic differences today. The vast chasms between Western views on freedom of expression and Muslims' distinctive respect for the Prophet of Islam is not easy to bridge. It is not only in Europe but also in such places as Nigeria in western Africa (Boko Haram) and Iraq-Syria (ISIS) that Muslim terrorists have been running amuck. Al Qaeda's involvement in the destruction of the Word Trade Center Towers in 2001 and Taliban atrocities in Afghanistan are other instances of once unthinkable acts.[16] The rise of radical terrorist groups has led to uncertainties and fear in much of the world. In this book, we speak of three types of radicalization in recent world history. The three types are to be correlated with the three questions just raised:

1. A secularist radicalization which led to the French and Bolshevist revolutions (still in evidence in various types godless nations such as in North Korea);
2. Islamic radicalization driven to oppose secularist types of godless radicalization as well as other faiths;
3. Both of these types of radicalization are addressed in this book with Lonergan's GEM-FS radicalization which fosters local-global community consciousness. Lonergan's moderately radical, transformative method "transvalues values"; it can help remedy blind radicalisms that have driven some to extremes.

Our answers to the above three questions are thus framed in terms of radical renewal. "Radical" points to the roots. There are both good and bad forms of radicalization. Thomas Merton and Pope Francis have embodied laudable forms of radical change--being converted to the good.[17] The Second Vatican Council radically updated the Catholic Church's rootedness in the Good News. Terrorists embody frightening radicalizations. As if in a cult-like trance, ISIS terrorists seem fascinated by wantom killing.[18] Our "radical" efforts to bridge Christian-Muslim-secularist stances invoke the roles of mercy in the world religions. Mercy is more than mere benevolence; it could radically help remedy many ills. "Blessed are the merciful for they shall obtain mercy" characterized St. Francis' ministry. It now guides that of Pope Francis. GEM-FS is qualified to help people renew our complex modern world. For Lonergan, "conversion" leads to generous responses in living self-giving values, in a new openness to faith, in fresh outlooks upon mankind and upon the universe."[19] This view prompts us to apply GEM-FS transvaluations-of-values perspectives in the light of today's complexities. We shall study how GEM-FS can help remedy cultural impasses by accessing and developing an ethical secularity in touch with merciful hearts and minds.

A Universally Verifiable GEM-FS Approach that Can Help Remedy Many Various Impasses

This book is based on a conviction that Lonergan has articulated a universally verifiable GEM-FS to critically ground human understanding and an ethical integrity. GEM-FS can help humans discover and live a spirituality able to resolve the uneasy tensions that have emerged among religious believers, and to jointly find ways of working with convinced secularists. An encompassing GEM-FS can be helpful in addressing said tensions (which stem from religions' sometimes contradictory demands and claims),[20] as well as in diagnosing life as it is actually lived in capitalist and socialist countries. Everything in the developed world has been more or less influenced by postmodern secularism. Some have "bought into" this secularism; the danger is that of getting blinded by an unexamined secularism and succumbing to it. Fundamentalists, who want no part of atheist secularism, often feel "justified" in opposing it violently as happened with the Hebdo killings in Paris. They feel that a frantic world where money rules has cut off its rootedness in the deeper realities which basic religious insights have revealed throughout the ages.

This Book's Double-Pronged, "GEM-FS" Theoretical-Practical, Global-Secularity-Ethical Strategy

Religious fundamentalists[21] are at a loss to understand postmodernist claims and may have ambivalent attitudes toward capitalism's flagrant injustices. In view of this, this book develops a double-pronged, "radical," theoretical-practical, religious-secular, apophatic-kataphatic ethical strategy. It aims to

1. present GEM-FS's operational range" (its *feasible* applicability to all fields) in some depth with a view to
2. deploy its practical applications with apt, conciliatory, but firm notions of religion and "secularity".

Our double-pronged strategy seeks to develop GEM-FS as a *generalized-empirical-method* template *"functionally specialized."*[22] For Lonergan, the functional specialties (FS) reflect the structure of our minds. Contrasting and integrating GEM-FS's generalized and functionalized capabilities as a "GEM-FS template" can help us build bridges between persons who hold moderate religious or secularist views; it can be compared to object-oriented programming—but with radical differences. A computer-generated template in software engineering has a sort of operational "self-transcendence": the template functions as a behavioral design pattern. One defines the program skeleton of an algorithm in what is called "a template method" while deferring some steps to subclasses.[23] The template lets one redefine certain steps of an algorithm without changing the algorithm's structure.[24] Two radical differences between computer-generated templates and what we call a "GEM-FS template" are

1. rather than standardizing the skeleton of an algorithm in a base class template method, in *Insight*, Lonergan studies how one can eventually reach intellectual and moral self-transcendence. *Method in Theology* (*MiT*) applies GEM as to the realm of religious conversion in functionally specialized (FS) ways.
2. In contra-distinction to computer operational algorithms, GEM-FS self-transcendence operates on ethical-moral-spiritual-theological-interfaith levels where self-transcendence is in "tension" with immanence. In object programming's algorithms, there ensue applications of abstract notions to programming; a GEM-FS template's generalized and specialized capabilities permit us to course between theory and the complexities of addressing Buddhist, Christian, Muslim, secularity encounters.[25]

The Role of "Understand-Judge-Act Subtemplates" to Complement Our Main GEM-FS Strategy

This book's double-pronged strategy explores and applies the radical implications of self-transcendence. It also develops practical "understand-judge-act subtemplates" to *apply* GEM-FS to societal problems in ways pioneered by e. g. liberation theologies. These subtemplates are indirect *applications* of GEM-FS developed in *Insight* and *MiT*. People in general, do not have the time nor expertise to address all relevant nuances. Our see-judge-act-subtemplates embody an implicit bridging method used by people of good will and common sense over the ages.[26] They hinge on simple, *implicit* "GEM-ways" of applying a sound method to various religious or secular problems.[27] After introducing, in Part One, Lonergan's "sophisticated" *generalized* empirical method (GEM) developed in his *Insight*, Parts II and III will apply GEM to various situations and problems using the eight-step functionally *specialized* (FS) method he outlined in *MiT*. Throughout the text we shall speak of GEM-FS as Lonergan's "Third-Way method," one which is somewhat "secular" in nature but open to faith and religion. To be "viable" in the real world, a GEM-FS template and its see-judge-act subtemplates must be applicable to the many injustices in a world in which rich persons and nations tend to get richer while the poor barely survive. This means that a GEM-FS template--a thoroughly philosophical method-- must also be able to help remedy injustices while attempting to bridge seeming religious incompatibilities; we shall use the see-judge-act method as a "practical" type of GEM-FS subtemplates to do so. Seeing-judging-acting-reacting to injustices are a way to collaboratively promote peace. People can, on the other hand, see, judge and act-react wrongly.

Lonergan was concerned more about method than content. Our GEM-FS template focuses more on how method may be related to global institutions and processes than on exploring the many claims of the world religions. We intend to apply a GEM-FS template and see-judge-act subtemplates to concrete problems facing humanity—problems which have not yet been tackled with large-enough a brush so as to be effective in bringing dialogue and needed "compromises" to establish a just peace in the world.

Lonergan, the Radical Visionary: The Role and Import of the Data of Consciousness in GEM-FS[28]

This book's GEM-FS bridging attempt develops Lonergan's theory-praxis vision as outlined in his *Method in Theology*. It appeals to Buddhists, Christians, Muslims, secularists, to all people of good will able to recognize so as to deal with the various human biases.[29] It is also in this sense that a GEM-FS template functions as a generalized theory-praxis method applied to bridge differences (inasmuch as they can be bridged) between the world religionists and secularists.[30] This book thus tries to show how Lonergan's lifework can have important applications in our lives. Using GEM-FS, it first studies various processes operative in nature and in the human mind. Through an ethical strategy, it then seeks to construct a bridge of understanding between different human worlds divided by their beliefs, values and practices. We turn to examine one of Lonergan's radical breakthroughs—his teaching on the data of consciousness.

In reaction to Kant's vestigial empiricism, the philosophers Bergson and William James introduced the "data of consciousness" as a way to complement the data of sense scientists use in their theories. Since Lonergan's metaphysics builds on judgments that lead to self-affirmation (judgments based both on the data of sense and of consciousness), GEM-FS metaphysics[31] is not subject to Derridean deconstruction aimed at self-identity as understood in Western metaphysics. "Insight," the modern term for "conversion to phantasm," initiates us into the deeper meanings of "conversion." It is not a matter of deconstructing words but of reaching beyond words with both heart and mind. How can GEM-FS help us transform badly distorted realities in conciliatory ways? This broad question needs to be answered piecemeal. Our double-pronged strategy focuses on GEM as "being generalized" in two radical, "transvaluing" manners:

1. It attends to both the data of sense and the data of consciousness.
2. The latter involve not only a genetically related series of "sublations"[32] from data through understanding and judgment to decision and action, but also the need for an ongoing series of dialectically operative methods grounded in decisions and actions aimed at promoting the human good and overcoming alienation.[33] It is what we name a GEM-FS transformative praxis of heart and mind.

Lonergan's radical *generalization of data* (integrating the data sense with those of consciousness) is arguably a theory-praxis revolution. One might say that all of Lonergan's work in method is "praxis" in so far as it is concerned with the question of *what we do* when we know. Lonergan himself acknowledges a more transformative sense of praxis in which decision and action precede and ground a knowledge of value. This, too, presupposes his original blending of the *transformative* nature of the data of sense and of the data of consciousness.[34] Taking our cue from this notion of a transformative praxis, this book deploys two transformative phases (mediating and mediated)[35] as outlined in Lonergan's *MiT*. With Jim Kanaris, we stress GEM-FS's decentering-recentering aspects which lie at the core of human realities.[36] Kanaris notes "the presence we have of ourselves is a constitutive presence because, not despite, the fact that it is a decentering presence. Our presence to ourselves as subjects is a constitutive presence of human subjectivity . . . in the sense "that it brings us closer to ourselves as engaged in a process which can provide us with access to the intelligible universe." (Ibid, 28). Kanaris rebuts claims of Continental thinkers that our presence to ourselves is merely that of a deconstructive metaphysics of presence.

The recent terrorist events in Paris, Syria (ISIL), Nigeria (Boko Haram) and other places testify to our human divides. How can one possibly bridge such extremes? A starter is for people of good will (and deep scholarship) to find answers by becoming aware of their deeper self. Admirers of Zen Buddhism such as Thomas Merton have been able to build bridges between Christianity and secularism. Merton's bridging ability led to his social activism as based on deep prayer. He taught many to look deep within themselves. Meditation and spiritual reading helped him find keys to his East-West bridging efforts. Wise Christians know that one can be both a Zen

Buddhist and a good follower of Jesus. One can help counter violence by "witnessing" with Muslims as did Charles de Foucauld--although he was killed while living among the Tuareg in the Sahara in Algeria. He lived life radically in exemplary Christian-praxis fashion. It is easy to blame religions for their past mistakes or for present terrorism. Foucauld and Merton's mystic insights let them pioneer interfaith encounters; they did not provide a full rationale for doing so. GEM-FS helps us understand the past so as to adapt to present and future needs. A problem is that education today, such as occurs in Muslim madrasahs, fosters a parroting of learning instead of educating the heart, mind, and soul. GEM-FS, as a holistic transformative praxis, helps us educate both our hearts and minds.

A "GEM-FS Secularity-Template" Correlates the Scientifically Objective with Authentic Subjectivity

A GEM-FS template is very much open to spirituality and to cooperation among the world religions. It proceeds from the principle that GEM is a secular method explaining how subjects arrive at objectivity. It moves from being a secular method to one that shows how the apophatic and the kataphatic can be related through an ethical secularity. Agreeing with Charles Taylor's search for a needed secularity in our postmodern world, we embrace both religion and secularity. Secular*ity* implies a retreat of religion from public spaces.[37] Even if many people view secular*ism* as linked with a sharp decrease of religious belief and practice in much of the world, with Taylor we admit that many people *have ceased to think* that religious theism should now be the unchallenged norm. Theism is now "*one option among others--* "not the easiest to embrace".[38] One has to concede that belief in God is no longer axiomatic; there are alternatives. Still, the alternatives cannot ignore ethics nor "the good." Our "GEM-FS-secularity bridge" seeks to retrieve the mystical roots of Christianity and Islam so as to help correlate the structure of the human good on the object side with that of the dynamic structure of human knowing on the subject side. Meeting secularity halfway, it correlates humans' religious, ethical and scientific roles. Husserl's "bracketing" method concentrated on essence but ignored contingence in an effort to reach an objective evidence. Positivists and behaviorists underestimate or reject subjectivity.[39] Lonergan detects and refutes "the ambiguities underlying naïve realism, naïve idealism, empiricism, critical idealism, and absolute idealism. (*MiT*, 265). He develops GEM-FS so that it can account for the common features underlying mathematics, science, philosophy, ethics, secularity and theology, revealing an objectivity that "is the fruit of attentiveness, intelligence, reasonableness, and responsibility." (Ibid).

To counter social constructivist views of how humans interact, Lonergan develops three levels of the human good: the particular good, the good of order, and value. Cooperative actions follow "some settled pattern, and this pattern is fixed by a role to be fulfilled or a task to be performed" within institutional frameworks such as the family, society, the state, the law and religious groupings. "They constitute the commonly understood and already accepted basis and mode of cooperation. They tend to change only slowly for change, as distinct from breakdown, involves a new common understanding and a new common consent." (*MiT*, 48). For social constructionists, on the other hand, "what appears to be natural or obvious to people may not represent reality, so it remains largely an invention or artifice of a given society."[40] GEM-FS is a systematic method for building bridges of understanding between different human worlds--this is what motivates this book. Like Merton, Bede Griffiths and other spiritual East-West bridge-builders, Lonergan taught us to reflect deeply so as to unravel the mysteries of our own deeper self. By so doing so, one can find transpartisan keys to building bridges between humans. Such bridges' transpartisan viewpoints transcend cultural differences and divisive religious beliefs. One seeks to ascertain how Buddhism, Christianity, Islam, contemporary science and modern types of skeptical secularisms may arrive at some forms of consensus. Such bridges potentially *lie within* each person, but they must be actualized.[41] One of this book's aims is precisely to find keys to reach persons' deeper self.

Besides the role of the good in GEM-FS, the way we mediate meaning is important. Lonergan argues that meaning is mediated through the patterned structures of our cognitional operations. Operations are "immediate when their objects are present" as in the case of seeing, hearing, etc. "But by imagination, language, symbols, we operate in a compound manner, immediately with respect to the image, word, symbol; mediately with respect to what is represented or signified . . . We come to operate not only with respect to the present and actual but also with respect to the absent, the past, the future . . . " (*MiT*, 28). Meaning grasped through the conscious subject's operations, introduces one to a world mediated by meaning and motivated by value. The world mediated by meaning is the world revealed through the memories of others, through the common sense of various communities through literature, through the works of artists, scholars and scientists, through the experience of holy people of every culture, and through the reflections of original thinkers. (Ibid). Human consciousness interacts with reality—not as an enclosed, self-contained entity--but as an entity-in-relation. Higher cultures develop reflexive techniques to control and safeguard meaning such as in an alphabet, dictionaries, grammars, logic, hermeneutics, philosophies. Consciousness can be theoretically or scientifically differentiated; it can be differentiated aesthetically corresponding to different worlds mediated by meaning and various differentiations of consciousness. In each case but in differing ways, meaning mediates a different world of experience.[42]

This book examines different approaches to transcendence and immanence in the three world religions, in science, and atheism by adverting to the subjective side of acts of meaning and how such acts are also "objective." A person's individual life experience implicitly integrates earlier stages of his or her own life. Each person can transcend earlier stages of life and readjust to meet present needs. Such are some of the presuppositions informing our bridge. Lest we get ahead of ourselves, we need to try to understand the past so as to build a better, more peaceful future. A world bridge of the type we are attempting is not to be restricted to friendly GEM-FS authors' views on foundations that might *actualize* the bridge. More than being a "bridge of understanding," it speaks to persons' hearts encouraging them to engage in ethical, spiritual, cooperative "interventions" in the many socio-political problems facing humanity. Such interventions rooted in an authenticity / الصحة (*as-sehah*) common to Buddhism, Christianity, Islam and ethical secular thought are aimed to help heal societies.[43] One must appraise past and present Buddhist, Christian, Muslim and secular events, while addressing readers unfamiliar with Lonergan.

Assessing the Radical Differences between Computer Programming and a GEM-FS Template

To return to the radical differences between computer programming and a GEM-FS template, let us correlate said differences with the double-pronged bridging strategy informing this book. Lonergan's GEM-FS Third Way of the mind and heart is based on human freedom. We correlate human freedom and its operational range with humans' recurrent, related operations. This correlation involves our use of a principle of an ethical secularity in tune with modernity but also rooted in the various traditions we are studying.[44] Secularists tend to underplay the vast differences between human operations and computer-generated algorithms due to unacknowledged secularist presuppositions. GEM-FS's Third Way, on the other hand, explores the radical differences between algorithms and a *genuine secularity*--differences that partly stem from the principle of the operational range of human freedom. This book's GEM-FS template studies, applies GEM-FS's normative operations with the hope of clearing a way for ethically applying secularity in practical ways. For us, secularity means to live in ways differentiated from religious living; it does not necessarily imply being atheist or anti-religious. As transcultural,[45] GEM-FS stresses the historical fact that people have asked religious questions; most cultures have left marks of people being conscious of a strong, apophatic Unknown. In answer to non-Westerners' complaints about western modes of thinking, we turn to briefly explore our version of a practical GEM-FS "see-judge-act" method--an important part of Lonergan's Third Way.[46] We do so recalling Alvin Toffler's words in his *Future Shock*: "Technocrats suffer myopia . . . (They) think about immediate returns, immediate consequences. They are premature members of the now generation."[47] GEM-FS helps bridge hearts and minds not with myopic hopes but through deep-minded pursuits of mercy and truth rooted in spiritual awareness.

Applying a GEM-FS Bridge's See-Judge-Act Subtemplates to Humanity's Search for Peace

Our double-pronged, theoretical-practical, apophatic-kataphatic strategy seeks to apply GEM-FS in feedback fashion to the many threats facing humanity. "Functional specialization distinguishes and separates successive stages in the process from data to results."[48] Rather than dividing tasks among members of a collaborating group", the FS involves a series of eight-fold tasks shared in complementary fashion among members of a collaborative group. The tasks may be assigned to various persons; the overall aim and final product of any functionally specialized "project" are thus shared. Lonergan recognized the need to separate tasks in the eight FS while interrelating them. GEM-FS and see-judge-act practical subtemplates together give us double-pronged ways to deploy the generalized and specialized aspects of our minds and hearts. *MiT*'s first mediating phase is complemented in the mediated phase by morally engaged persons using various technologies. The mediated phase's last four FS take into account how GEM's conversions can "make a difference" in lessening the evil impacts of the "isms" haunting the world. This book *partly* deploys the FS's mediated phase in practical see-judge-act subtemplates (in FS 6).

For Lonergan, there is a "need for division" in engaging in any scholarly discipline. What is new is his conception of the branches of theology as functional specialties (FS) "as distinct and separate stages in a single process from data to ultimate results." In speaking of the two phases for deploying the eight FS, Lonergan notes that there is a "radical difference between the two phases" in each of which, there are four ends corresponding to the four levels of conscious intentional operations. If these eight ends exist, then there are eight different tasks to be performed and eight different sets of methodological precepts that have to be distinguished. . . . Each of the eight has its proper excellence. None can stand without the other seven. . . . If all of the eight are needed for the complete process from data to results, still a serious contribution to one of the eight is as much as can be demanded of a single piece of work." (*MiT*, 137). While this is true, our radical GEM-FS bridge interlinks the heart of contemporary, variously dependent religious-secular processes. It notices the inbuilt links between our cognitional *opera*tions upon which GEM-FS pivots. Etymologically, co-*opera*tion implies people using their *opera*tions so as to co*opera*te. In referring to the FS, Lonergan means intellectual col*labor*ation. For us co*opera*tion and col*labor*ation both mean "working together." In this book, "to apply GEM-FS in feedback fashion" means to work together to fashion bridges of mercy based on the inbuilt self-corrective process of our cognitional operations.

Searching for Quasi-Global GEM-FS Bridges of Mercy to "Radically Reconcile" Religions and Secularity

Our double-pronged strategical GEM-FS template seeks to integrate Lonergan's generalized-specialized GEM-FS by deploying both the theoretical and practical aspects of his method. GEM-FS can be used to enhance understanding between religious and secular persons. GEM-FS stems from Lonergan's extensive study of the conditions required for human understanding and for ethical action. Mere understanding cannot solve the problems dividing humans. Committed, coordinated actions are needed.[49] We deploy GEM-FS, situating the world religions within today's realities of an ever-growing secularization (notably in the Western world) *also* using see-judge-act subtemplates that addresses some of the issues dividing mankind today; the subtemplates are a greatly simplified, practical version of GEM-FS.[50] That is, we aim to develop a GEM-FS bridge of mercy" which seeks to reconcile religions and secularity using both GEM-FS and a simplified see-judge-act version of it. We seek to identify authentic notions of secularization that can help mediate between Christian and Islamic mercy so as to avoid unnecessary conflicts. We touch on Buddhism somewhat indirectly. Buddhism can help underpin a radical bridge of mercy, since mercy is one of its core values. Our GEM-FS template strives for a quasi-global GEM-FS bridge of mercy" reconciling religions and secularity. Such a bridge depends on the cooperation of millions of ordinary persons and of leaders apt at using a see-judge-act method to solve problems. GEM-FS helps us reconcile the complementarities[51] between subjectivity and objectivity, between the apophatic and kataphatic on a global scale. While most human communication is "phatic", involving verbal and non-verbal ways that establish relationships rather than convey ideas, this book also stresses the virtue of mercy. We speak of the need for both verbal and non-verbal (apophatic) bridges of mercy to forgive if not undo past hurts.

For the first time in American history, religious belonging is now on the decline. The trend began after 9/11 when people started suspecting that religion can be a source of divisive intolerance.[52] This book seeks insights into divided, seemingly incompatible mentalities: those of different cultures, ideologies, cults. It seeks to build a bridges with a "visionary" GEM-FS that respects human differences. It offers a method based in part on mercy for those wishing to overcome divisive ideological misunderstandings. Instead of harping on an atmosphere of moral panic (afflicting some naïve forms of religion), it explores a GEM-FS bridge of mercy. Such a bridge may escape atheists' ken due to their inability to account for the sources of mercy. On this topic, one may invoke the insightful reflections of St. Thomas Aquinas.[53]

In his *Summa Theologica, Secunda Secundae*, Question 30 "On Mercy", Aquinas asks "Whether evil is properly the motive of mercy?" He responds: "Mercy is a kind of sorrow. Evil is the motive of sorrow. Therefore, it is the motive of mercy. ... Mercy is heartfelt sympathy for another's distress, impelling us to succor him if we can." Mercy (*misericordia*) denotes a man's compassionate heart for another's unhappiness... Unhappiness is opposed to happiness: it is essential to beatitude or happiness that one should obtain what one wishes; for, according to Augustine (*De Trin.* xiii, 5), 'happy is he who has whatever he desires, and desires nothing amiss . . . It belongs to unhappiness that a man should suffer what he wishes not.'"[54] Aquinas adds that "Since sorrow or grief is about one's own ills, one grieves or sorrows for another's distress, in so far as one looks upon another's distress as one's own."

If indeed, a double-pronged bridge between the world religions and secularism is possible, such a bridge may help remove some of the mistrust between believers and unbelievers. There is a growing awareness of the need for global cooperation not only to thrive but even to survive. This is due to such factors as an ever-growing human population, the globalizing of commerce, a greater access to technology, etc. Perennial human desires to undo undue restrictions and utopian visions also play their roles. Our bridging project comes on the heels of what has transpired since September 11, 2001. The West has sought to cope with "pan-Islamism" and jihadist terror. Some argue that Islamist terrorist "successes" are partly due to the ineffectiveness of the political left in Western democracies.[55] Western feminists are incensed over Islamic countries' mistreatment of women.[56] Lest our bridging projects backfire, we seek to foster open dialogue based on shared experiences and reflective awareness which is at GEM-FS's core.

In view of the heightened awareness of humanity's divided-divisive mentalities, this book seeks to bridge some of the divides but not metaphorically. Consider urban development. When towns are situated on opposite banks of a river, they build a bridge.[57] Bridges facilitate commuting, but also cause people to notice their differences. Our bridging effort seeks to address religious-secular divides by first bridging hearts,[58] then minds through GEM-FS's operational range. It calls for a transformative praxis. Lonergan spent his life trying to help us understand and act in keeping our world's realities—as did the Buddha, Jesus and Muhammad in their own day. Lonergan has shown how and why appropriating one's own "rational self-consciousness" is key to bridging divides; it is a basis for bridging philosophical, ethical, and even political and economic thought. Lonergan's way of dealing with disparate disciplines can help us uncover GEM-FS's socio-political dimensions while promoting justice.[59] If the post-Vatican Catholic Church has been torn between progressives and traditionalists, GEM-FS helps us find a middle way between the two. It helps us look beyond "Islamophobia"[60] while respecting secularity. Its investigation of the differentiations of consciousness among humans to include the realms of interiority, culture and science[61] is a key for respecting all traditions while making efforts to bridge their differences. We do not speak pejoratively of any tradition. Rather, we investigate the causes and implications of human divisions so as to heal them. There is a rising Islamophobia in the West, but, there are many peace-loving Muslims who reject terror. We invoke the apophatic and faith so as to lay a ground for explaining how GEM-FS respects traditions while kataphatically addressing Buddhist-Christian-Muslim-secularity differences.

A First Subtemplate-Example of How to "See-Judge-Act"

We now wish to initially apply GEM-FS in keeping with this book's effort to bridge religious-secular divides. The Young Catholic Worker's "see-judge-act" method,[62] pioneered by Pierre Cardijn in Belgium in the 1920's, helps people stand back from a situation. Reflecting on a situation before jumping in and taking action helps one develop critical judgement about situations. As with Lonergan's eight specialties or ends[63] in his *MiT*, so various stages or steps in see-judge-act subtemplates overlap and intermingle.[64] Still, they all retain their distinctive, unique functions—as well as their complementary aspects. These distinctive yet complementary aspects in see-judge-act and in *MiT*'s eight FS are what makes a bridge such as ours possible. Two of the foundations which this book invokes for an "effective world bridge" are that of an implicit "apophatic universalism" as well as the roles of heart and mind.[65] We outline various theoretical aspects of GEM-FS as well as its possible practical see-judge-act subtemplate applications (see FS 6). That is, we want to show that GEM-FS can be implicitly applied to concrete situations. This book's "how-to, hands-on" application in FS 6 aims to help bring believers and "non-believers" into closely-coordinated projects. One might say[66] that in the see-judge-act method, the "see" aspect does not meet the criteria Lonergan established for the first two levels of conscious intentionality. Still, the everyday world also prizes good judgments; it needs responsible actions. GEM-FS, for its part, needs to be supplemented by practical "see-judge-act" initiatives. responding to pressing social needs.

In the mediated phase of our FS approach, using the see-judge-act format in FS 6 we shall illustrate how GEM-FS can be applied in concrete situations such as in responding peacefully to the tragic incident in Garissa Kenya where in March 2015, over 140 Christian students were murdered by Muslim extremists. Our GEM-FS strategy thus aligns itself with practical see-judge-do methods so as to show GEM-FS's practical side. Lonergan's method is not just theory. It deploys a self-corrective inbuilt praxis.[67] Our see-judge-act subtemplates suggest ways to recover the "quasi-forgotten" experience of an "apophatic universalism" which had been more or less taken for granted in traditional religions.[68] When properly exercised, a self-correcting GEM-FS template and its subtemplates can help enable effective cooperation on the part of thinkers and doers so as to build bridges for the present and future in the light of the past.

Understanding the Past so as to Erect Viable Bridges Today

The Islamic - Secular encounters now occurring in Europe has led to much violence. This leads thoughtful people to ask: "What are we to do about Islamic terrorist violence—just hope that it might go away?[69] Are we to "pragmatically" ignore what does not touch us directly? Or, is there a way to bridge the sometimes totally different, mutually antagonistic assumptions of the Islamic and secular worlds?" Lonergan's GEM-FS probes deeply into human understanding, ethics and spirituality; it offers a key for addressing the underlying causes of the terror facing us in the 21st century. It clarifies a subject's operations regarding values based "on a personal appropriation of what occurs when making value judgments, on a discovery of innate moral norms, and on a grasp of the meaning of moral objectivity."[70] It helps us conceptualize for oneself what occurs in value judgments and "for expressing to others the grounds for one's value positions." (Ibid). Carefully attending to how Christians, Muslims and secularists form their value judgments is both needed and helpful in building bridges between secularists and believers. We turn to briefly summarize GEM-FS. Our aim is to suggest how Lonergan's major book, *Insight*, laid a ground for his second major work, *MiT*, which focuses more on persons' hearts than their minds in developing the eight FS. The present book examines these eight FS in its attempt to build bridges between Buddhists Christians, Muslims and secularists[71] in a world of instant communication.

*2. AN ALL TOO BRIEF A SUMMARY OF LONERGAN'S GENERALIZED EMPIRICAL METHOD (GEM).[72] AN OVERVIEW OF THE PROBLEM OF "KNOWING": FROM PLATO AND ARISTOTLE TO HUSSERL AND LONERGAN

Plato's view of knowing as an intellectual gazing on ideas is incomplete. It has caused untold confusion across the centuries. Perhaps it is not Plato, but those who have misread him who cause the confusion. The critical question that arises as to the Platonic view of knowing is: "what is the importance of the individual particular thing?" Hence it has been called the problem of the abstract (universals) and the concrete (particulars). This way of asking the question is misleading--based on a false presupposition. Lonergan uses an inverse insight to avoid the confusion. He asks not how does the universal idea relate to the particular. He investigates the knowing process and asks: "What am I doing when I am knowing?"

In answer to Platonism, Aquinas turned to Aristotle who had modified Plato's intelligible essence attained through ideas referring abstractly to an object (e. g. tree). There is an "actual existence" that needs to be verified empirically (this tree). For Aristotle and Aquinas, full human knowing requires both idea (insight-intelligible form) and experience of a sensible individual. The distinction in Aquinas (which he found in Avicenna's writings between "essence and existence") is at the heart of his philosophy and theology. It influenced Lonergan's cognitive theory which distinguishes between being intelligent and being reasonable. An insight understands an "essence"; "existence" is affirmed in a judgment.

In his *Posterior Analytics*, Aristotle lists two different types of questions we ask. That is, when we ask, "What is X?", we want to understand the essence of "X", and when we ask, Is it so?, we want to know if "X" is actually real (or, are we only *thinking* of "X"). In Latin, Aquinas called the "essence" component the *quidditas* = whatness, (Aristotle's "τὸ τί ἦν εἶναι).[73] The "existence" component for Aquinas is the *Veritas* = Truth, affirmed in a reasonable judgement. Lonergan wrote that in his *Confessions*, an account of his conversion to Christianity, Augustine (educated as a neo-Platonist), discovered the *Veritas*, or existential component of the Christian message. He discovered it when understood and grasped the reality of what St John meant in his Prologue (1, 14) by "*Kai o Logos sarx egeneto*": "And the Word was made flesh".

In *Insight*, Lonergan studies the role of insight in human knowing. He illustrates acts of insight not by quoting Aquinas but by devoting his first five chapters to the way insights actually occur. Many thinkers in such fields as mathematics, philosophy, theology, ethics, and the social sciences influenced him, including Edmund Husserl (1859-1938).[74] Husserl had been inspired by Franz Brentano (1838-1917) who had tried to adapt Aristotle's works to the modern condition with particular emphasis on the Scholastic notion of intentionality. Phenomenologists attempt to describe human experiences (and the "things themselves") without metaphysical speculations. Husserl focused on human cognitional operations and their intentionality. Linking our conscious intentional operations in various fields of human endeavors and applying GEM-FS's operational range to an ethical secularity are central aims of the present book.

In *Insight*, Lonergan faults phenomenology for being too focused on scientific description at the expense of a valid scientific explanation.[75] This resulted in a phenomenological "abstract looking from which the looker and the looked-at have been dropped because of their particularity and contingence." (*Insight*, 440). Lonergan helps us understand how inquiries in any field of study are related[76] to actual conditions of life. Description relates things to ourselves and to our senses while explanation relates things to one another within a universal viewpoint. (587). Explanatory understanding demands the creation of a theoretical language based on the various differentiations of human consciousness. This basic distinction between description and explanation is central to all of Lonergan's analyses. In the natural sciences, explanatory understanding is made possible by mathematics. In the human sciences, mathematics takes second place in relation to how humans actually understand and how they freely decide (316-21).

If Husserl helped bridge Greek and scholastic philosophy with modern philosophy, Lonergan helps us bridge Husserl's abstract[77] approach derived from mathematics with insights into how all we humans in fact use our conscious intentional operations in all facets of our lives. Like Ricoeur, he was interested in the "capable human being." Both men dwelled on human abilities, but also on how vulnerable we are in our thoughts, in our activities; they rejected claims that one's self is immediately transparent to self or that one is fully one's master. Self-knowledge presupposes one's relations with others in the various worlds or spheres of influence one is involved in. In *Insight*, Lonergan closely examines the process of how a person comes to self-knowledge. In doing so, he develops his generalized empirical method (GEM). *Insight*'s four chapters on metaphysics recapitulate the explicit emergence of metaphysics "in the minds of particular men and women" (426). This involves a methodical pedagogy. Lonergan concludes: "The preliminary stage ends when the subject reaches an intelligent and reasonable self-affirmation. Such self-affirmation is also self-knowledge. It makes explicit the pursuit of the goal that has been implicit in the pure desire to know. From that explicit pursuit there follows the directives ... of reorienting both one's common sense and scientific knowledge, and... of integrating what one knows or can know of proportionate being through the known structures of one's cognitional activities" (Ibid).

Basic Pattern of our Conscious, Intentional Operations developed in *Insight*

Lonergan lists the following as the "basic pattern of operations": seeing, hearing, touching, smelling, tasting, inquiring, imagining, understanding, conceiving, formulating, reflecting, marshalling and weighing the evidence, judging, deliberating, evaluating, deciding, speaking, writing. (*MiT*, 6). We are all familiar with these operations. Note that all of them are intentional-- a potentially misleading term. Usually one thinks of "intentional as being roughly synonymous with the adjective "deliberate." Lonergan does not imply that intentional operations are deliberate; rather, he refers to the fact that each of these operations requires an object. For example, one cannot see without seeing something, nor can one imagine without imagining something, and so on. The "something" in each case is what Lonergan calls the object. "To say that the operations intend objects is to refer to such facts as that by seeing there becomes present what is seen, by hearing there becomes present what is heard, by imagining there becomes present what is imagined, and so on, where in each case the presence in question is a psychological event. (*MiT*, 7). Operations[78] imply an operator--that is a subject who is conscious by way of his/her four intentional operations. Lonergan describes a subject's movement through the operations on the empirical, intellectual, rational and responsible levels as being respectively that of experiencing, understanding, judging and deciding. Our consciousness expands when from mere experiencing we turn to the effort to understand what we have experienced. Thirdly, in coming to know there emerges within the content of our acts of understanding the question as to whether one is merely dealing with a bright idea or whether one judges one is really on to something; one endeavors to settle what really is so. Fourthly, when one judges that one has judged correctly as to the facts, one begins to deliberate on what we are to do about them (*MiT*, 9). Every act of knowing involves a pattern of experiencing, understanding, and judging. The fourth level, of deciding,[79] while extremely important, is not constitutive of knowing. We come to know many things without making any decision about what to do with them. The first three patterns in knowing may be summarized as follows:

1. Experiencing. If someone is in a deep coma, or is in a dreamless sleep, he/she cannot come to know anything. Experiencing is part of knowing. But, contrary to empiricist philosophers' claims, in itself it does not constitute knowledge. What we experience is, of itself alone, nothing more than scraps of data.
2. Understanding. To the data of our experience we put the question, "What is it?" (the "question for intelligence.") Answers come through insights. We have an insight whenever we come to understand something. Merely arriving at an insight does not constitute knowledge. In trying to understand, one may arrive at correct answers but also at incorrect ones.
3. Judging. With regard to an insight, one asks "Is it so?" This is the question for reflection. It is here that one judges whether there are adequate grounds to support our initial insights. The question for reflection is answered with further "reflective" insights that should lead to correct judgments.

Let us expand on these three cognitional operations by putting into context how Lonergan arrived at his cognitional theory. In *Insight*, Lonergan asks and answers three basic questions (see *MiT*,25):

1. "What am I doing when I am knowing?" (The cognitive, psychology-based question). In order to know how we come to know anything, we must pay close attention to the things going on in our consciousness. Each one must examine his/her consciousness and the mind's processes of knowing. One observes how people actually operate when they formulate and verify ideas. Scientists consider data (the first step in knowing). The data are not divorced from how a mind operates as it asks questions so as arrive at answers. Cognitional theory identifies, distinguishes and relates the sets of acts we perform[80] whenever we know in mathematics, in natural and human sciences or in every day commonsense living.
2. "Why is doing that knowing?" (The epistemological question). *Insight* argues that genuine human knowledge is based on one's personal self-appropriation and an affirmation of one's own rational self-consciousness. It invites readers to appropriate their own conscious operational acts of experiencing, understanding, judging and deciding—in theology or any other discipline.[81]
3. "What do I know when I am knowing?" (The metaphysical question that transposes Aquinas' cognitional theory into contemporary contexts). GEM-FS is a generalized, transformative method that can help a person access his/her conscious intentional operations and data of consciousness in ways that interact with other persons while correctly handling various kinds of data.[82]

These three basic questions must be addressed in that order. Lonergan's GEM (a cognitional theory) is influenced by the method of inquiry as pursued in the sciences. So as to rethink the Cartesian *cogito ergo sum*, in *Insight*, chapter 11, readers are invited to affirm their own existence—not with a mere *cogito*, but through a judgment based on reflective insights. Later in *Insight*, Lonergan explores an epistemology and a metaphysics that reject the a priori presuppositions of Kant and Husserl. Like many modern philosophers, Lonergan disagrees with the Scholastics, with Leibniz and Christian Wolf who presumed that a rationalist metaphysics has priority over epistemology. He reverses formerly taken-for- granted hierarchies in said philosophies. He transforms the metaphysics of Aristotle and Aquinas by situating it within his GEM methodical context. He argues that Gilson's immediate realism cannot be mediated. Gilson is left (by his own admission) to dogmatically affirm his realism in the face of Kant's denial of such a possibility. Lonergan prefers Emerich Coreth's version of immediate realism which can be mediated--but he corrects Coreth on some points.[83]

This book seeks to apply-extend the first basic question to ask "what are we doing when we try to build bridges of mind and heart that can help face the many challenges confronting humanity and the planet?"

Lonergan extended and applied the reach of his explicit metaphysics[84] by developing *MiT*'s eight FS. Early in *MiT*, he notes that his use of our four basic operations of e. g. hearing, inquiring, reflecting, deciding refer to transitive operations which are the operations of an operator or subject. The operations are conscious and they intend objects. Lonergan appeals to the successful sciences[85] to form a preliminary notion of method. GEM goes "behind the procedures of the natural sciences to something both more general and more fundamental, namely, the procedures of the human mind." (p. 4). Lonergan discerns in the mind's procedures "a transcendental method, that is, a basic pattern of operations employed in every cognitional enterprise." This method is relevant in approaching "other, more special methods appropriate to particular fields." (Ibid). "Just as operations by their intentionality make objects present to the subject, so also by consciousness they make the operating subject present" to self (8). Lonergan uses the adjective, "present" (of an object to the subject) but he does so "ambiguously, for the presence of the object is quite different from the presence of the subject . . . The subject experiencing himself operating......is that very operation which besides being intrinsically intentional, also is intrinsically conscious." (p. 8). Explicitating the data of one's consciousness is to be done "not by looking inwardly, but by recognizing in our expressions the objectification of his subjective experience." (p. 9). This is not a covert, secretive process but an implicit one waiting to be worked out, developed by a subject.[86]

Our text aligns GEM with *MiT*'s eight FS because these eight FS build on our reduplicative cognitional knowing-doing operations. The data of consciousness are what makes GEM-FS unique[87] in that they enable its reduplicative structure both within one's consciousness and as grounding the FS process. GEM-FS highlights how our minds generate the specialized (FS) methods of the sciences or scholarly disciplines. GEM-FS delves into questions of meaning, progress or decline in history and religion. It acknowledges the proper autonomy of the sciences and scholarly disciplines, but sublates them within higher viewpoints of faith-heart language. Having briefly situated *Insight*'s historical genesis--later applied in *MiT*--we continue our basic account of GEM's cognitional theory. Our aim is to apply GEM-FS, an original and challenging method, in "down-to-earth" ways so as help heal secular-religious issues.

GEM-FS as a "Mind-Heart Language" that Apophatically Helps Integrate Many Aspects of Reality

Lonergan's transposed metaphysics follows upon epistemology which in turn depends on understanding one's own knowing. GEM metaphysics, a transcendental integration of heuristic structures,[88] helps ground, unify other knowledge. (*Insight*, 410-616). GEM-FS gives us a language and a way to integrate academic disciplines as well as the realities of one's internal and community-social life in general. Its "radical" Third Way bridges the apophatic and kataphatic. In GEM-FS, feelings may function as either operators[89] or integrators. "As operators, they represent our initial response to possible values, moving us to pose value questions. As integrators they settle us in our value judgments as our psyches link our affects to an image of the valued object. Lonergan names this linkage of affect and image a symbol."[90] One must distinguish the use of a flag as a symbol from Lonergan's meaning of symbol as *an event in consciousness*. "The concrete, functioning symbols" suffusing "our psyches can serve as integrator systems for how we view our social institutions, various classes of people, and our natural environment, making it easy for us to respond smoothly without having to reassess everything at every moment. Symbols can serve as operators insofar as the affect-image pair may disturb our consciousness, alerting us to danger or confusion, and prompting the questions we pose about values." (Dunne, Ibid).

As to a possible GEM-FS role in integrating the heuristic structures informing local-global communities, one may refer to Akeel Bilgrami's integration of political, moral, and epistemological themes. One should integrate phenomena so as to find new possibilities for thought and action but also to dis-integrate "deeply and often invisibly integrated phenomena, through whose integration alternative possibilities for thought and action are foreclosed. We can see here the Janus-faced nature of this integrating style of thought: one side shows its normative orientation, the other its genealogical orientation."[91] For Bilgrami, the "irreducibly normative relations between subjectivity and the world are shaped by a 'history and tradition' which form the contexts in which perceptions of value and the demands those values make on us can exist."[92] It is important to identify the contexts within which human subjects respond to normative properties in the world. "Failure to recognize the normative character of the world implies that the only 'place' for normativity left, if anywhere, is within the subject" (Ibid). For Bilgrami, the human subject is somehow "enchanted" from within." (Ibid). As does Lonergan, Bilgrami helps us integrate our lives' subjective and objective aspects. GEM-FS is reinforced in this regard by its ability to incorporate apophatic sources within us with the kataphatic realities of daily life. Any "bridge" between religion and the secular depends on an awareness of hidden commonalities, on a center of gravity within the human mind and soul. Just as there are centers of gravity in the galaxies and the universe as a whole, so each human person needs a "center of gravity" for heart and mind. Both Lonergan and Bilgrami help us search for his/her center of gravity which includes one's background and sociocultural involvements.

Lonergan's Critical GEM-FS Realism Requires a Change of Mind by Living Out the Operations

Lonergan referred to GEM as a critical realism—partially grounded in the Aristotelian-Thomist traditions. Such a realism seeks to ground knowing and valuing in a way analogous to what Kant had attempted. But he avoids both Kant and Husserl's notions of intuition. Lonergan considered intuition to be "the same as seeing" which is why he avoided it. His point was that "insights are a dime a dozen and most of them are wrong. You have to have an awful lot of before you get anything that is really considerable."[93] Intuition short-circuits insight and judgment. GEM traces to their radical roots the sources of the meanings and values that constitute personality, social orders, and historical developments. GEM-FS explores the ways such meanings and values are distorted. It proposes a framework for collaboration among disciplines to overcome basic philosophical distortions that negatively affect our lives. It aims to promote sound ways of living. *Insight* analyzes the change of mind involved in doing science and its implications. Adequately analyzing science, far from justifying positivist claims of scientific understanding, reveals the need of a critical realism that can integrate all the sciences while addressing the question of God and grounding moral and religious concerns. A key to all this is a critical realism, a change of mind regarding mind itself.[94] As distinguished from Husserl's intentional phenomenology, GEM is based on human awareness not only of sensed experiences and feelings but also of other mental acts such as imagining, inquiring, understanding, questioning,[95] hypothesizing, formulating, marshalling evidence, judging and so on. GEM stands to the data of consciousness as the empirical method stands to the data of sense. Just as there are data about the material universe studied in the natural sciences, so there are also data about the working of the human mind. For Lonergan, the data of consciousness are as ascertainable as are the data of sense in the natural sciences. They are the starting point for the knowing of knowing; they constitute its justification. Generalizing the notion of data to include the data of consciousness as well as those of sense is pivotal to GEM. It helps account for disciplines that deal with humans as makers of meanings and values. From the compound data of sense and of consciousness,[96] one ascends through hypotheses to verification of the operations by which humans deal with what is meaningful and what is valuable. Further, GEM, a "generalized empirical method" (*Insight*, 96) can be functionally specialized.

Insight shows that genuine human knowledge is a personal self-appropriation of one's own rational self-consciousness. It invites readers to appropriate his/her own fourfold process of conscious intentional operations of experiencing, understanding, judging and deciding. It considers a very wide range of problems such as philosophy, mathematics, natural science (especially physics), ethics, psychoanalysis, literature and theology. Coming to insights in any field has both distinctive and similar patterns. *Insight* helps a reader come to "understand understanding"; it focuses on knowing's dynamic structure, on that structure's invariant patterns shared by all knowers in whatever discipline they might venture. Its program is succinctly stated: "Thoroughly understand what it is to understand, and not only will you understand the broad lines of all there is to be understood but also you will possess a fixed base, an invariant pattern, opening upon all further developments of understanding." *(Insight*, 22).

This book correlates human operations operative in members of any and all religions or in secular persons. It may be that the thrust and reach of the operations is "reduced" in secular persons to the extent that they reject out of hand forms of (self-)transcendence--thus short-circuiting a full GEM-FS operational range.)[97] So that followers of world religions or of an authentic secularity[98] can effectively cooperate in building bridges, we deploy the eight FS which reflect the structure of our minds. Our aim is to integrate GEM-FS's generalized and functionalized capabilities as a "GEM-FS template" operative in both religious and secular persons. Unlike object-oriented programming, a GEM-FS template is open to operational "self-transcendence". A GEM-FS template pivots on the data of consciousness allowing genetically related series of sublations from data through understanding and judgment to decision and action. These are grounded in heartfelt decisions and actions aimed at promoting the good[99] and overcoming alienation; an implicit premise is the role of *human* schemes of recurrence (*Insight*, 72, 485).

The Importance of Human Schemes of Recurrence and of Heart-Healing Vectors in GEM-FS

GEM-FS is a critical realism requiring changes of heart and mind. It utilizes two types of "schemes of recurrence," those of a series of *events in nature* and those of *human operations* leading to cooperation. This book's double-pronged strategy focuses on human operations' operational range and how they can be applied so as to heal. The emergence of human schemes of cooperation follows a self-correcting or "self-organizing criticality" (e. g. in physics). This yields a process of 1) existing human schemes that give rise to 2) questions about how to do things better. In turn, this gives rise to 3) insights for improvement and to 4) actions that modify the schemes. Other questions and insights may follow. What distinguishes human schemes of recurrence from natural ones is that their emergence and survival depend upon acts of human intelligence and choice. We should implement the schemes of cooperation in our professional and daily lives.[100] Human schemes of recurrence depend on implementing the common good and living universal values,[101] as when we address the complexities of mass migrations and the resulting clashes. In dealing with complexities,[102] GEM-FS interrelates what goes on within our hearts and minds.[103] Relying on universal values, this book asks how GEM-FS's mediating-mediated phases can help build bridges between religions and the secular. GEM-FS's distinction between faith and beliefs[104] is a key to such bridging efforts. Christian and Islamic beliefs can be divisive, whereas faith helps unite minds and hearts. We seek to evaluate today's complex religious-secular realities so as to lay foundations to reconcile authentic convictions. We stress the role of the heart in preparing a fertile ground for bridging what on the surface may seem contradictory claims. We seek a "middle way" between faith, beliefs and an ethics that seeks to bridge differences by way of the common good. Needed bridges can best be founded in hearts responsive and devoted to realistic appraisals of spiritual-cum-ethical-secularity principles.

Correlative to human schemes of recurrence[105] and the role of the heart in GEM-FS are its "healing and creating vectors in history." Lonergan's grasp of history and faith helps him postulate such vectors in history whereby one deploys the heuristic structures used in human endeavors. In spelling out the vectors, Lonergan analyzes the development of the modern sciences as an example of self-transcending human consciousness. One moves from attentiveness to experience to refined understanding to critical judgments—a process probed in *Insight*'s examination of mathematics and the natural sciences. This leads to an overall view of world process as an emergent probability guiding both the dynamic[106] worlds of nature and human affairs (*Third Collection*, 100-09). For Lonergan, it is important that we understand correctly how the sciences are linked. Unfortunately, human biases and moral failures militate against the smooth functioning of human intelligence. This provokes decline. GEM's cognitive analysis can mediate between Christian-Islamic-secularist standoffs in that its analysis of consciousness as an ethical, moral "ought" focuses on the facts of a situation. For example, the growing threat of Islamic terrorism and the refugee crises it has spawned calls for an 'ought' of appropriate public policies so as to defuse the crises. In Europe, Germany has shown the way by accepting close to two million refugees in recent years. Unfortunately, biases can blind people and lead them to close their hearts due fear and economic interests.[107] This has impeded the ability of such Catholic nations as Poland to admit any ethical "ought" in dealing with the situation. The global challenge of violence calls the world to explore how all might participate in such an endeavor of caring for the refugees of war. Our book enlists interdisciplinary theories and practical efforts so as to promote changes in organizational norms, beliefs, and practices.

For GEM, the notions of good and evil are useful for expressing moral conclusions "if rooted in intelligent analysis, dialectical encounter, and personal conversion."[108] It relies on dialectical encounter to expose the oversights when 'good' and 'bad' are used to categorize actions in the abstract.... The complexities of one's situation involve both its own history and how observers view this history. "Darwinian, Hegelian and Marxist views of history are largely genetic, insofar as they support the liberal thesis that life automatically improves, and that wars, disease, and economic crashes are necessary steps in the forward march of history.... GEM declares an end to this age of scientific innocence. It regards this thesis of progress" as based on approximate understandings "of actual situations," (ibid) of the dynamics of historical decline and possible factors of recovery by which bias and its objective disasters are reversed.

*3. HOW GEM-FS CONVERSIONS MAY HELP PEOPLE OF GOOD WILL FOSTER A GLOBAL SECULARITY ETHICS [109]

Lonergan's first major work, *Insight*, develops GEM by explaining how insights occur in science, mathematics or academic disciplines—as well as in human commonsense. GEM is a "secular-apophatic" method *applicable* to the study of religion or of any other discipline. GEM-FS's development of intellectual, moral and religious conversions exemplify Lonergan's lifelong quest to bridge problems that may arise between religiously- or secularly-oriented persons. As to the conversions, Lonergan refers to Joseph de Finance's vertical exercise of freedom which consists of "a set of judgments and decisions by virtue of which we pass from one horizon to another, in such a way that the new horizon represents not just a broadening or a deepening of the preceding one, but rather its overturning. Through this overturning, a radically new beginning occurs in one's conscious life,"[110] as when one is converted:

- Intellectual conversion explains how humans can objectively study "reality" by overcoming the spontaneous and deeply rooted myth that regards knowledge as a kind of intuition, and reality as an "already out there now" corresponding to the animal movement of extroversion.
- Moral conversion "consists in a change of our decisions and choices, from satisfactions to values. A person no longer makes self the center of its aspirations. One becomes a self-transcendent person, capable of real love and of genuine collaboration.

- With religious conversion, one places the center of one's life in the transcendent mystery of God. (*MiT*, 40). Religious conversion often leads to better loving interpersonal relationships. As a radical change in our consciousness, it adds a new meaningful reality that broadens the meaning of the intelligible, the true, and the value innate to our spirit. It supplies one with a new dimension of meaning and a new horizon, "a new principle of knowledge and decision." (Ibid). Values seem worth devoting one's life to.

Reflection on conversion supplies theology with "a foundation that is concrete, dynamic, personal, communal, and historical." Just as reflection on a scientist's operations "brings to light the real foundation of the science, so too reflection on the ongoing process of conversion may bring to light the real foundation of a renewed theology,"[111] and of the subsequent phases of theology, e. g., for "formulating and affirming the true Christian doctrine, understanding its content in some way, and communicating it in an appropriate and effective way to various kinds of people." (Sala. Ibid).

GEM-FS's treatment of the conversions can help humans find convergences of horizons. "Conversion as lived affects all of a man's conscious and intentional operations. It directs his gaze, pervades his imagination. . . . But as communal and historical, as a movement with its own cultural, institutional and doctrinal dimensions, conversion calls forth" reflection. (*MiT*, 131). Lonergan studies the horizons within which this can occur, including those of foundations. We are exploring how Buddhism, Christianity, Islam and secularity define their horizons, arguing that opposed horizons can be reflected on, bridged. For Lonergan, religious conversion presupposes moving from the first mediating phase of the FS to the second mediated phase. "Conversion occurs, not in the context of doing theology, but in the context of becoming religious." (*MiT*, 268). The context on the conversions can help us evaluate "secularism" so as to e. g. establish contexts for the sorely-tried Muslim refugees to adapt in new European homes and for Europe's new right extreme parties to find more conciliatory attitudes by transvaluing their values. There is an urgent need for conversion inasmuch as many claim that Islam is incompatible with democracy.

Comparing Peter Berger and Charles Taylor on "Secularism"

Comparing the respective views of Charles Taylor and Peter Berger on secularism can help us appreciate the wide range of GEM-FS' applicability and its operational range. Taylor views secularism as a naïve form of anti-religion; his thesis on a secular age is more compatible with GEM-FS than is Berger's which holds that secularism is *opposed* to religion. While we interpret Taylor's view of secularity as one that can help bridge the religious with the secular, Berger writes that since Nietzsche's proclamation of the "death of God" in the late 19th century, it was assumed that religion would soon pass from the scene. Instead since the 20th century, "the alleged fact became increasingly dubious" even as a description of what is happening at the beginning of the 21st century. Religion has not been declining. In fact, in many parts of the world there has been "an explosion of religious faith."[112] Many had predicted religion's decline due to the progress of science which would replace "the irrationality and superstition of religion. Not only Nietzsche but other seminal modern thinkers thought so--notably Marx (religion as opiate of the masses) and Freud (religion as illusion)."[113] For Berger, the two great figures of classical sociology, Durkheim and Weber, also erred on this point. "Durkheim explained religion as nothing but a metaphor of social order. Weber believed that... 'rationalization', the increasing dominance of a scientific mindset, would destroy the 'magical garden' of premodern worldviews... Durkheim, an enlightened atheist, saw secularity as progress. Weber was not happy about what he saw: 'ostensibly the imprisonment of modern man in the 'iron cage' of rationality. But ... both agreed on what was supposedly happening. Not to put too fine a point on it, they were mistaken. Modernity is not intrinsically secularizing." Ibid).

A validation of GEM-FS as a secular method promoting the conversions gives an alternative to Berger's religion-vs-secularism scenario. Rather than attack secularism, Berger could benefit from the Taylor- Lonergan view that secularity is a state of being separate from religion;[114] secularization is a process that has been progressively adapted by Western societies since the French Enlightenment. Since secularity does not exclude interiority, there is a very broad bridge between it and the various world religions.

Taylor's *A Secular Age* (2007) explores what it means to be spiritual in a secular age. While many today agree that we live in a secular age, it is unclear how "secularity" affects spirituality. Taylor aims to clarify these issues by giving a historical account of the secularization of Western cultural and social orders. He depicts what it means to inhabit a secularized society. He clarifies the conditions of the experience of and the search for the spiritual in our current age.[115] For some people, 'secularity' refers to the retreat of religion from public spaces. For perhaps a majority, it refers to a great decrease of religious belief and practice, especially in Western Europe. Taylor offers us a third meaning, namely "a move from a society where belief in God is unchallenged and indeed, unproblematic, to one in which it is to be understood to be one option among others, and frequently not the easiest to embrace". (55). Belief in God is no longer axiomatic; there are alternatives. This type of secularity[116] has had a major impact on spirituality. It affects "the whole context of understanding in which our moral, spiritual or religious experience and search takes place..., the implicit, largely unfocussed background of this experience and search". (56).

For Taylor, spiritual life may require going through an experience of "fullness": how can one's life be good, whole as it should? Fullness may include an unsettling experience breaking through our ordinary sense of being in the world or an experience in which "our highest aspirations and our life energies are somehow lined up, reinforcing each other, instead of producing psychic gridlock." (59). Such a sense of fullness can be interpreted as do theists (Jews, Christians, Muslims) or in non-theistic ways (Buddhists, Daoists). For theists, the sense is often the fullness that comes to them within a personal relationship with the divine. Non-theistic believers tend to experience a transcending of the self, opening it out.

Taylor delves into the background frameworks that constitute human agency and personhood, and how approaches to spiritual life have changed. Pre-modern, naive frameworks have given way to reflective ones. Belief in God is now one option amongst others--for some the most plausible option, for others, a very implausible one. Taylor notes (12, 73) that the default option in modernity is unbelief or exclusivist humanism. Buddhist theories of "emptying", of "nothingness" provide a further default option, one that calls for distantiation from relativist presuppositions; such a mystical-ethical distantiation is compatible with Christianity as well as "secularism". This shift in background has produced "the secular age": it is not just a shift in beliefs, but a shift in terms of experience and sensibility. It determines the context in which we live our spiritualities. Some kinds of immediate, naive experiences of fullness are no longer accessible to us moderns. Instead of a world in which the place of fullness was "unproblematically outside of or 'beyond human life'", we have moved into a conflicted age in which this construal is being challenged by many. (71). Secularity refers to a new context within which the spiritual life nowadays takes place. It constitutes a shift from pre-modern naive acknowledgements of the transcendent. This is very different from past shifts, where one naive horizon replaced another. Taylor challenges simplistic views of secularism, "the subtraction thesis," which believes that to the extent that science is added to a culture, religion is subtracted (79). We need a more radical analysis of how the secular age arose. Taylor asks "why was it virtually impossible not to believe in God in, say, 1500 in our Western society, while in 2000 many of us find this not only easy, but even inescapable." (25). He answers with a historical-philosophical sketch of how changes in mentality happened over between the 16th and 21st centuries. *A Secular Age* does not offer a usual historical narrative of events; rather, it traces how ideals, social trends and motivations[117] arose which over time brought about today's secular western mentality --in North Atlantic world of Western Europe, North America and the regions influenced by this geographical area.

Taylor is not interested in minor changes in mentality, but in what emerges when "we take into account the fact that all beliefs are held within a context or framework of the taken-for-granted, which usually remains tacit, and may even be as yet unacknowledged by the agent, because never formulated." (13). He relies on Wittgenstein, Heidegger and Polanyi who each analyzed the background frameworks of unformulated concepts underlying a given mentality. As to views on secularity today, Taylor notes that it is "a matter of a whole context of understanding in which our moral, spiritual or religious experience and search takes place." (4). He links his understanding of this issue to Heidegger's notion of what is already implicit[118] in our ordinary pre-ontological understanding of Being; to Wittgenstein, who speaks of a taken for granted "background picture" of the world; and to Polanyi's work on the role of "tacit knowing" which underlies our explicitly formulated knowledge. Taylor thinks that unless we are reflectively aware of the influence of this tacit background on our thinking, we remain "naïve" because our mentality will be controlled by what remains unacknowledged assumptions. These conceptual backgrounds are not eternally fixed, forever static. Over time, they shift and slide around, like the banks of a river.[119] There has occurred a shift in background leading to our secular age. This shifting or disrupted background can be tested historically: for example, by examining how the conceptual distinctions between the immanent and transcendent, or natural and supernatural, were understood in the 16th century, and how they are understood today. Taylor concludes that our contemporary secular age is not necessarily non- or anti-religious, even if it differs tremendously from 16th century forms of religion and their assumptions.[120]

In his earlier *The Sources of the Self: The Making of the Modern Identity*, Taylor had attempted "to write a history of the modern identity . . . what it is to be a human agent: the senses of inwardness, freedom, individuality . . . in the modern West."[121] Exploring the inescapable, often inarticulated moral frameworks within which contemporary moral values exist, he postulated three axes underlying moral frameworks such as our beliefs about the values of human life, the kind of life deemed worth living and the dignity humans accord themselves based on their perceptions of their roles in society. He argued that in our contemporary societies, our modern moral frameworks are now invisible. Utilitarians want to calculate the greatest good for the greatest number while Kantians reason towards moral maxims that would be universally acceptable. For Taylor, both of these groups fail to ask why the particular goods constitute the greatest good. He faults those who espouse forms of reductive naturalism but cannot avoid making qualitative distinctions as to the goods guiding their lives.[122] Past moral frameworks, which viewed man as God's creature, are now fractured. Countless other moral frameworks have emerged. Reductive naturalists object that these frameworks are simply re-interpretations of various understandings of the natural world and man's place in it. Some argue that such moral frameworks were mere passing modes of interpretation which no longer have valid or helpful bearings on human existence. It may be that Taylor would fault Berger for not realizing that transvaluations of values for the good are possible today.

Cultural Overreach and Imperial Violence: Secularity Can Help Defuse Secularist Shortcomings

Recent events suggest that Islamist attacks are directed against our all-too-secularized world; however, there is also a cultural/economic/technological violence from the secular world directed against those who disagree with such strong versions of "secular" as an anti-religious atheism. There is a pressing need to evaluate the West's often-self-righteous devaluation of religion that have led to terrorist "reprisals." Sam Harris[123] compares religion to mental illness. He dismisses even religious moderates for diluting the role of reason. He promotes science as a universal moral guide, an idea that resurrects proposals made by such men as Auguste Comte and John Dewey who saw moral progress as dependent on the scientific method. Unlike GEM-FS, such atheists overesteem "reason", losing sight of the fact that the heart is also important. Our effort to evaluate devaluations or falsifications of religion turns on both mind and heart.

Empire and mercy exemplify opposed attitudes toward polity. Mercy informs the teachings[124] of the world religions. However, secular societies' loss of transcendence[125] and the fundamentalist views afflicting Christianity and Islam, have led to dysfunctional confrontations. The "secular" is a complex phenomenon. One reason why we seek to apply GEM-FS to the secularization problematic is that it is also partly rooted in scientific (secular) reason, in how scientists ask and resolve questions. GEM, contrary to naïve assumptions that the secular is simply "bad", is *itself at its core* a secular method. Secularism is a problem; the secular as such is not. We present a Charles Taylor-rooted notion of secularity informing a "secular GEM" which Lonergan's FS and their operational range develop in sound ways.[126] The history of the 20th century (and earlier centuries) suggests that the "secular world" easily succumbs to pressure groups; it does not have sufficient human motivational resources to maintain political or social neutrality. It, too, can be intolerant towards human groups that differ in their beliefs, values or religious practices. It is for this reason that with Taylor we explore "secularity"[127] for its tolerant, merciful openness to all views.

Theorists of secularism argue that socio-political institutions should be neutral toward religious views but such neutrality seldom occurs. Competing pressure groups use "secularism" as a façade to directly or indirectly establish their own thought-world. Secular theory has no defense against determined in-group ideologues infiltrating a society for their own purposes, defining those who are "in" and those who are "out". The pattern of recurring conflicts amongst humans seems to argue against the possibility of an ideal state in which neutrality and tolerance are the core values and practices. There are countless examples where out-groups, who do not conform to the dominant in-group, are daily confronted from the dominant ideology in the form of mocking, exclusion, suspicion, and violence. North Korea is a primary example. With Pope Francis, we invoke mercy as a universal value. Before he became Pope Francis, Cardinal Bergoglio took initiatives to help students face life's harsh realities. His wisdom is a practical, merciful one building bridges between persons of good will.[128] As pope, he has continued to speak a welcoming, secularity-friendly language of mercy that refuses to condemn. A GEM-FS template also invokes mercy so as to help Christians, Muslims and secularists cooperate with persons of good will.

If the West (with Reason) Fears Islam, GEM-FS Trusts Wise Persons of Good Will

Peter Kreeft notes that many Christians today fear a violent Islam,[129] witness the 3,000 victims of 9/11. "Yet many Muslims, most Muslims in the West, and the vast majority in America, want to be our friends, not our enemies in our battle against our real common enemy, which is sin, Satan, selfishness and secularism. If those are not our real enemies, then Jesus and all the saints were fools. Why do Christians believe our irreligious media's picture of Muslims as hate-filled, violence-prone, ignorant, superstitious, irrational, fanatical terrorists?"[130] To the secular Western media, the only good Muslim is a secularized one, while the only good Christian "is a de-supernaturalized, modernized, liberalized, compromised, rationalized one—especially one who worships the gods of the Sexual Revolution (the old one--not the new one expressed in John Paul II's Theology of the Body). To let the media define a religion for us is idiocy. The secular media fear Islam because they think it is the reason, or the rationalization, for nearly all the terrorism, murder and wars in the world today; and because it is deeply religious. The media believe these two things naturally go together. They are wrong." (Ibid). Showing that they are wrong is part of this book's task which offers a GEM-FS alternative open to all religious traditions and the secular.

Recognizing Islam's Flexible and Inflexible Sides "through the Eyes" of a GEM-FS Secularity Bridge

The life and legacy of the prophet Muhammad often leads western observers to "view Islam as having an unbending set of rules, as being the most rigid religion in the world. There is however, a flexibility in Islam which is one of the reasons it could spread so effectively from Arabia through Asia and Africa, allowing local practices to remain as long as they didn't contravene its basic tenets. Islam is not necessarily "a rigid set of one-size-fits-all edicts.

Interpretations run the gamut"[131] from bans on women driving in Saudi Arabia to giving women the right to hold top political office as has happened in Pakistan and Bangladesh. Islam's largest sect, the Sunnis, is decentralized. It lacks an organized clergy which allows its followers to go from scholar to scholar until they find an opinion that matches their own.

"To reform, Islamic societies needs more Islamic education, not less. The Prophet Mohammed warned his followers against blind faith. A famous anecdote tells of his coming across an Arab nomad walking away from his camel, having neglected to tie it up. When he asked the man why he didn't secure the beast, the man said, 'I put my trust in Allah.' Muhammad's pithy answer was: 'Tie your camel first—then put your trust in Allah.'" (Ibid). Unfortunately, today the likes of ISIS have overlooked this injunction.

As opposed to the Prophet's realism, let us consider ISIS' original name given it by its initiator, Abu Musab al-Zarqawi: "*Tawhid* and *Jihad*." The name implies using force to achieve unity. Zarqawi was a former petty criminal radicalized in Jordan. His medieval barbarity was too much even for Al Qaeda.[132]

Another troubling side of Islam's inflexibility may be noted in several narratives in *Leaving Islam*.[133] The book relates cases of Muslims whose eyes were opened when they read the Quran--attentively. The Quran seemed to go against their conscience, offended common sense or revealed impieties disguised as submissive piety. A case of the latter is recounted by Anwar Shaikh in his "Autobiography of a Dissident." Shaikh writes that he had read the Quran many times, but in carefully rereading *sura* XLIX, he was struck by the passage "Do not raise your voices above the voice of the Prophet." He notes: "It is supposed to be Allah telling the faithful to behave well in front of the Prophet. All of a sudden something struck me like lightning. I said, "Why is it really for Allah to tell people to show reverence to Muhammad? Can't Muhammad tell the people these things himself? God was acting as a servant to Muhammad.'" (287). Shaikh then decided to read the entire Quran critically and rationally. When he did so, he realized the Quran "did not appeal to me anymore . . . It is at that time that I started thinking about the nature of prophethood itself." Prophethood "is the ratchet with which someone raises himself above the status of God . . . He even wants to be greater than God." (Ibid). A GEM-FS secularity bridge respects priorities.

Lonergan bridges Abstract Science with Insights into Human Potentialities and Limitations

Lonergan, concerned about today's loss of transcendence, argued that the proper grounding for human wisdom (*philosophia*) is to be found in "self-appropriation." *Insight* shows how intelligent and reasonable persons come to know. Personal knowledge can in principle be attained in any human culture—religious or secular. Bridging such vast cultural-religious domains as Christianity and Islam with *secularist* views can best be done through an adequate notion of *secularity*. This book attempts to do so by recognizing the diverse historical realities of Christianity and Islam and by suggesting ways to modernize religious traditions with the challenges of a relevant secularity. This involves deploying GEM-FS's operational range. Self-appropriation includes an integrated understanding of the truth. As opposed to the usual understanding of the scientific method, GEM pays equal attention to the data of consciousness and of sense--this is why it is called a generalized method. GEM-FS is in the first instance a secular method based on the dynamic process of human cognitive operations. It was born out of Lonergan's revision of Husserl's original views on the intentionality of our consciousness. He faulted Husserl's focus on scientific description at the expense of scientific explanation. Linking our conscious intentional operations in all fields of human endeavors is one of GEM's breakthroughs. If Husserl had helped bridge Greek and scholastic philosophy with modern philosophy, Lonergan helps us bridge Husserl's abstract approach derived from mathematics with insights into how all we humans, in fact, use our conscious intentional operations in every aspect of our lives. Having elucidated that GEM--as a *secular* method based on how we use our cognitive operations in daily life or in doing mathematics, science, etc--Lonergan showed in *MiT*, how his method can be applied to religion. As to the several ways scientists, theologians or other academics "function," GEM-FS speaks of the dynamic unity of a subject in process of development. The fact that insights 1) both help maintain the schemes of human living and 2) constantly bring about transformative new schemes helps make GEM-FS a method for transformative adaptations between seemingly contradictory ways of thinking. This book pivots on GEM-FS's transformative praxis—its repeated calls to foster trust because based on deeper realities often lost sight of in our busy world.[134]

"Functional Specialization" (FS) Pivots on a Diphase, Self-Correcting GEM-FS Questioning Process [135]

"GEM-FS" is an umbrella term linking several key notions informing our text such as submitting to the truth and a global ethics' foundations.[136] Trying to understand the concrete universe involves our ability to question. GEM does not simply ask questions about this or that; it explores questioning itself. The set of questions this book asks and the set of operations to be performed in fostering understanding between Christianity and Islam differ greatly. This is due to Christianity's acceptance of the critical investigation of its Scriptures and Islam's opposite tendency. For Islam, the hadiths and even fatwas[137] have an authority that go much beyond the role of Tradition and Church Councils in determining the authenticity and roles of Christianity's sacred texts. Such a difference not only has a decisive role in how Christianity and Islam help guide their believers in daily life but also in how they may be open to dialogue with other religions or with secularists.[138] GEM-FS provides a series of potentially important bridges to help us deal with many human problems. Its foundational method helps humans arrive at knowledge and make decisions in everyday life or in the various disciplines. All humans in any culture come to know through the fourfold, reduplicative feedback process Lonergan clarified in GEM-FS.[139] On the basis of this reduplicative fourfold process, the various human disciplines can engage in FS transcultural bridges. Such bridges are transformative ones--powerful helps in our age of constant change. Their effectiveness derives from humans' ability to appropriate their own knowing-doing operations. An inclusive GEM-FS addresses human limitations which therefore require self-transcendent,[140] foundational conversions.

Our as-inclusive-as-possible GEM-FS template addresses human limitations. The Greek term used in the New Testament for a heart-felt conversion is *metanoia*. It points to a new state of mind cleansed of self-preoccupation and self-aggrandizement. The *metanoia* process opens wide the pathways of the heart and mind to the larger picture of the unlimited Universe in which every point of view can be understood as part of the unfolding Cosmos. Since the Universe is so magnificently complex, it cannot be fully comprehended by any one point of view, whether philosophical, scientific, or theological.[141] Therefore we cannot but question. In this book, we question how GEM-FS may help bridge religion and secularity. GEM-FS' dynamic process, first outlined in *Insight*, was clarified in *MiT* which explains how eight inter-related questions arise in any collaborative effort. Each question is answered in its own way according to the level of intentional consciousness one is addressing in each of the eight FS. Whether one is still in the mediating phase of the first four FS or has moved on to the last four FS in the mediated phase, the process of questioning always plays a pivotal role. Making progress in any GEM-FS collaborative effort is the result of finding new answers to the complete set of eight inter-related questions outlined in *MiT*.

Muslims submit to the transcendent Allah. Christians submit to God from the heart so as to love God and neighbor with all their soul. Scientists submit to the processes of Nature before "discovering" anything. We must not forget that all humans potentially or actually have a "dark side" to them. Addressing that dark side both personally and collectively requires that we use the full panoply of human questions so that we can critically wed faith and scientific thinking. Submitting in the above senses paradoxically frees persons to understand one another and to cooperate, even while acknowledging the "dark side."

Questioning, so important to GEM-FS, plays a vital role in our effort to build Buddhist-Christian-Islam-secular bridges. We thus pose such questions as: Why do Islamic - secular interfaces often lead to violence? What can a global secularity ethics do about it?[142] Shall we ignore the reasons that lead to violence, hoping that "time will heal"? Shall we just agree to differ? While rejecting the violence of Al-Qaeda and ISIS, we note that they stringently oppose secular trends. Nor can we ignore the fact that there exist some cultural/economic/technological forms of secular intolerance which would nudge faith and beliefs aside. Worse, strong "secular" versions--such as a militant atheism that persecutes religious believers--tragically limit the possibilities of human progress. In fact, they restrict the operational range of effective, responsible freedom. As will be shown in Parts 2 and 3, GEM-FS deploys the full operational range of human possibilities including practical, ethical see-judge-act subtemplates which, we argue, can, should be equally operative in Buddhist, Christian, Islamic, secular or common sense points of view.

Transition from our GEM-FS Template's Background Issues to its Actual Commitments

Taking our cue from *MiT* (which first outlines background issues before engaging in GEM-FS's mediating-mediated phases), we now turn to the two mediating and mediated phases for deploying the eight FS. This book studies the birth and evolution of Christianity and Islam, their violent encounters as well as peaceful cooperation during the Middle Ages so as to suggest policies whereby these two religions might address today's secularist tendencies. Consistently with our double-pronged strategy, we appeal to Buddhism to illustrate GEM-FS's operational range founded in part on an openness to the apophatic,[143] and to extend the operational range of freedom among humans. A genuine secularity involves its own operational range of (authentic) freedom which can help bring it "in sync" with the world religions in an effort to build the type of "world bridge" we seek.

II

Sketching a GEM-FS Bridge's MEDIATING PHASE as Outlined in *MiT*'s First Four Specialties[1] : Probing into Buddhist-Christian-Muslim Teachings so as to Best Broach a Global Secularity Ethics

Part one briefly studied the GEM "secular" process, arguing that it offers a general template to relate today's scientific methods to religious beliefs and traditions. We now turn to delve into the functional specialties (FS), that is, into *MiT*'s mediating-mediated phases. Our aim is to discover "GEM-FS ways" to promote Christian-Islamic cooperation so that they can jointly address our secularized, postmodernist world. To a lesser extent, we appeal to the Eastern views of Hinduism and Buddhism to help us situate the importance of conversions[2] In doing so, we call to mind some benevolent traits that can be found in the world religions and in secularity such as the quality of mercy, courage and a willingness to change. Such shared traits play important, if somewhat implicit roles in our bridging efforts.

THE FIRST MEDIATING PHASE EXAMINES THE PAST TO DIALECTICALLY PREPARE A WAY FOR THE MEDIATED PHASE

In *MiT*, the first four Functional Specialties (FS) constitute the *"mediating phase"* which focuses on the past. Our book's mediating phase (FS 1-4) is meant to help the reader understand the past of Christianity and of Islam so as to prepare a way to relate these two traditions to today's secular realities. One must not forget the colonial powers' mistakes in recent centuries, the ensuing reactions, nor the role of an apophatic mysticism and ethics exemplified in Gandhi[3] who united Hindus—but in doing so led to the secession of Pakistan from India. In FS 3, we shall note how GEM-FS helps us evaluate such issues. In FS 4, Dialectics, we shall consider what has been done to redress past mistakes while indicating how self-transcending persons in secularity-oriented nations can be a key to "living out" the GEM-FS *mediated* phase which confronts the future. We shall argue that persons able and willing to live a merciful secularity are a key to bridging misunderstandings and fostering reconciliation.

Chapter One

First Functional Specialty

Researching[1] Data on Christianity, Islam and an Ethical Secularity

There are now millions of Muslims living in Western European countries. Many of them do not want to or cannot understand how they could integrate themselves in their new found "homelands" which include both Christian and secular-atheist elements. Belligerent acts such as the destruction of New York's World Trade Center's twin towers in September 2001, the terror of the "ISIS-Caliphate" and the violent attack on Charlie-Hebdo in Paris in January 2015[2] stand out in a spiral of Islamic attacks against the West. For their part, such leading Western countries as France and Germany are being challenged as to how to accommodate millions of Muslim immigrants. Backlash movements such as the National Front in France and Pegida in Germany have taken to the streets and ballot box in opposing further Muslim immigration. Expressing Westerners' anxieties, Michel Houellebecq's best-selling satiric novel *Submission* imagines France in 2022 with a Muslim president. How may a GEM-FS ethical secularity be relevant to such issues? This book is rooted in a radical theology of the heart that would transcend words' destructive powers.

A BRIEF OVERVIEW OF BUDDHIST-CHRISTIAN-ISLAMIC BEGINNINGS AND OF THE RISE OF SECULAR SOCIETIES

1. Buddhism's Two Main Traditions: Theravada and Mahayana

There are two main traditions in Buddhism. Early Buddhism (Theravada or "teaching of the elders" still practiced in South Asia) gave way in Eastern Asia to Mahayana (Large Vehicle). Nagarjuna (circa 220 CE) the founder of Mahayana, spoke of *anatman* (one's true nature as non-self). Buddhist 'wholeness' (the interrelatedness of all phenomena) is described with the paradoxical phrase that all things are 'empty' (being 'nothing' in themselves, they must be grasped as part of an interrelated whole). Consonant with our stress on the apophatic, all Buddhists point to the limitations of language. The whole is 'beyond knowing'; still, we can arrive at some form of enlightenment free from the limitations of language. Mahayana Buddhists teach that things are 'devoid' of existence, 'empty.' Emptiness is related to ultimate reality. By 'negating' the reality of things, they mean that they are devoid of existence. Paradoxically this implies the interrelatedness of all things.[3] Nagarjuna rejected both the absolutist and the nihilist interpretations of Buddhism. He rejected the absolutists' contention that, because the ultimate nature of reality transcends the rational, all meaningful discourse is impossible. He also rejected the nihilist claim that nothing really exists. His solution is to reject the assumption that reality can only be characterized through the categories then current in Indian metaphysics. His is a type of relational, inter-individual[4] philosophy. The 'emptiness of all phenomena is not that of utter ineffability nor of utter non-existence: it means the need to go beyond conventional reality so as to arrive at Buddhism's ultimate truth.

2. From Jesus to the Christ

The death of Jesus on the cross would by any worldly standard have meant the end of his "movement." The Messiah was not supposed to die a shameful death at the hands of the Romans. The Kingdom of God preached by Jesus had not arrived. In the face of an apparent ignominious defeat, his disciples scattered. The *Acts of the Apostles* do relate his followers' conviction that something had happened. Saul, miraculously converted to be the Apostle to the Nations, helped spread the belief in Jesus' rising from the dead. Already in the early days after the death of Jesus, his followers had begun to meet regularly to celebrate the Eucharist which commemorated the death and resurrection of Jesus. He was proclaimed to be "the Christ" (the Messiah). Christian communities arose in Judea and other parts of the Roman Empire. These communities organized themselves under the guidance of deacons, priests, bishops and a Pontiff residing in Rome. After three centuries of growth, punctuated by repeated persecutions, in 313 Diocletian's Edict of Milan formally legalized Christianity within the Empire. In 325, Diocletian himself presided over a group of church bishops at Nicea and other leaders who defined the nature of God for all of Christianity. The emperor wanted to eliminate confusion, controversy, and contention within the church. The Council of Nicea affirmed the deity and eternality of Jesus Christ and defined the relationship between the Father and the Son as "of one substance." Thus 300 years before the appearance of Muhammad, the stage had been set for the Christian-Islam confrontations as to the dogma of the Trinity that have led to innumerable claims, counterclaims and the deaths of uncounted millions of persons.

3. Islamic Beginnings: The Umayyad and Abbasid Dynasties

The Prophet Muhammad was born around 570 AD. For decades, he lived a completely private life, being engaged in trading caravans centered around Mecca on the west of the Arabian peninsula. Stemming from the tribe of the Quraysh and familiar with local polytheistic religions, he often retreated to a cave in Hira, a mountain far removed from the polytheist bustle of the pilgrim city of Mecca. He received his first revelation at the age of forty—22 years before his death.[5] Persecuted in Mecca for trying to share his revelations, he emigrated (the *hijirah*) to Medina in 622. This is reckoned as the beginning of Islam. In 630, he marched into Mecca and began a series of military campaigns. After his passing, the first two Caliphates were short-lived. The Umayyad Caliphate under founder Uthman ibn Affan began to expand toward the West, bringing much of North Africa, the Mediterranean and southern Europe under its sway. The fourth Caliphate, the Abbasids (750-1258), turned East. It ruled from Bagdhad. Being for a time the world's largest empire—Islam at its zenith—it was in contact with the Chinese and Indians as well as with the Byzantines. This enabled them to adopt and synthesize ideas from diverse cultures.

4. Secularity in a Now Transhuman or Hypermodern World

Following upon postmodernism there has arisen a hypermodernist, artistic-literary movement in which the form of an object has no context distinct from its function. Rather than focusing on the "truth" or non-truth of the social, it focuses on questions of extraneous vs non-extraneous. As opposed to modernity, an object now has its reference point in the form or attribute of an object. The new attribute-driven world is marked by the rise of technology. It fosters a convergence between technology and biology, between information and matter. A founder of hypermodernism, Paul Virilio, argues that new technologies can overcome natural limitations. He dismisses an object-driven past in favor of a flexible, attribute-driven heuristic. While modernity held out the hope of reasonable, historical change when dealing with complicated issues, hypermodernists or transhumanists[6] seek to break free of historical traditions. Virilio appropriated geometry from Husserl's phenomenological tradition to attack the postmodern turn. He agrees with Husserl that geometry's origins are not to be found in a search for first geometers. This is not a philological question but one of "reactivating the original activities contained within geometry's fundamental concepts."[7] Postmoderns have lost these 'origins' because they no longer have access to the "human surrounding world". (Ibid). As Husserl suggests, this world "is the same today as always," but this 'sameness' is problematical in digital cultures. For Husserl, the problem is that there is a 'turn' from the surrounding world to one of idealizing, spiritual acts of 'pure' thinking which create 'ideal' objects. Modernity has cut itself off from the original world leaving only idealized objects empty of meaning." (Ibid). Put in terms of our GEM-FS bridging project and its FS 1, whereas some in the West have embraced hypermodernity, the data show that there is an urgent need to interpret secular and religious texts so as to assess their impact today. In many nations human consciousness and politics are not sufficiently differentiated from the religious domain.[8] In pursuit of a global secularity ethics, we turn to interpretations of conflicting data so as to assess their impact. There is a clear need for a pluralist secularity ethics that can transvalue values but this has to be contextualized in the light of conflicting interpretations.

Chapter Two

Second Functional Specialty

Interpreting Religious Scriptures, Democracy, and Secularism so as to Avoid Misunderstandings or Resentment

One should interpret Islam in ways that respect Muslims' felt need for cultural identity in vastly different Western nations. Many Westerners are repelled by what they see as Muslims' intolerance in countries where they are in the majority (Saudi Arabia, Iran, Turkey, Pakistan[1]). For their part, Muslim immigrants in the West insist on being free to practice and propagate Islam. While short-term responses to militant "Islamism" may be needed in various regions of the world, this book looks at the long-term in addressing Christian-Islamic paths for cooperative dialogue (paths that existed[2] before Islam undercut the role of philosophy in favor of Mullahs' interpretations of sharia law).[3] One could hardly think of two more different Sunni Muslims than Rumi, the genial, renowned Sufi poet, and the ISIS leader Abu Bakr Al-Baghdadi who summons his followers to a pitiless jihad against Shiite "heretics", Christians, Jews, and Kurds. GEM-FS helps us address religious conflicts irenically rather than in partisan fashion. Instead of focusing on secularist-Christian laws or sharia, this book seeks to bridge divides between the world's religions and anti-religious secularist types of thought. Many new interpretations are needed.[4] Unlike the Catholic Church which updated its interpretations of Scripture and canon law, most Islamic leaders still interpret Islamic tradition in ways that fail to meet modern life's exigencies in a pluralist world.[5]

We argue that secularity, with its flourishing of democratic institutions (though far from perfect), does provide the best political context for religious truths to work themselves out. It allows religious truths to have an implied role emergent in secular law. The tensions between theism and a polity of secularism can be worked out. The tensions are based on a false dichotomy in that the question of what constitutes e. g. true catholicity has a hidden premise of being open to democracy. For example, both in Europe and in the U.S., rightist (religious) elements fear an "Islamic takeover." Such fears ignore the very tenets of "democratic" religious freedom, failing to understand that the relative peace experienced in a "secular society" is founded on both religious and secularity principles. This is in contrast to ongoing conflicts caused by would-be theocratic claims in some parts of the world. Secularity presupposes outgrowing biases. A religious consciousness lacking religious conversion or moral principles can result in ISIS extremism and its murderous sociopaths. They grab onto religious doctrine without understanding its essential meaning. Lonergan helps us interpret doctrines correctly. His cognitional theory is built on intellectual conversion, (self-appropriation leading to self-affirmation). As GEM-FS is empirically-based, data or evidence must always be interpreted. Human knowing is essentially open to self-transcendence, to the truth of religious meaning. Today, we are challenged to dialogue and share values in an increasingly secularized world.[6]

CONTRASTING CHRISTIAN AND MUSLIM INTERPRETATIONS OF REASON AND OF REVELATION WITH A FOCUS ON *TAWHID*, THE ONENESS OF GOD, AND TOLERANT DIALOGUE[7]

For the Islamic scholar Umar Abd-Allah, the numinous world, the Ultimate, is ontologically imperceptible to us humans. To believe in the unseen, according to the Qur'an, is the most "essential requirement of those who would seek guidance." This requires "acceptance of the three fundamentals: the absolute oneness of God (*at-tawhid*), the institution of prophecy (*ar-risala; an-nabuwa*), and the coming of the hereafter or return (*al-ma'ad*). . ... To believe in the unseen is not to know the unseen or even to desire knowledge of it beyond these fundamentals and the subsidiary beliefs connected to them" since for Islam, God alone is the knower of the unseen and the visible. This implies 'God's Lordship' (*rububiya*) which he shares with no created being." Man has the means to "know the perceptible" for the Quran "clearly directs him to make it the object of his speculation and investigation. But he has no means of delving into the unseen and knowing anything about it ... except through the vehicle of prophecy."[8]

Some denounce (not incorrectly) certain outdated laws of Islam, but "Muslims who constantly have the feeling that they should be ashamed of their religion will increase their need for cultural self-assertion.... The Quran itself makes explicit links to pre-Islamic biblical prophets such as Abraham and Moses... Despite these links, however, it is much debated within Islam whether Mohammed's encounters of the numinous were mystical or physical." (Lee, ibid, 118). This may prompt memories of the Islamic world's outrage when Pope Benedict XVI told his audience in Regensburg, Germany, that faith without reason gives rise to fundamentalism, even violence. This speech, however, must be nuanced by an earlier one that Ratzinger had given, when still a Cardinal, in a 2005 address in Subiaco, Italy where he called on Christians and Muslims to engage in self-reflection. He held up the profound correspondence between Christianity and the Enlightenment which led to modernity, a heritage that both sides must defend."[9]

A problem in the history of Islam keeping it from accepting religious pluralism today is that Sunnis now reject both *ijtihad*, defined as a process of legal reasoning, and a hermeneutics through which a jurist *rationalizes* law on the basis of the Quran and the Sunna. But if one is no longer allowed to exercise one's discretionary opinion on the basis of the knowledge of a legal precedent, reason is belittled.[10]

For Robert Reilly, only the restoring of reason to Islam can undo the spiritual pathology driving young men to terrorist acts. Most likely, the Christian West and Islam will remain incompatible because "we" believe in man's power to reason, while Islam does not. Reilly believes that Islam must be reformed. Failing this, jihadist Islam and the Christian West will remain in mortal conflict. Reilly doubts that dialogue is possible with those who reject tolerance due to the denigration[11] of dialogue resulting from the 10th century struggle between Mu'tazilites rationalist theologians and the traditionalist Ash'arites. The Ash'arites insisted that reason is subordinate to revelation; while accepting the Mu'tazilites' cosmology, they rejected their theological principles. Sadly, the Ash'arites won. There is much in the Quran that speaks to and from the heart, but it is a speaking in which beliefs trump needed interpretations of a tolerant faith. With Lonergan, we argue that beliefs should not overlook the deeper common roots of an apophatic faith. An eye of love can transcend divisive beliefs which have pitted e. g. Sunnis and Shiites against one another.[12]

THE UNENDING STRIFE BETWEEN SUNNIS AND SHIITES (SHIA)

The most fundamental divide in Islam, that between the Sunnis and Shiites goes back to conflicting historical claims. It began with the debate of who should succeed the Prophet Muhammad. Some argued that leadership should be awarded to qualified individuals while others insisted that the any legitimate ruler should be of Muhammad's bloodline. Abu Bakr, a companion of Muhammad, was named first caliph (leader of the Islamic community) over the objections of those who favored Ali ibn Abi Talib, Muhammad's cousin and son-in-law.[13] Ali became the fourth caliph in 656 but he ruled only five years before being assassinated. The caliphate, previously based in the Arabian Peninsula, then passed to the Umayyad dynasty in Damascus and later the Abbasids in Baghdad. Shiites rejected the authority of these rulers. In 680, soldiers of the second Umayyad caliph killed Ali's son, Husayn, and many of his companions in Karbala (in modern-day Iraq). Karbala became a defining moral story for Shia. Sunni caliphs worried that Shia Imams—the descendants of Husayn, who were seen as the legitimate leaders of Muslims,[14] would use this massacre to capture the public imagination and topple monarchs.

This fear resulted in the further persecution and marginalization of Shias. While Sunnis triumphed politically in the Muslim world, Shiites continued to look to the blood descendants of Ali and Husayn as their legitimate political and religious leaders. However, even within the Shia community, there arose unending differences over the proper line of succession. Islam's major schism, now 1,400 years old, does not account for all the political, economic, and geostrategic divisions feeding various conflicts. It does offer one angle for understanding some of the underlying tensions. The tensions have, for example, influenced during the past decades Sunni Saudi Arabia's competing for leadership in the Islamic world with Shiite Iran. The two nations have used the sectarian divide to further their ambitions while creating unending conflicts in such nations as Syria, Iraq, Lebanon, Bahrain, and Yemen.[15]

THE CHALLENGES OF DEMOCRACY IN LIGHT OF A TRADITIONALIST ISLAM AND SECULARIZED WESTERN SOCIETIES

This book seeks to bridge misunderstandings, but there are limits to such bridging which would require transformations of fundamentalist convictions. An inclusive faith stance (as opposed to restrictive beliefs) is needed. Mysticism can be a help but it is not tolerated by e. g. Wahabbism in Saudi Arabia. A first step for bridging misunderstandings is to address cultural gaps as done, for example, by a Louis Massignon. Some claim that Vatican II has complicated the Church's mission to preach the gospel by her outreach to non-Christians and secularists--leading to a polarization of the Church.[16] There are tensions between the proponents of evangelization and advocates of interfaith dialogue. The reality of a polarized Church calls for an examination of the history and present states of many philosophical, cultural, ethical, societal, interfaith and theological issues. Internal conflicts within Islam and Christianity have mirror images in the misunderstandings and conflicts that arise between believers and non-believers. A second step for bridging misunderstandings is to study the attitudes of Western and Islamic nations as to the nature of democracy. While Western secularism may or may not have answers to humans' religious impulse or to moral depravity, democracy can only function when religious freedom is recognized and ethical codes are respected. As democracies emerge, encouraged "from above" and embraced "from below", the needed transitions from authoritarianism to democracy may gradually occur in Islam. How best preserve the good in Islamic traditions while transforming what is contrary to democratic forms of government? One may hope that an ethical secularity may be reinforced by the natural law tradition.

Postmodernists have exposed the pretensions of modernity –its constructs of meaning in history, its rejection of mystery, its lapses into scientism, historicism and relativism. Lonergan's notion of progress and decline can help us avoid modernity's pretensions. It helps us discern, in the wake of modern science and historical scholarship, the differentiations of interiority and ways to (re)discover the self through renewed integrations of the spiritual, the intellectual, the moral, and the historical.[17] Can GEM-FS and natural law help moderate religious persons and proponents of secularity find solid grounds to agree?

A. Moderate Muslim Views of Natural Law as a Potential Bridge with Modernity

Natural law is the theory that some laws are basic and fundamental to human nature—being discoverable "by human reason without reference to specific legislative enactments or judicial decisions."[18] It stands in contrast with human-made positive laws which are conditioned by history and subject to continuous change. Natural law originated with the Stoics who believed that the basic moral principles underlying "all the legal systems of different nations were reducible to the dictates of natural law. This idea became particularly important in Roman legal theory, which eventually came to recognize a common code regulating the conduct of all peoples and existing alongside the individual codes of specific places and times." (Ibid). In contrast, to these lofty principles, the reality is that many Muslims in Europe honor shariah more than local laws—a fact that Muslim leaders living in Europe should not tolerate. Western politicians want to avoid isolated "parallel" Islamic communities. A GEM-FS historically-informed "global ethical secularity" would appeal to natural law traditions rooted in the history of both Europe and Islam.

The meaning of "the Islamic World" is not easy to delineate due to its historical and cultural diversity[19] as well as its geographic spread. Yet, there are some consistent characteristics in Islam. In his *Islam Past, Present & Future*, Kung uses five paradigms to discuss the changes that have occurred throughout Islamic history, highlighting both the unity and diversity of the

Islamic world. He seeks to bridge traditional Islam views with modern secularist thinking. Other attempts to build bridges between the Christian and Islamic worlds are based on St. Thomas Aquinas' study of natural law. Anver Emon studies natural law from an Islamic perspective in an attempt to bridge medieval Islamic thought and postmodernist views.[20] Russel Powell's study of social justice and natural law notes that "Lonergan moves from the individual subject to universal insights rather than presuming to deduce universals a priori, without regard for history, culture and individual experience."[21] Human rights and social justice are good starting points for meaningful dialogue. "If Muslims and Christians mutually acknowledge and defend basic human dignity as a consequence of commonly held natural law conclusions, reconciliation is more likely." (Ibid). Premodern Sunni Muslim jurists theorized about the authority of reason amidst competing theologies of God. Today, some have contrasted natural law and postmodernism which dismisses natural law in modern societies.

B. The "French *Malaise*" that Discounts the Potential Help of Natural Law as a Cultural Bridge

Postmodernists tend to swim in a nihilist sea rather than tuning to the apophatic insights which mystics have shared crossculturally over the millennia. They rule themselves out of court[22] when they deny reason's ability to reach certain truths; they use reason to deny its validity. For Lonergan, one cannot use reason to claim it is unable to reach certainty since this is self-contradictory. For us, a prior condition for interreligious-secularist discussions is that all parties try to understand one another. One must give reasoned arguments to justify one's basic code of behavior or the laws or traditions on which one bases one's behavior. Natural law is important in bridging heart and mind so as to arrive at some modicum of understanding and a tolerant peace. One must *not* let one's kataphatic beliefs obscure or substitute for the apophatic faith or the generosity of converted hearts. Because postmodernists are ignorant of the profundity of the apophatic in spiritual life, they wind up rejecting natural law.[23] This ignorance has provoked an ever-increasing series of clashes between the proponents of the sacred and the secular that according to Tom Heneghan "is slowly pulling European society apart." He adds: "At first glance, Irish Catholics voting for same-sex marriage, British Muslims living according to sharia and French secularists chasing symbols of faith from the public sphere would seem to have little in common. Some seem to be drifting away from religion, others towards it." Heneghan cites a European study on religion alleging "a deeper link that goes beyond Catholicism, Islam or atheism. They all reflect the tensions that arise in secularized societies because of the contemporary disconnect between religion and culture."[24] We seek to bridge such a "disconnect."

Olivier Roy writing about a secular Islam, argues that there is "in the modern disconnection between faith communities and sociocultural identities a fertile space for fundamentalism to grow. Instead of freeing the world from religion, secularization has encouraged a kind of holy ignorance to take root, an anti-intellectualism that promises immediate access to the sacred and positions itself in direct opposition to contemporary pagan culture."[25] Religion then seems ever weirder and unmanageable. Secularism "has fostered the emergence of shallow fundamentalisms "in reaction to societies seen as pagan." (ibid). Until recently, Christianity was a central part of Europe's cultural landscape. Even atheists, still familiar with faith, shared certain moral values with the believers around them. But no longer. The laws on same-sex marriage "show we are in an anthropological change. The Thomist vision of a natural law that both believers and non-believers can accept is finished . . . Contrary to Protestantism and Islam, which can imagine themselves without roots in the dominant culture" (think of evangelicals and Salafists), the Catholic Church has insisted that faith "should be rooted in the culture." Combining universalism and a cultural anchoring was the Church's great success. It still "considers European culture to be of Christian origin, so it has a harder time than other religions with this divorce from the dominant culture." (Ibid). France's gradual tightening of its *laïcité* policy reflects this loss of religious culture in secular society.[26]

Despite the French *malaise* induced by *laicite* and postmodernism, we argue that a natural law approach can serve as an intermediary for a bridging project of heart and mind. In principle, it is not of capital importance which tradition, theology or theory (Biblical, Quranic or secularist) one relies on to justify one's use of reason or the validity of one's code of behavior, as long as one is able to provide reasonable arguments to justify one's actions. For example, when secularists say that they believe in the importance of "enlightened reason and rational scientific method," they are declaring which tradition of thought informs their position. Muslims and Christians have equivalent stands. But when engaged in an intercultural "bridging" discussion, the actual reasoned arguments secularists give to justify the basis of acceptable behavior, and the extrapolation from those arguments to a general (legal) code of behavior, is vitally important. This is so because it allows participants to engage with one other by means of those reasons. While often there will be no agreement with the content of another's argument, at least, they can all agree as to why some action need be taken or not; the agreement is in the human practice of giving reasons. Accepting that natural law is common[27] to all peoples—Christian or non-Christian-- is helpful when one has to combat a postmodernist nihilism partially rooted in Nietzsche's claims.[28]

B1. Postmodernism and Atheism in Europe—Nietzsche's Influence

Friedrich Nietzsche was a precursor of postmodernism. His atheistic philosophy exalted will above reason, power above weakness. His *Thus Spake Zarathustra* (1883), outlines some of his main ideas:

- the "will to power," (the desire for self-mastery and self-transcendence);
- the "*Ubermensch*" or "'overman" as a courageous, creative individual; and
- "the Death of God": belief in God or future life are disguises for cowardice and failure in this life.

For Nietzsche, all values are baseless, one must create a purposeful future. "The last man" will be the self-satisfied man who no longer seeks to transcend himself, but settles for material well-being: "One has one's little pleasure for the day and one's little pleasure for the night: but one has a regard for health".[29]

For Sydney Ahlstrom, postmodern man is "post-historic, one-dimensional."[30] He no longer takes his own historicity seriously. Eschewing tradition, he fears the grip of the past and is pessimistic about the future. Postmodernists seem to reject reason itself. Modernism, a child of the Enlightenment, fed upon a belief in progress and an exaltation of reason. Postmodernists exalt unreason. Michel Foucault praised "madness" as "man's ultimate truth",[31] arguing that as leprosy was conquered and disappeared, society needed a stigma to fill the void and to populate the empty leprosaria. Madness was chosen. For Foucault, the Enlightenment's belief in reason brought with it an unhealthy denial of unreason, the dark side of the human soul. He concludes that "madness" is "man's ultimate truth" (82), and that "unreason has belonged to whatever is decisive, for the modern world" (285). This means, for him, that "through madness… the world is forced to question itself… the world is made aware of its guilt" (288-89).

B2. The Role of Values and the Sacred in our Lives is Being Threatened

Louis Roy has pointed out the cultural ambiance which makes it difficult for college students in the West to address the complex problems of ethical development. In the West, "the separation between facts (to be recognized by everybody) and values (left to individual preferences) has generated what has been called 'emotivism'[32] which is typical of an individualistic conscience. For such a conscience, "values are a matter of personal choice and cannot be rationally discussed. This stance entails ignorance of relevant information, unexamined principles of conduct and hidden agendas in the minds of many students, especially with respect to their goal of quickly becoming successful and wealthy." (Roy, Ibid).

Robert Coles' interest in the transcendental has led him to examine the value of the sacred in our daily lives as reflected in his benign work with troubled children. He approaches the "most significant of mysteries", that is, our relations "to a possible God and ultimate judge." He asks: "What are the chief differences between secular and sacred as they affect our personal lives, the wide world around us, and especially as they impinge upon the state -- the government that orders our existence and permits our continuance while it simultaneously attempts to impose on us its notion of the 'sacred'?"[33] Piaget,[34] Kohlberg and Lonergan have also realized that we humans are mired in various crises because we have lacked the vision and courage to live the advanced stages of human values such as the sacred. Our hope is that humans will have the courage not to forget that the universal values of an ethical secularity are indispensable in facing the modern threats to daily life all too often distorted by postmodern atheists.

B3. Postmodernist Atheism in the Light of the Polymorphism of Consciousness and Authenticity

The theme of atheism versus religious creeds complements the faith-beliefs distinction.[35] A sort of moral panic seems to surround naïve forms of religion. Such naïve forms had degenerated over the centuries into superstition. Secularists today have a field day accusing religions of its involvements in various forms of evil such as the witch hunts in the West. Today's enlightened Christian and Muslim thinkers distance themselves from such troubling episodes. GEM-FS's operational range—a notion not sufficiently stressed in Lonerganian circles—may help us understand such a distancing. This book correlates how human operations operate in religious and secular persons. We shall ask whether the thrust and reach of the operations is "reduced" by secularists inasmuch as they reject out of hand forms of self-transcendence, thereby short-circuiting GEM-FS's full and complete operational range.[36]

Richard Rorty called the philosophical idea of knowledge a mental mirroring of a mind-external world; he sought to pragmatically deconstruct the correspondence theory of truth from any overarching structure of rationality.[37] What is the origin of such a pessimist skepticism towards reason? Some scholars trace postmodernism to the tragedies of the two World Wars. Alister McGrath sees the primary cause of postmodernism to lie in "the trauma of the Holocaust which shattered the pretensions and delusions of modernity".[38] He defines postmodernism as "a cultural sensibility without absolutes, fixed certainties or foundations." It takes delight in pluralism and divergence. . . in an inbuilt pre-commitment to relativism ... mark[ing] the end of the possibility of fixed, absolute meaning" (184-85). As opposed to such an attitude, a GEM-FS bridge studies an interfaith-interdisciplinary ability "inbuilt" within humans.

Atheists such as Richard Dawkins and Christopher Hitchens ask whether religion has a future. They sell their books to audiences "all too easily fixated on past errors. Their readers are fed hindsight 'wisdom' that fails to realize that religion, too, has come a long way"[39] in apologizing for past evils. Such evils had betrayed the essence of the gospels' Good News and the mercy-filled verses of the Quran. Viewed as a relic of superstition, religion is often demonized, misrepresented. Atheistic books such as Dawkins's *The God Delusion* or Hitchens's *God Is Not Great* are in vogue. Are not atheists' attempts to ignore or "undo" humans' self-transcendent side naïve? Do they not overreach with their theoretical arguments?[40]

Young people attracted to ISIS' sense of "meaning" will only be persuaded otherwise when offered a plausible sense of radical meaning. Saints and holy persons are witnesses of the roots (radix/radicality) inscribed deep in their hearts—as Francis of Assisi learned. Mainstream churches fail to the extent they let themselves be comfortably co-opted by the dominant culture's instrumental rationality (the opposite of radicality). At our core, we are made in the image of a jealous God. (*Exodus* 34: 14). That each one "has a wild side" points to an implicit desire for the radically true, the good, the beautiful. Lacking a deep sense for the good dehumanizes one. Young persons are impressed by the beautiful; remembering one's impressions of childhood can help an adult sort through his/her polymorphism of consciousness.[41]

For Lonergan, philosophic evidence is within a philosopher's self. One cannot avoid experience, renounce intelligence, desert reasonableness. Yet, scientists who turn to philosophy tend to ignore some aspects of their personal development and values. They may be attracted by "the range of recent philosophies that rest on the successive attempts to formulate a symbolic logic, for a deductivism offers the security of an impersonal and automatically expanded position." (*CWL* 3, 454). They might "seek a new integration of the sciences in works written by individual scientists or by commissions of scientists" for they are accustomed to believing scientists. They hope for a new philosophy that can be named not philosophy but science." (Ibid). Still, one can hardly hope "that the unification of the sciences will be effected correctly because it is the work of scientists." They are "not made of a different clay from mere philosophers." They are not exempt from the polymorphism of consciousness which makes it difficult to correctly grasp the ambiguities residing in such terms as knowledge, reality, objectivity." (Ibid).

GEM-FS, based on our cognitional operations, promotes authenticity. Throughout history, Christians, Muslims and secularists have used their cognitional operations for different, sometimes contradictory ends, but they all had to rely on their similarly functioning operations to do so. The challenge today is to adapt historical realities to the modern world. Here authenticity plays a large role. For Lonergan, an authentic person struggles to be attentive, intelligent, reasonable, and responsible. This precarious and ever-developing state depends on long, sustained faithfulness to the transcendental precepts (*Third Collection*, 8). There is a twofold authenticity: the minor one of a person obeying the rules of the tradition that nourishes one, and the major one[42] that justifies or condemns the tradition itself (*MiT*, 80). The minor authenticity leads to a person having to judge as to his or her operations. The major one depends on specific examples of transcending or advancing a tradition by developing the positive and eliminating the negative elements within it (*Third Collection*, 120-21). Having achieved authenticity, one can easily fall back into inauthenticity. (*MiT*, 110). In *Insight* (453-54), Lonergan contrasts a philosopher's authenticity with a scientist's reasonableness. While the latter is a consequence of the reasonableness of all, a philosopher's reasonableness is grounded on personal knowledge and commitments. One cannot settle philosophical issues by appealing to experiments performed by someone else or "by referring to the masterful presentation of overwhelming evidence in some famous work. Philosophic evidence lies within the philosopher himself. It is his own inability to avoid experience, to renounce intelligent inquiry," to be unreasonable in reflection. "It is his own detached, disinterested desire to know…his own advertence to the polymorphism of his own consciousness. It is his own insight into the manner in which insights accumulate in mathematics, in the empirical sciences," or in common sense. A philosopher strives for the dialectical unfolding of his desire to know in its conflict with other desires. This is the key to one's philosophical development; it reveals one's ability to adopt the stand of traditional or new philosophical schools. "Philosophy is the flowering of the individual's rational consciousness in its coming to know and take possession of itself. To that event, its traditional schools, its treatises, and its history are but contributions; and without that event they are stripped of real significance." (454).

B4. Grounds[43] for Being a Radically Authentic Person in Christianity, Islam, Buddhism or Secularity

There are Christians, Muslims, and secularists striving for major authenticity.[44] It is such pivotal persons who can help bridge the abstract notions called "Christianity," "Islam", "secularism." They respect true assertions as opposed to ideological ones. Consistent in their beliefs, they follow their conscience, striving to be authentic within the tradition into which they were born and raised but are open to dialogue with persons of other traditions. They differ from unauthentic persons who use their tradition's symbols – texts, images, rituals – to legitimate their attempts to satisfy desires other than the desire to know truly and to act conscientiously. In GEM-FS, one who has not appropriated one's own tradition is unlikely to be aware of it. So he/she does not recognize the difference between the kind of Christian, Muslim or Buddhist one is and what a genuine Christian, Muslim or Buddhist is. "My unawareness is unexpressed. I have no language to express what I am, so I use the language of the tradition I unauthentically appropriate." I thereby devalue, distort, water down, "corrupt that language." (*MiT*, 80). It is not altogether clear within Christianity, Islam, or secularism just what it is to be an "authentic"[45] member of a tradition. Many traditions contain sects, each of which has defined itself in opposition to one or more of the others on the basis of which one is authentic. Sect leaders denounce other sects as heretical, as having deviated from the "authentic" tradition in one or more truly important ways.[46]

Thomas Merton believed that he would be less of an authentic monk if he excluded the "experiential knowledge" of various non-Christian influences in his life. He noted in his *Journal* that two eminent pioneers in Catholic-Muslim relations, Louis Massignon and Charles de Foucauld "were both converted to Christianity by the witness of Islam to the one, true, living God." In 1966, Merton stayed up late on the 27th night of Ramadan to pray in solidarity with Muslims; later, he met the Algerian Sidi Abdeslam Sufi master at Gethsemani. Merton sensed that he and "Sidi Abdeslam were able to communicate beyond the translated words.... It was like meeting a Desert Father or someone out of the Bible,"[47] he wrote. Merton had also pursued a very personal correspondence since 1960 with a Muslim student of Sufism in Karachi named Abdul Aziz, who had read Merton's *The Ascent of Truth.*[48] Bede Griffith noted that by 1964 Merton had anticipated Vatican II's *Nostra Aetate*, asking, "How can one be in contact with the great thinkers and men of prayer of the various religions without recognizing that these men have known God and have loved Him because they recognized themselves loved by Him?"[49] As to the salvation of non-Christians, Merton wrote to Aziz: "Obviously the destiny of each individual person is a matter of his personal response to the truth and to the manifestation of God's will to him, and not merely a matter of belonging to this or that organization. ...Any man who follows his faith and his conscience, and responds truthfully and sincerely to what he believes to be the manifestation of the will of God, cannot help being saved by God . . . Personally, in matters where dogmatic beliefs differ, I think that controversy is of little value because it takes us away from the spiritual realities into the realm of words and ideas. In the realm of realities we may have a great deal in common, where in words there are apt to be infinite complexities and subtleties which are beyond resolution." For Merton, what mattered is "to try to understand the experience of divine light. . . that God gives us even as the Creator and Ruler of the Universe. It is here that the area of fruitful dialogue exists between Christianity and Islam."(Ibid).

As to the Christian doctrine of the Trinity, Merton tried to find a spiritual common ground: "The question of *Tawhid* (the confession that God is one) is of course central and I think that the closest to Islam among the Christian mystics on this point are the Rhenish and Flemish mystics of the fourteenth century, including Meister Eckhart, who was greatly influenced by Avicenna. The culmination of their mysticism is in the "Godhead" beyond "God" (a distinction which caused trouble to many theologians in the Middle Ages and is not accepted without qualifications) but at any rate it is an ascent to perfect and ultimate unity beyond the triad in unity of the Persons." Merton's search for grace in non-Christian religions led him to write to Czeslaw Milosz in 1962: "I cannot be a Catholic unless it is made quite clear to the world that I am a Jew and a Moslem, unless I am execrated as a Buddhist and denounced for having undermined all that this comfortable and social Catholicism stands for" such as the regimenting of cassocks or birettas. (Ibid). Merton's broad historical interpretation of authentic religion and worldviews give us a good entry to evaluate the vast subject of Christian-Muslim encounters for the past 1,400 years.

These encounters between Christians and Muslims as well as their encounters with secularized societies bring us back to the theme of radicality. GEM-FS is indeed radical. It turns on the transformative horizons of conversion. We have touched on Merton, Massignon and Charles de Foucauld, and on how Lonergan radically generalizes data to include those of sense and of consciousness--which enables us to recenter ourselves. GEM-FS judgments can enable us to radically reevaluate the present. Famous Muslim bridge-builders such as al-Ghazali, ibn Al-'Arabi and Rumi embodied a positive radicality—one that differs totally from that of Islamic terrorists.[50] It is for the latter to reevaluate acts of violence based on distorted beliefs. Supposedly "radicalized" young Muslims do not know what radicalization is in the good sense.

Perhaps Merton who wanted "to be as a good Buddhist"[51] can help us find the balanced type of radicality our world needs; his fertile mind may have discerned how a secular, agnostic or even atheistic Buddhism may help bridge religious and secular claims. Secular Buddhists interpret Buddhist texts in a rationalist way. One may explore human experience as understood from the perspective of Nagarjuna's philosophy of emptiness.[52] This, too, can help define the meaning or purpose of life despite its being agnostic. In principle, the Buddha sought to help humans be authentic. Nagarjuna and Merton's broad cultural groundings can be useful in reinforcing GEM-FS rejection of flawed views of "civilization".

B5. A Flawed "Clash of Civilization" Thesis and Interpretations of Cultural Differences[53]

Huntington's "Clash of Civilizations" thesis is problematic in that civilizations are "portrayed as playing the roles that nation-states played during the Cold War, ... seen as monolithic blocs acting on the geopolitical scene rather than as living and evolving organisms."[54] After the Sep. 11, 2001 attacks in New York, Rene Girard, known for his anthropology of violence, saw in that tragedy a "'mirror image rivalry' of an unprecedented scale. ... The resistance to the current globalization process emerging from different parts of the world and the various Islamist armed actions. . . are motivated not because of their intrinsic differences but because they are similar to what they fight against. 'They fight us because they look more and more like us.'" Girard saw Bush and Bin Laden as "'mimetic twins" striving for global impact and using a religious terminology based on binary logic (Crusades/Jihad, Good against Evil, etc.).[55]

Leaders were concerned about how they should respond to the ISIS attacks in Paris on November 13, 2015. This mindless slaughter of over 130 persons by a Muslim gang shocked the West. It led to rounds of solidarity and soul-searching. Some asked whether this atrocity would turn public opinion?[56] As to a response, we appeal to Lonergan's view that faith has the power of undoing decline. Decline "inflicts on individuals the social, economic, and psychological pressures that for human frailty amount to determinism. It multiplies and heaps up the abuses and absurdities that breed resentment, hatred. . ., violence." (*MiT*, 117). Neither propaganda nor argument, but rather religious faith can "liberate human reasonableness from its ideological prisons. Hope can help us resist the "vast pressures of social decay. If passions are to quiet down, if wrongs are not to be. . . merely palliated, then …human pride (has) to be replaced by religious charity, by the charity of the suffering servant, by self-sacrificing love." (ibid). It is a fact that Islamist as well as Christian and Jewish neo-fundamentalist' movements see themselves primarily as political actors rather than as spiritual movements. The fear of the Other is often based on the ignorance of the Other. This should prompt us to study more about natural law, the spirituality of Islam, its arts, its poets, writers, its times of being tolerant as it was in Spain for 700 years and partly in the Ottoman empire until the beginning of the 20th century." We must learn what transcends national borders. FS 3 history sets the stage for properly evaluating our mutual histories and aims.

Chapter Three

Third Functional Specialty

GEM-FS Judgments of Value[1] and Historical Perspectives

REFLECTING ON, EVALUATING SOME NOTED CHRISTIAN
AND MUSLIM THINKERS AND PRESENT REALITIES

A. Comparing Two Key 18th Century Figures: Muhammad ibn Abd al-Wahhab and Benjamin Franklin

Wahhab (1703-1792) and Franklin were contemporaries during the "Age of Enlightenment", but their "enlightenments" could hardly have been more different. Wahhab, born in Arabia, travelled widely in surrounding Islamic countries. In 1736, he began to strongly attack Sufism's inner mystical experiences. Upon his return to Arabia, he wrote the *Kitab at-tawhid* ("Book of Unity"), the main text of *Wahhabiyah* puritan doctrines which emphasize the absolute oneness of God (*tawhid*). Adopting the fundamentalist interpretation of Hanbali's traditional School of Law and the theology of Ibn Taymiyyah, Wahhabism means by *tawhid*, "to make one." It utterly excludes any analogy or quality in creation that reflects God. Except for the Quran, it "invalidates" the possibility of any holiness. Saudi Arabia's adoption of Wahhabism has led to many tensions with the West despite much ongoing petrodollar-based commerce.

Benjamin Franklin (1706-1790) was a renowned polymath, author, printer, political theorist, politician, freemason, inventor, civic activist, an influential and well-travelled statesman-diplomat. It is debated whether he was more of a deist than a Christian. For us, he was a pioneer of secularity. Wahhab and Franklin embodied some of the antipodal belief-scientific worldviews this book is trying to bridge. Even on the question of mysticism, the two men diverged. While Franklin, a Rosicrucian, helped design the occult-mystical [2] Great Seal of the United States, Wahhab tolerated no form of mysticism. As opposed to the de facto incompatibilities between a Wahhab and a Franklin, we invoke some "patron saints" of a GEM-FS bridge such as the efforts of scholars that predate and postdate the two men's careers.

B. Muslim Scholars Were the West's Benefactors during the Early Middle Ages

Western universities owe much of their foundational knowledge to the philosophical and scientific enterprise undertaken in the Arab world during the early Middle Ages – in major intellectual centers that included Baghdad, Cordoba and Cairo. During Islam's Golden Age, Muslim, Christian and Jewish scholars collaborated to create the first medieval encyclopedias. The resulting synthesis of Greek, Roman, Persian, Hindu, and Arabic scholarship became the foundation for the medieval universities of the West-- beginning about 1100 with the medical faculty of Salerno.[3] The Greek classics did serve as the basis of both Muslim and Western learning and their ensuing dialogues. This type of fruitful dialogue needs to be revived so as to include both mysticism and secularity tenets. GEM-FS is partly rooted in secularity. In *MiT*, Lonergan explores the human good, the various aspects of meaning and mysticism. Implicit here are the work of Islamic and Western medieval thinkers. Lonergan pioneered seminal bridges between religious hearts and the minds intent on (secular) knowledge. We argue that al-Ghazali is one of the "patron saints" of converted, apophatic-kataphatic engagement compatible with secularity tenets.

C. The Arab Spring in Tunisia, Egypt and Syria and the Ensuing Islamic-Secular Conflicts

The Arab Spring began in 2011 in Tunisia with a young man burning himself to death in protest of police mistreatment. Tunisia, saved by a National Dialogue Quartet (recipients of the 2015 Nobel Peace Prize) is the only country to have responded reasonably to demands for change. The Quartet, formed in 2013, has helped stabilize democracy in Tunisia in spite of political assassinations and a looming civil war. It helped steer Tunisia toward a constitutional system of government guaranteeing basic rights for the entire population irrespective of religious belief. Still, many young Tunisians have joined ISIS. Sadly, other Middle East nations such as Egypt and Syria have fared much worse than Tunisia. Following the Arab Spring, Egypt underwent much turmoil. General al-Sisi, having deposed the elected Muslim Brotherhood President Morsi, established a short-term doctrine for stability calling for 1) a more limited role for sharia (still enshrined in the new constitution) yet no longer to be interpreted by clerics at al-Azhar University, but by the government whose outlook is more secular than religious; 2) an electoral democracy with somewhat limited civil liberties, to satisfy both the demand for popular sovereignty and for an end to the endless chaos—strikes, demonstrations, skyrocketing crime--following the fall of Mubarak in 2011. It has limited the public role of the Islamists deemed to be "at war" with Egypt.[4]

Syria is the biggest victim of the Arab Spring. The Alawi-led government has been plagued by many rebel movements including ISIS which have devastated the country leading to mass emigration.[5] Observers now predict the end of the infamous 1916 Sykes-Picot's Agreement that set up the Arab states system. Tunisia's apt "transvaluation of values," in response to pressing needs, is a possible "model" for a GEM-FS bridge. As we now write in early 2016, the "Arab Spring" has turned into a catastrophe for millions of refugees. Some have made it to Europe whose people and infrastructures feel threatened. Such Catholic countries as Poland have been inhospitable. Self-centered personal or national responses want to ignore today's problems rooted in history. Refugees have been stranded in disastrous situations. FS 3 urges all Christians, Muslims and secularists to evaluate and judge our present global dilemmas. Is mercy to go abegging on the practical level? Can nations together salvage the ideals of an "Arab Spring"? We seek ways for humans to deepen their faith while being anchored in ethics and in a GEM-like metaphysics.

D. Needed Transvaluations of Values in Christianity, Islam and Secularity: A Bridge of Mercy

Nietzsche wanted to transvalue values, but he could hardly have anticipated how an ex-Muslim woman, Ayaan Hirsi Ali, a Somali-born Dutch-American writer-politician would harshly criticize Islam including its practice of female genital mutilation. Now an atheist who supports women's rights, she identifies more with the American *literati* than with the secular dissidents dying in Bangladesh and Pakistan, or jailed in Turkey and Iran.[6] She writes: "I am now one of you: a Westerner. I share with you the pleasures of . . . campus cafes. I know we Western intellectuals cannot lead a Muslim Reformation. But we do have an important role to play."[7] She is trying to transvalue Islamic values calling for a "reformation" in Islam. She asks: "Can religions be reformed through reason and logic?" This would require that Muslims learn to critically exegete the Quran as Christians have done to biblical studies. "We do have an important role to play. We must no longer accept limitations on criticism of Islam. We must reject the notions that only Muslims can speak about Islam, and that any critical examination of Islam is inherently racist. Instead of distorting Western intellectual traditions so as not to offend our Muslim fellow citizens, we need to defend the Muslim dissidents who are risking their lives to promote human rights… equality for women, tolerance of all religions and orientations, our hard-won freedoms of speech and thought." (Ibid).

In reviewing Hirsi Ali's book, *Heretic*, Tarek Fatah[8] writes: "Christians believe a snake in the Garden of Eden could speak to a human. Hindus are convinced a monkey once flew holding a mountain on the palm of his right hand. Muslims are certain Mohammed flew on a winged horse (undoubtedly inspired by Pegasus). The difference between Muslims and other religious believers is that many Muslims still believe in the mixing of religion and politics, whereas the rest of the world now uses faith mainly as a moral compass, rather than a basis for legislation." (Ibid). Transvaluations of values in Christianity, Islam and secularism are needed. A GEM-FS Third Way of the heart and mind helps us integrate our emotions in sound ways. Its apophatic, value-laden sources can help Christians, Muslims and secularists transvalue values in ways that avoid ideologies and promote mutual respect and fruitful collaboration. It recognizes forms of secularity that allow faith or personal convictions to become moral compasses. It is a bridge of mercy, one that, in theory at least, is common to the world religions and to some secularists.[9] One of this book's aims is to test how secularity (even secularism) can help lay a bridge of mercy in our world--a middle-ground position between believers and non-believers that integrates their values and emotions.

Lonergan's Third Way of the Heart and Mind:
A Bridge of Mercy Integrating Values and Emotions

If for many people today, beliefs now mostly serve as a "moral compass", Lonergan's Third Way helps us transvalue values in Christian-Muslim-secularist encounters. Mark Doorley has noted the role of feelings in Lonergan's work.[10] He reflects on how "uneducated" people have often taught him much about an existential or moral commitment to God. How did they arrive at such a deep knowledge of God? The answer is that each spoke from the heart; it was in their "guts" (xiii). This is important. Lonergan was interested in how the human good is to be realized through the cooperative efforts of human beings under the sway of God's grace.[11] His reflections on such cooperative efforts led him to wonder about human feelings. Moral effort is not merely rational; feelings "are involved as well" (Doorley, xv). GEM-FS's transvaluation of values adopts a middle ground between emotivism and rationalism. It denies that our emotions are either separate from or superior to reason. Rather, the emotions play a key role in practical reasoning, but the balance is not an easy one to strike. Neither Aquinas nor the *early* Lonergan quite achieved this balance for both tended toward rationalism. Even *Insight*'s study of our conscious intentional operations all too often treats our feelings as obstacles to an unrestricted desire to know. *Insight* does recognize the importance of feelings in decision-making. It was the influence of Max Scheler and Dietrich von Hildebrand that helped the later Lonergan develop a typology of feelings and their roles[12] in our lives. He began to approach human realities through the prism of the heart. His Third Way of the heart and mind helps us integrate our emotions. Doing so can help all persons (religious or secular) orient their lives through transformative love purifying the pleadings of our hearts. It is well when practical persons realize the need for an integrative theory such as GEM-FS. The great world religions owe much to the heart. One must not overly get caught up in details thus losing the overall impact of GEM-FS' Third Way which helps us put secularity in perspective. This Third Way's apophatic base helps lead to an ethical love-in-action. It relativizes "ideological isms" such as predatory capitalism, Macchiavellism or a secularism not in tune with secularity. Its ethics is open to universal values but resists moralism, media hype or biases that trivialize or belittle sound achievements. Moreover, it is consonant with the insights of some of the most profound Christian mystics and philosophers in the realm of human interiority and holiness such as Jean-Luc Marion's rereading of Denys the Aeropagite.[13]

E. Overcoming Biases in Religious Teachings to Help Erect Inclusive Apophatic-Kataphatic Bridges

Universities should strive to have religious traditions taught in as pluralistic a way as possible. Religious texts could be written with a holistic goal in mind. The Christian story of the Good Samaritan or Muhammad's inclusive Medina Charter could serve as models for this. A danger is that political and religious leaders manipulate teachings to serve their agenda. For example, a government in South East Asia formerly discouraged the Buddhist teaching of being content with a simple life—not good for the economy. Academically, theologians' interpretations tend to differ from those of religious studies departments. There is a lack of inter- and intra-disciplinary cooperation. A global secularity ethics can foster trust and lead to legitimate forms of cooperation based on enlightened understandings so as to accept differences. Professors from different departments should be partners, doing justice to value-laden teaching, recognizing the limits of "value-free" research. Presently, there is not enough dialogue or interaction between economics and theology departments. As a result, neither religious nor secular ethical views are fully understood or judiciously applied in economic theory. A human-rights ethics, respecting both religious and secularity values, would reinforce the roles of values and virtues.

Religious teachings have been sources of inspiration for ethical reforms (abolition of slavery, justice and peace). How can religious traditions today learn to speak to present needs, live ethically, be fortified in today's pluralistic societies? A secular ethics is not in conflict with religious ethics. Both strive to foster understanding and oppose evil. History can deepen our understanding of why, for example, among Africans everything has a religious aspect, which renders notions of secularism moot. Instead of stressing differences, one should respect contextuality. In FS 5, we shall investigate how mystics of many traditions can help us live apophatic-based ethical love. But first, in FS 4 we explore how a GEM-FS bridge dialectically balances apophatic-kataphatic and secularist realities to point us in the right direction.

Chapter Four

Fourth Functional Specialty

Dialectics¹ Pointing to Where We Need to Go: GEM-FS' Apophatic-Kataphatic Ability Can Help Integrate Secularity with the World's Religions

Unfortunately, religious fundamentalists of all stripes tend to paint themselves into positions that pit one against the other.² A GEM-FS bridge of mercy's logic of the heart would do well to recall the quality of mercy—esteemed by Christians and Muslims and praised in Portia's soliloquy in *The Merchant of Venice*:

> The quality of mercy is not strain'd,
> It droppeth as the gentle rain from heaven
> Upon the place beneath: it is twice blest;
> It blesseth him that gives and him that takes.

This book addresses both GEM-FS theoretical and practical issues as it seeks to balance emotions and reasoning. Its see-judge-act subtemplates complement our GEM-FS template—practical ways to address some of the realities plaguing our modern world: the super-rich ever extending their share of wealth and leftists' reactions;³ religious fundamentalists' divisiveness; Muslim immigrants in Europe marginalized in enclaves. Our apophatic-kataphatic strategy reaches deeply into GEM-FS's operational range so as to deploy its religious and secularity aspects. There are various ways to show how GEM-FS' third way of heart and mind can help bridge the divides between Christianity, Islam and secularism despite conflicting historical hopes and interpretations.⁴ All too often efforts to bridge human divides have been derailed.

Matthew Lamb's study of how Aquinas approached Christian Scripture can help us evaluate how modern and postmodern thought have derailed the search for wisdom—a derailment that this book tries to salvage with an ethical-spirituality. "Wisdom has to do with the apprehension of order,"[5] that is how we come to understand that spacetime is an ordered whole present in the divine eternal now. Coming to terms with divine eternity as the source of order and meaning in history is intrinsic to wisdom. Lamb shows how Augustine wedded the Platonic concern for human intelligence *as spiritual* to the Christian commitment to the word of God *as true*. Such a commitment entails that history itself is a field of divine meaning." (Ibid). This book traces parallel developments in Muslim philosophy and its derailment by jurists. Augustine had taken "intelligence in act as the analogue for approaching the mystery of God, whose loving understanding creates and orders the meaningful totality of times and places" (Ibid). We argue that, on the Islamic side, bridge-building Sufis such as Ibn al-'Arabi, al-Ghazali and Rumi laid apophatic paths for Muslims to deal with complex kataphatic problems of the type Aquinas addressed on the Christian side. While Aquinas' synthesis helped lay metaphysical foundations for modern science, Islamic legal scholars cut off from valid metaphysical underpinnings have laid barriers to dialogue.[6] Augustine's spiritual path became possible only because he had been converted morally, intellectually, and religiously. Lamb argues that unless we, too, are converted we will be unable to reach up to the mind of Augustine. "Christian wisdom depends upon a deep personal transformation, which involves, among other things, intellectual probity as a form of purity of heart. Boethius and Thomas Aquinas were worthy heirs of Augustine, but their achievement was derailed by voluntarism and nominalism, where divine power and will eclipsed divine wisdom as the key categories for conceiving God's relationship to the world. This derailment leads directly into the modern project, preoccupied with power relations and convinced that divine sovereignty and human autonomy compete in a zero-sum game." (Ibid)

RECENT INITIATIVES TO OVERCOME THE DERAILMENTS OF DIALOGUE: EFFORTS TO BRIDGE RELIGIOUS DIVIDES

Maria Hornung has pointed to how persons engaged in interfaith dialogue must probe their worldviews, sets of values and ways of interrelating with others.[7] She envisions various ways to respond to another's world and describes some of the transformational processes this requires, such as individuation, a deeper sense of integrity, inclusivity of others, and an ability to constructively speak to global realities. She writes of a paradigm shift towards a global awakening, a transformed relationship and a global transforming of life and behavior. "The communion I experience with all – self, others, and the Earth – is profound. I sense that my care for myself is integral to the care of the whole." (Ibid, 59). One becomes irrevocably reshaped by a world in relationship. The traditional view of religious belief is that it helps explain life's ultimate meaning, providing a communal structure as to how to live "based on the notion of the transcendent with which the believers have a relationship (cult)."[8] It proposes a code of behavior as to all the psychological, social, and cultural dimensions of human life. The traditional view of religion is now challenged to respond to the pressing problems of globalization and terrorist attacks.

JOINT CHRISTIAN-MUSLIM CONSULTATIONS AFTER THE NOVEMBER 12-13, 2015 ATTACKS IN BEIRUT AND PARIS

A few days after a series of terrorist attacks devastated Beirut and Paris in November, 2015, Muslim and Christian leaders gathered in Paris to discuss possible religious peacemaking roles in education and in promoting dialogue to put an end to violence around the world. Episcopalian Bishop Pierre Whalon, an engaged GEM-FS scholar, hosted at his Cathedral a panel of Muslim theologians from the World Union of Experts of Islam for Peace and Against Violence. "There are acts of violence committed" such as those in Paris, "that can be attributed to a false teachings of hatred" said Sheik Mustafa Rashed president of the Union. "We want to update this sort of teaching, now that we have done a complete evaluation of it. We are at a turning point. We cannot rewrite the Qu'ran, but there is enormous latitude in the interpretation of its verses. Those that evoke violence must be contextualized in light of history; they are no longer applicable."[9] Rashed, in effect, is here expressing views in conformity with FS 2 and FS 3. For Rashed, "there are 660,000 hadith [sayings], but only 2,240 are true. There is an immediate action to take, and another that is very long-term – a reform of Muslim teaching. That has never before been done ... We have launched a reform coming from inside Islam to train imams who reject violence." (Ibid).

Whalon, for his part, noted that the teachings of all religious traditions are susceptible to extremist views and violence. "Christianity has no moral high ground historically. The wars of religion in the seventeenth century left a third of Europe's population dead, all in the name of the Prince of Peace. Dialogue is the only way forward." (Ibid). These reflections on the post-Paris attacks reflect this book's calls to overcome dogmatic Christian-Muslim fundamentalisms with hearts converted to faith and mercy. With Rashed, we argue that tackling rabid fundamentalist claims involves both short-term and long-term policies. Political leaders must address present problems. In European cities, Muslims are mostly confined to enclaves that marginalize, frustrate the young--some of whom react violently. Germany has been pioneering ways to help integrate young Muslims--its third-generation Turkish contingent--as well as its newly arrived refugees by offering them more educational opportunities. The migrations have polarized Germans. To deal with polarization, this book concurs with Rashed's proposal that would encourage Islam to reform its teachings. Such a reform must be undertaken by Muslims themselves—but it is not easy. Appeals by Professor Mouhana Khorchinide at the University of Münster to adapt Islam to modern Western societies have been met by threats from Salafist extremists in Germany. Erudite Muslim thinkers who have migrated to the West need counterparts in Muslim nations to develop paths for a tolerant Islam.[10]

Lonergan's "cosmopolis" may help address both short-term and long-term policies. Cosmopolis would "make operative the ideas that, in the light of the general bias of common sense, are inoperative" (*Insight*, 263). We call for new forms of world cooperation aimed to overcome human biases. The great Muslim bridge-builders, al-Ghazali, ibn al-'Arabi and Rumi knew how to radically adapt Islam to changing conditions. Muslim terrorists embody a wrong kind of radicality--a false notion of religion based on distorted beliefs in need of reevaluation. We stress Pope Francis' focus on mercy; humans need to overcome biases in ways that complement Charles Taylor's views on a needed secularity today. In doing so, we repeat that this book's stress on GEM-FS' normative pattern of operations includes the roles of the heart and of mercy so as to arrive at cumulative and progressive results. Our Third Way is founded on the apophatic developed in *MiT* as well as on the more kataphatic approach of *Insight*. It insists that humans' normative pattern of operations and their rules can and should lead to cooperation. Our GEM-FS template integrates the kataphatic and apophatic in ways that complement Charles Taylor's thesis.

HOW GEM-FS APOPHATIC-KATAPHATIC APPLICATIONS COMPLEMENT CHARLES TAYLOR'S INSIGHTS

This book's spiritual-ethical focus enlists mercy as well Charles Taylor's secularity approach. Taylor helps us reinforce GEM-FS as both a secular and religious method.[11] GEM-FS pivots on integrating the roles of the kataphatic operative in the mediating phase with the apophatic that informs the mediated phase. Taylor notes that every person and every society has a notion of what human flourishing is. One asks "what constitutes a fulfilled life?" or "what makes it really worth living?" Trying to answer such questions "define the view or views that we try to live by . . . . These views are codified, sometimes in philosophical theories, sometimes in moral codes, sometimes in religious practices and devotion. These and the various ill-formulated practices which people around us engage in constitute the resources that our society offers each one of us as we try to lead our lives." (*Secular Age*, 72). Taylor then asks "does the highest, the best life involve our seeking, or acknowledging, or serving a good which is beyond, in the sense of independent of human flourishing? In which case, the highest, most real, authentic or adequate human flourishing could include our aiming . . .at something other than human flourishing." Even "the most self-sufficing humanism has to be concerned with the condition of some non-human things" such as the environment. The issue is whether, in the final instance, they do matter. The Judeo-Christian religious tradition answers this question affirmatively. "In this tradition God is seen as willing human flourishing, but devotion to God is not seen as contingent on this. The injunction "Thy will be done" isn't equivalent to "Let humans flourish", even though we know that God wills human flourishing. (73).

Taylor argues that Buddhism is one tradition which takes us "beyond ordinary human flourishing." We can construe the Buddha's message "as telling us how to achieve true happiness, that is, how to avoid suffering, and attain bliss." But the Buddhist view is a revisionist one in that "it amounts to a departure from what we normally understand as human flourishing" that can be put in terms of a radical change of identity. Normal understandings of flourishing assume a continuing self, its beneficiary, or in the case of its failure the sufferer." In Buddhism, *anatta* (nothingness) "aims to bring us beyond this illusion"; *nirvana* "involves renouncing, or at least going beyond all forms of recognizable human flourishing." Despite this great difference in doctrine between Buddhism and Christianity, there is something similar, that is, "the believer or devout person is called on to make a profound inner break with the goals of flourishing in their own case." They are called on to detach self from one's "own flourishing, to the point of the extinction of self in one case, or to that of renunciation of human fulfillment to serve God in the other. The respective patterns are clearly visible in their exemplary figures. The Buddha achieves Enlightenment; Christ consents to a degrading death to follow his father's will." In both religions, a form of renunciation is required. "In the Christian case, the very point of renunciation requires that the ordinary flourishing forgone be confirmed as valid. Unless living the full span were a good, Christ's giving of himself to death couldn't have the meaning it does. In this it is utterly different from Socrates' death, which the latter portrays as leaving this condition for a better one." (Ibid). Here, Taylor finds an "unbridgeable gulf between Christianity and Greek philosophy." God wills ordinary human flourishing as is reported in great detail in the Gospels. Christ makes this possible for the people whose afflictions he heals. "The call to renounce doesn't negate the value of flourishing; it is rather a call to center everything on God, even if it be at the cost of forgoing this unsusbtitutable good; and the fruit of this forgoing is that it become on one level the source of flourishing to others, and on another level, a collaboration with the restoration of a fuller flourishing by God. It is a mode of healing wounds and "repairing the world" (I am here borrowing the Hebrew phrase *tikkun olam*)." (73-74)—acts of kindness to perfect the world.

Flourishing and renunciation cannot be collapsed into each other to make a single goal, by as it were, pitching the renounced goods overboard as unnecessary ballast on life's journey in the manner of Stoicism. "There remains a fundamental tension in Christianity. Flourishing is good, nevertheless seeking it is not our ultimate goal. But even where we renounce it, we reaffirm it, because we follow God's will in being a channel for it to others, and ultimately to all." (Ibid). Taylor is not sure that such a paradoxical relation exists in Buddhism which also has a notion that the renouncer is a source of compassion for those who suffer. There is an analogy between *karuna* and *agape*. Over the centuries in Buddhism there developed, "parallel with Christendom, a distinction of vocation between radical renouncers, and those who go on living within the forms of life aiming at ordinary flourishing, while trying to accumulate 'merit' for a future life." (75), a notion which was radically "deconstructed"[12] in the Protestant Reformation.

Taylor harps on the distinction between human flourishing and goals which go beyond it. He claims that the coming of modern secularity in his sense "has been coterminous with the rise of a society in which for the first time in history a purely self-sufficient humanism came to be a widely available option." That is, we now have a humanism that accepts "no final goals beyond human flourishing, nor any allegiance to anything else beyond this flourishing. Of no previous society was this true." (75). Taylor does *not* claim that modern secularity[13] is coterminous with exclusive humanism. (76). We agree with Taylor's two senses of "coterminous". For us, an ethical secularity is open to a transformative[14] self-transcendence. Taylor's two senses of coterminous mean that while secularity is coterminous with a "purely sufficient humanism", it is not coterminous with an *exclusive* humanism. Still, in practice this distinction tends to be overlooked or ignored; this ignorance has led to many confusions as to the role of a valid secularity.

If humanity is at present mired in a mud of confusing possibilities from which it is hard put to extricate itself, this book's complex double-pronged GEM-FS strategy requires mutual understanding and needed transformations. Its GEM-FS horizon detects both false and helpful attempts to extricate humanity from its present plight. Using see-judge-act subtemplates,[15] we distinguish between a secularism opposed to religion and a secularity able to address the need for mutual tolerance between religions and secularism.

Flannery O'Connor and Bin Laden are two persons who lived out their own version of a see-judge-act method. Neither of them was a philosopher or a theologian. Upon "seeing" modern trends, both judged that secularism can be nefarious; both acted according to their very different views. O'Connor was in the minority in opposing secularism. As did Dante, O'Connor boldly underscored human sinfulness, our need for divine grace.[16] She used dark humor in doing so. Bin Laden was transformed into a charismatic leader after his having been a callow young man who "couldn't lead eight ducks across the street."[17] Some observers, detecting Bin Laden's unresolved Oedipal problems toward his powerful and wealthy father, have explored the roles that various older mentors played in his growing radicalization.[18]

Today's secularist trends serve as one of the determining but not easily identifiable signs of the *malaise* which O'Connor and Lonergan (among others) knew could not be ignored. If persons like O'Connor and Osama bin Laden saw, judged and acted in their own ways toward what they perceived as unacceptable forms of secularism, we also appeal to philosophy to examine secularism, including its positive sides. In a way, Taylor's analysis implicitly employs various FS outlined in *MIT*. Reinforcing GEM-FS's mediating phase's dialectical efforts, Taylor's analyses are pertinent to dialogues among the world religions. His *Secular Age* traces three overlapping stages of a "secular" separation of Church and State:

A society is secular,

1. where its political government does not have religious authority;
2. when its public spaces and institutions do not require, or even exclude mention of religion;
3. where the conditions for religious belief are absent or where the mentality of the times excludes any serious consideration of religious values.

Secularists want to create religion-less societies. Many western societies went through the three above stages as they moved from the dominant religious culture of 16th century Europe, to contemporary non-(or anti)-religious culture of western societies, dominated by secular-techno-commercialism. Islamic history has been on a different trajectory. This difference leads us to ask how Taylor's notion of separation of Church and State can be helped by how Lonergan in his eight FS divides tasks. Here in Part Two, we develop the first mediating phase (FS 1-4) of the GEM-FS template. In Part Three's treatment of the second mediated phase (FS 5-8), we shall apply the GEM-FS template to concrete situations—giving special attention to what we call a see-judge-act method.[19] As to the future prospects of Christianity, we answer with a GEM-FS perspective. Our book's mediating-mediated phases would help lay a basis for a renewed "version" of self-transcendent Christianity "in touch" with other religions and secularity processes. Christians can help "mediate" between Islam and a secularism that most Muslims are unable to understand due to Islam's abandonment of philosophy.[20]

THE AGE OF SECULARISM AND THE RISE OF A COTERMINOUS ETHICAL SECULARITY

Taylor notes how the concept of "secular" in French (*laicité*) has undergone a significant change over the past three centuries. In the 17th century, "secular" was used grammatically as part of an internal dyad--words linked together as up and down, left and right, out and in. "Secular" was understood as inseparable from the meaning of "sacred". It was a temporal word referring to "this age or in time" from the Latin word, *saecularis*, as opposed to the Latin word for sacred, *Sanctus*, which refers to what is outside of time, the Divine. Earlier, "it was virtually impossible not to believe in God." (*Secular Age*, 56).

Christianity has consistently attended to ordinary human flourishing in deference to an inscrutable divine grace.[21] With deism, grace was eclipsed in that people endowed with reason and benevolence need only these faculties to carry out God's plan. God's providence, once a mystery, was now just God's plan. For Feuerbach, "the potentialities we have attributed to God are really human potentialities." (251). Taylor traces the eclipse of grace and providence through a series of developments. In the first development, secularity tended to be interpreted as if science has credibly deprived religious belief of its plausibility. In this view, secularity is just an inescapable consequence of the rise of science: religious beliefs get crowded out by science so that some now speak of the "death of God". Taylor refutes such explanations, which he labels "subtraction stories": the idea that modern humanity has liberated itself from earlier, confining horizons, illusions, or limitations of knowledge. For Taylor, secularity is not just the result of a gradual disenchantment.[22] Rather, it arose out of a newly invented self-understanding. Such a self-understanding is not a theory about ourselves but a lived understanding, "the construal we just live in, without ever being aware of it as a construal or – for most of us – without ever even formulating it". (30) The new self-understanding arose "as buffered, bounded selves required new inner sources of moral power. During the Enlightenment, one of these new sources proved to be disengaged reason, freeing us from our narrow perspective and allowing us a view of the whole, thereby kindling a desire to serve that whole" (64). Science could now pursue objective truths with universal validity (universalization).

In the second development, through the practice of introspection, a rich vocabulary of interiority developed. Humans began to see themselves as having inner depths. Even more strongly, the depths which were previously located in the cosmos, the enchanted world, were now placed within. (91). Spiritual life began to refer to how one accesses or reaches those inner depths (psychologization).

A third development is that in Western societies, a culture of "authenticity'" or expressive individualism arose. People have been encouraged to discover their own fulfillment. The last half-century is dubbed by Taylor "the age of authenticity". The individuality that characterized modernity has shifted into a widespread expressive individualism. Each one of us has his or her own way of realizing our humanity. It is important to find and live out one's own way. Many forms of therapy encourage their clients to find themselves, realize their true self. In the context of expressive individualism, it is not necessary to embed our search for the sacred in any broader religious framework. Doctrinal issues seem irrelevant. One can only connect with the sacred through passion and deeply felt personal insight. The spiritual as such is no longer intrinsically related to society. The spiritual path becomes a personal search (individualization).

These three trends of universalization, psychologization and individualization came together in the development of the concept of "religious experience". In order to shield religion from the discoveries of science, a distinction was made between the diverse cultural manifestations of religions, and the universal experiential ground of religion. For the latter, the term "religious experience" was coined.[23] In this book, we focus on people's inner depths so as to retrieve a sense of divine presence in our lives.[24]

Poland and the Residual Christianity in the West; Radical Christian-Islamic Renewals in Africa

This book seeks to apply GEM-FS-transvaluing perspectives to traditional cultures in the light of today's complexities. We have been asking how GEM-FS could help remedy some of today's cultural impasses. It is "clear" to a Kaczynski and his "Law and Justice" Party in Poland that a somewhat militant secularism must be confronted.[25] The party's success in the 2015 election led to reactionary laws that in effect manipulate constitutional provisions as to the judicial process and the freedom of the press. At issue in Poland is whether secularity is "coterminous" with the rise of a society in which a purely self-sufficient humanism is desirable. The issue arises less in Islam due to its traditional cultural-political perspectives. A GEM-FS transvaluing heart-mind perspective finds a more auspicious model in Africa where a sense of religion and community is alive. Faith shines in Africa--immersed as it is in genuine religious sensitivity.

CAUTIOUS REALIST OPTIMISM AS WE TRANSITION FROM *MIT*'S MEDIATING PHASE TO ITS MEDIATED PHASE

Today's globalization and its many crises call for caution. The flow of refugees now "haunting" European nations are a case in point. As of this writing, the European Union is in disarray. Rightist parties in Europe now flourish due to fears of Muslim immigrants; they argue that Muslims fuel poverty and violence.[26] Muslim terrorists accuse the West of decadent perversions. A largely de-Christianized West has lost its grip on the Christian virtues that had nurtured it. We recall Sheik Rashed's words that the Quran has an "enormous latitude" for reinterpretation of teachings that have been falsely seized upon by terrorists.

Our radical theology of the heart seeks to transcend words' destructive powers through a GEM-FS global ethical-secularity bridge. It calls for foundational, non-fundamentalist ways to interpret religion. A key to such a radical theology is our stress on apophatic faith as being the source of all genuine religious kataphatic beliefs. On this point, Nicos Mouzelis and William Franke are helpful. Mouzelis notes that Freud practiced a type of apophatic "self-analysis." A subject does not construct what is to be done in rationalistic a way; it emerges spontaneously, "unproblematically." Mouzelis calls this "apophatic" as "opposed to Giddens' cataphatic, affirmative ... reflection."[27] For Franke, apophatic thought is the "missing mean between radically secular and radically orthodox theology."[28] It enables unprejudiced dialogue among religious faiths and secular cultures. This parallels this book's approach. Secularity, can serve as the criterion of an authenticity that undercuts rabid secular-atheist contentions even if the apophatic is fathomed by only a small minority of humans—those attuned to God's love. Freud, Franke and Mouzelis can help us extend the effective role of the apophatic in our lives. Christian churches have different levels of efficient organizations. Muslims are grounded on the Quran, but Islam's various traditions conflict with one another. GEM-FS is modelled in humans' creative process; we do realize that many human actions are rooted in illusion, bias or the lust to dominate. One wishes that the messages of Jesus and Muhammad would not be undermined as in fact they have been. GEM-FS can help fulfill the need for policies of tolerance in all nations (see FS 6). GEM-FS lays the ground for such policies in FS 5 which supplies GEM-FS models and general and special categories based on a transcultural base.

Prior to modernity, "very few people could be recognized as individual human beings, as separated from their collective and religious belonging, such as Jews, Muslims or Christians as far as the Mediterranean and European areas were concerned."[29] A focus on the individual began in Italy during the Renaissance. On the positive side, it is strong, innovative individuals who have changed society. Today, Western individualism and secularists' vague, tempting appeals[30] influence humans' daily lives. In transitioning from *MiT*'s mediating phase to its mediated phase, we seek to link GEM-FS *personal* psychic, intellectual, moral and religious conversions to *vastly complicated political* processes ruling our lives as well as to the conflicting meanings of "liberal" in the English language. Thomas Hill Green (1836-82) balanced the usual emphasis on individualism prevalent in liberal thought with a stress on the "organic" society and the value of community ethos. With Green, we stress that persons have obligations towards the community. As to John Stuart Mill's ideas on liberalism, they must be understood in the context of the historic circumstances in his lifetime, including the highly unequal socio-economic consequences of the industrial revolution. In contrast to Western individualism,[31] Muslims remain devoted to their prayer (*salah*) commitments which places Allah, the Merciful, at the center of their communal lives: individuals are rooted in the community. Buddhists still have a deep respect for *sangha* monastic communities and the socio-ethical implications of the *Dharma* (cosmic law and order).[32]

Can Lonergan's third way of self-transcendence[33] of heart and mind and his transformative praxis help Buddhists, Christians, Muslims and secularists meet one another in needed, mutually beneficial encounters? We turn to GEM-FS's mediated phase which calls all persons to initiate future changes beginning with one's own deeper self.

III

Sketching a GEM-FS Bridge's Mediated Phase as Outlined in *MiT*'s Last Four Specialties: Toward Enabling Needed Transformative Changes[1] among the Religions and Secularity

In Part Two's chapters 1-4, we stressed that interiority-based conversions are indispensable for bridging religion and secularity; we noted that see-judge-act subtemplates can help conduct dialogues between Christians, Muslims and secular persons with the view of empowering one another. Chapters 5-8 on the last four FS outline ways in which such empowering can be effectively pursued. All actors in a vast dialogue such as this book undertakes should understand the deep historical and social-cultural implications that have led to the sometimes contrary claims of believers or secularists. The Middle East and Europe have been shaken to the roots by war, uncertainty, migrations. If, as we noted, conversion implies transvaluations of values, *MiT*'s mediated phase challenges us further; its foundations lays a base for coalitions of the willing in search of adequate answers that may help empower a tolerant future.

Chapter Five

Fifth Functional Specialty

Foundations¹ and Its Underlying Premises

EVALUATING-DIFFERENTIATING THE FOUNDATIONAL
SCRIPTURES OF CHRISTIANITY AND ISLAM

Our text's GEM-FS template focuses on our four "knowing-doing" operations which it interlinks in various theoretical and practical ways. GEM-FS's openness to both secular and faith-based commitments helps us address concrete problems. Its openness helps us critically compare the founding Scriptures and authoritative texts of both Christianity and Islam. The Holy Texts and their stories recite Divine-human encounters. Within these scriptural frameworks—which provide the meaning-giving structures in the subconscious of individuals, communities, and cultures— human beings determine their destiny on earth in the here and now and in the hereafter. From this perspective, religions' Holy Texts can be considered foundational to cultures and their peoples. They are sacred compendiums—the stories of cultures and peoples, their sufferings, conflicts, joys, hopes, loves, beginnings and ends; they tell how these stories interweave the human and the Divine, the sacred and the profane, and, ultimately, timeless life. Recalling the imperative of these dimensions of religion and culture for human existence, in this book we consider a range of conflict situations and explore whether and how dialogue may play a pivotal role in bringing about transformation at the personal, societal, and global levels.² An ethical secularity knows that Christianity and Islam both have adherents who seek prayerful communion with God. However, words and beliefs can get in the way and provoke conflicts. Our ethical secularity, buttressed by the apophatic roots of a "union" with God, seeks to transvalue "kataphatic-secular" conflicts with mercy.

THE APOPHATIC OF MYSTICS AND THE FURTHER ROLE OF INTERIORITY

For Lonergan, a person is changed for the better through intellectual, moral and religious conversions which "revolutionize" one's thinking and basic commitments. In implementing the GEM-FS revolution, conversion, as "foundational reality" (*MiT*, 267), helps one evaluate the past so as to guide the future with needed changes. GEM-FS foundations also depend on one's cognitional operations from which all human knowledge and culture arise. This book on Lonergan's Third Way of heart and mind asks how persons might be converted to living a merciful, ethical secularity. It develops GEM-FS' insight-based critical realism and explores its transformative potential when applied to cultures and to academic disciplines. It adverts to personal horizons of development needed to lay viable grounds for developing the human good. The human good requires personal actions and community developments informed by history. Foundations for applying the human good in societies means moving from mere "information-sharing" to ways of viably deploying GEM-FS so that it can help effectively improve our modern world.

There is potentially in human beings an immanent frame of a transformative apophatic presence linked to the transcendent.[3] The gradual disenchantment with religion in the West has led it to stress nature over the supernatural. 'Nature' is an independent domain studied by scientists to be explained on its own terms. We noted earlier that Charles Taylor is following a long Christian tradition in retrieving an "apophatic impulse". He is not alone in insisting on the need of a sense of the ineffable in a postmodern, secular world.

Two French-speaking Catholic philosophers, Louis Dupre and Remi Brague have stressed the role of interiority. Dupre replies to a world which has lost its sense of divine presence with a mysticism of negation. He proposes an apophatic model of mystical experience "where spiritual emptiness, transfigured in the night of divine absence, becomes a space of transcendence." On this view, the transition from atheism's pure negation of the sacred to the paradox of divine-absence-and-presence in apophatic mysticism is a conversion from the modern "'conquering, grasping' attitude towards the real to a contemplative receptivity to the core of being and selfhood at the heart of each creature."[4]

Brague seeks to recover Europe's cosmopolitan conviviality by rethinking the meaning of universality's "claim" upon us as that of "an inescapable human concern."[5] His proposal is guided by apophatic traditions but more specifically "by deconstruction and critical theory, which I take to consist, in crucial respects, in adaptations and extensions of apophatic thinking in the postmodern world.... What is at stake in apophatic thinking is a universality without any definitive or definable content, a universality that consists instead in an attitude of radical openness toward all others." (Ibid). We argue that the proposals of both Dupre and Brague reinforce, even "exemplify" a GEM-FS-inspired ethical secularity.

We may extend Brague's transformative apophatic by adverting to the Mahayana-Buddhist Diamond Sutra of the "Perfection of Wisdom" genre which emphasizes the practice of non-abiding, non-attachment. In the sutra, the Buddha helps a pupil unlearn his limited notions of the nature of reality and enlightenment, stressing that all forms, thoughts and conceptions are ultimately illusory. Since one cannot be enlightened through them, they must be set aside. The sutra focuses on four main points: "giving without attachment to self, liberating beings without notions of self and other, living without attachment, and cultivating without attainment."[6] Still, we know that few persons reach the high pinnacle of apophatic universalism or are capable of truly integrating the realities of heart and mind in their lives. The supernatural and the transcendent may have slipped from modern consciousness but apophatic experiences, when had, give glimpses of what many have lost today. *MiT*'s second mediated phase turns on recovering such apophatic experiences, that is, formulating an immanent frame of a "transforming apophatic presence" (the realm of interiority) in ways that offer a solid transition to future possibilities. Of course, the hopeful apophatic optimism of a Brague or a Massillon is all too often undermined by political realities. If we contrast the respective Buddhist and European notions of "enlightenment", Buddhism speaks to the heart[7] so as to be freed from illusions. The French enlightenment sought to free minds from superstition. GEM-FS can enlighten both hearts and minds.

For Fritz Williams, "Suffering and joy teach us--if we allow them" He asks how might we make the leap of empathy which transports us into the soul and heart of another person? "In those transparent moments we know other people's joys and sorrows, and we care about their concerns as if they were our own."[8] In its own way, this book, too, is a leap of transformative empathy. Both heart and mind underly GEM-FS's empathetic foundations; all humans can potentially speak from the heart. Not seldom, academia obscures empathetic ways for finding and integrating the ways of heart and mind. The FS as presented in this book are partly grounded in Lonergan's metaphysics. FS 5, foundations, formally understood and put into practice, is a key for linking the heart and mind informing Christian, Muslim and secular thought. This book's see-judge-act subtemplates complement a more formal GEM-FS template. This is not just an academic exercise; rather, it foundationally deploys the eight FS in ways that academically depend on the work of many Lonergan scholars with a view to integrate their various approaches. A crucial aspect of integrating GEM-FS in both academic and everyday life is distinguishing between faith and beliefs, a distinction that helps spell out the crucial apophatic-kataphatic complementarities[9] this book stresses.

ANALOGIES BETWEEN THE APOPHATIC-KATAPHATIC AND FAITH-BELIEFS HELP GROUND GEM-FS' BRIDGE OF MERCY

Lonergan writes (*MiT*, 115-17) that "faith is a knowledge born of religious love." He cites Pascal's remark that the heart has reasons which reason does not know--adding that by the heart he understands "the subject on the fourth, existential level of intentional consciousness and in the dynamic state of being in love." In sum, besides knowing "there is another kind of knowledge reached through the discernment of value and the judgments of value of a person in love. . . Faith and progress have a common root in man's cognitional and moral self-transcendence. To promote either is to promote the other indirectly."

In FS 5, we seek to show how the apophatic of mystics and faith are needed to bridge the contradictory teachings and beliefs of the world's religions and opposed secular claims. With W. Cantwell Smith[10] and Lonergan (*MiT*, 123) we distinguish between faith and beliefs so as to help mediate between differences among religions and between religious and secularist claims. The faith-beliefs distinction leads to a "praxis" enabling GEM-FS to link the dynamic structure of knowing with the structure of the good. Faith transcends, but does not negate beliefs in dogmatic expressions. Dogmas deal with theological problems raised in particular historical eras; "mystery" is the fundamental nature of human consciousness in the face of the temporal and contingent nature of human existence. Religious people express their faith in terms of an ultimate; secularists tend to speak solely in ethical terms. What counts is practicing the justice of God's Kingdom which is within each one of us while remaining connected to the "Ultimate".

Analogously to Gabriel Marcel's distinction between Problem and Mystery, faith is an archetypal ground of human consciousness that enters as a realm of Mystery in one's life. In the realm of faith, love precedes knowledge (*MiT*, 123). Accepting God's loving initiative in the world can embolden humans even to the point of heroism. A mystical eye of love penetrates beneath the surface of life's sordid aspects. FS 5, foundations, outlines feedback relationships[11] between the apophatic and the kataphatic. Some great mystics, nursed in in the apophatic realm, channeled it to address pressing problems as did St. Catherine of Siena. In 1377, she helped Pope Gregory XI return from Avignon to Rome. In her writings, she gives us insights into her mystical experiences, "the affection of love," accompanied by grace. This requires "sincere counsel without any respect of persons." Having crossed the bridge of mercy, she turned to assist others.[12] As to a way and bridge of

Divine Mercy in Islam, Imam Sadiq, a descendant of Ali born c. 700, wrote "that on the Day of Judgment, Allah shall look upon one with mercy if one has been merciful. Only the merciful can cross the Bridge of Sirat "which passes from the top of Hell."[13]

The Buddhist, Christian and Islamic traditions all allude to bridges of mercy. Buddhists speak of the role of Kannon Bodhisattva, the goddess of mercy who comes in many forms and manifestation to assist people in distress in the earthly realm. With mercy she bridges the heavenly and earthly realms.[14] The three world religions reveal how mystics apophatically channel mercy and influence kataphatic life. The question is how GEM-FS might extend the three world religions' potential bridges to the secular world.

IN-DEPTH ATTEMPTS TO RECONCILE BASIC COMMONALITIES IN THE WORLD RELIGIONS AND SECULARITY

On the surface, Buddhist, Christian and Islamic traditions differ greatly; but in their depths, they reflect analogical efforts to transform the human heart and mind for the better. Comparing Buddhism with Christianity, James Finley notes: "There is the free fall into the boundless abyss of God in which we all meet one another, beyond all distinctions, beyond all designations. This is the oneness that includes all distinctions."[15] For Finley, Buddha's four noble truths embody Buddhism's distilled essence. We do have to respect Buddhist-Christian differences. However, emphasizing the four noble truths as universal principles of spiritual awakening and fulfillment is helpful. This book seeks principles for doing so. Finley suggests that each of the noble truths is present in the teachings of Jesus and in the writings of many Christian mystics. In fact, one can only realize the relevant Buddhist-Christian complementarities when one prays and reflects in depth. This book explores how the world religions in their genuine strivings can build faith bridges among their adherents and with secularists. This involves promoting a viable ethical secularity.[16] As we shall note in FS 8, communities are needed to catalyze structural transformations.

GEM-FS'S SECULAR-RELIGIOUS FOUNDATIONS RECONCILE SEEMINGLY CONTRADICTORY METHODS

The loss of transcendence within secular societies, on the one hand, and the various fundamentalisms afflicting Christianity and Islam, on the other, have produced dysfunctional forms of life. The reality is that "secularism" and "secularization" are complex phenomena. We argue that GEM-FS is partly rooted in modern, scientific-secularist reason, in how scientists ask and resolve questions. We do not assume that the secular can only be bad. GEM-FS is at its core a "faith-based secular method" in dialogue with secularism. Secular methods abound today; secularism is a problem when it turns dogmatic. GEM-FS is also a transformative method. Christianity, Islam and secularity guide people's daily lives in different ways. We focus on how these three entities may be open to dialogue with one another while respecting traditions and needed changes in today's world. Christians are to render to Caesar what is his while not forgetting what is God's. For Muslims, the Quran, hadith and fatwa are daily guides. Further questions arise between those who have embraced secularity's differentiations of mind and culture and those who have not. Within such contexts, secularity emerges differently and has different emphases. Having shown in *Insight* how GEM is primarily a secular method based on how humans use their cognitional operations in daily life, in doing mathematics and science, etc., Lonergan showed in *MiT* that his "secular method" can and should be used in the religious sphere. Whether in science or in the way theologians and other academics "function", GEM-FS speaks of the unity of a subject in a *dynamic* process of development". GEM-FS dynamism helps make it a method for radically transformative adaptations to seemingly contradictory ways of thinking.[17]

Both Charles Taylor and Lonergan have noted the practice of introspection through which a rich vocabulary of interiority has developed. In FS 5, foundations, we call attention to what is at the center of the GEM-FS template, namely an interiority that is common to not a few Muslim and Christian mystical writers. We seek to lay a ground for FS 6's "see-judge-act subtemplates" which illustrate with various examples how "GEM-FS interiority" can be applied. Lonergan studied the formal relationship between science, spirituality and ethics.[18] This helped him develop a holistic philosophy[19] which reconciles religious and scientific views. *Insight*'s first five chapters list many instances of how insight functions in modern science and mathematics. The transition of the early to the later Lonergan is characterized by a critical junction in the shifts from ancient and medieval thought to modernity--a junction that offers a possible junction-bridge between religion and secularity. Lonergan notes in *MiT* that models "stand to the human sciences, to philosophies, to theologies, much as mathematics stands to the natural sciences......(They) are interlocking sets of terms and relations." (284). This notion of interlocking sets of basic terms and relations treated as models is one that we rely on in our attempt to develop transcultural, interfaith categories not divorced from a needed mercy.

HOW INTERIORITY AND MERCY HELP BRIDGE A GLOBAL BUDDHIST-CHRISTIAN-MUSLIM ETHICAL SECULARITY

Lonergan's *Insight* explains human understanding manifested in our unrestricted desire to know. "The transcendental notions are our capacity for seeking and when found, for recognizing instances of the intelligible, the true, the real, the good. (*MiT*, 282). This unrestricted desire, we argue, implies a *further unrestricted ethical-spiritual desire to act*[20] in merciful ways on the part of sensitive humans whether they be Christians, Muslims or secularists. This book develops this latter desire which complements Lonergan's unrestricted desire to know--thus extending GEM-FS's diphase operational range. GEM-FS's operational range is partly dependent on how Lonergan derived the general and special categories founded in a common transcultural base. All humans share in that transcultural base. "What is transcultural is the reality to which such formulation refers, and that reality is transcultural because it is not the product of any culture but rather the principle that begets and develops cultures that flourish, as it also is the principle that is violated when cultures crumble and decay." (283). *The Epistle to the Romans* 5, 5 refers to God's gift of love—a (transcultural) gift lived more or less authentically[21] "in the many and diverse religions of mankind." (Ibid). If it is apprehended "in as many different manners as there are different cultures, still the gift itself as distinct from its manifestations is transcultural... For being-in-love is properly itself, not in the isolated individual, but only in a plurality of persons that disclose their love to one another." (Ibid). Theological categories are transcultural[22] "only in so far as they refer to that inner core. In their actual formulation, they are historically conditioned and subject to correction." (284). For us, mercy is an integral part of that core.

Our brief summary of Lonergan's view on God's gift of love to all humans suggests that a GEM-FS template foundationally pivots on that gift. It serves as a junction between religions and an authentic secularity. Still, what is an "authentic secularity"? Here we return to Brague's effort to recover Europe's cosmopolitan conviviality. He seeks to rethink "the very meaning of universality which for him is an inescapable human concern." He sees it as impossible to have a secular society to the extent that it lacks a "transcendent horizon." Failing such a horizon, "society cannot endure."[23] Brague's claim is "brutal and paradoxical." He insists that "a purely secular society simply cannot survive in the long run...The term secular society is tautological, because the ideal of secularity is latent with the modern use of the term society.... Whatever comes after secularism... won't be a 'society' any longer but rather another way for us to think about and give political form to the being-together of human beings." (Ibid). Brague traces and faults the use of the term secularism by Holyoake (1817–1906). John Stuart Mill used it in his work *The Principles of Secularism* (1859).[24] In *On Liberty*, after mentioning the religious principles that can motivate human action, Mill speaks of "secular standards" (for want of a better name).

This book develops an alternative to Brague's harsh view by invoking the insights of Lonergan and Taylor on authentic secularity—itself implicitly grounded in divine mercy. Some, on "principle", refuse to acknowledge the divine. For Christians and Muslims, authenticity and mercy are important, though all too often honored more in the breach than in observance. Our "junction-bridge" between Christianity, Islam and secularity depends in part on the implications of the human creative process. Our GEM-FS template is informed by an interiority common to Buddhists, Christians, Muslims and authentic proponents of secularity. On the practical level of see-judge-act praxis, there emerges a creative impulse, examples of which we shall give in FS 6. For Brague, secularism is a contradiction in terms, but we seek to transmute it into a valid ethical secularity. A ground for this emerges in William Franke's "apophatic universalism."[25] Franke contrasts the historical roles of Greece, Rome and Islam. "Apophatic universalism," very different from Hegel's dialectic in the *Phenomenology of Spirit,* can be interpreted "as an heir and a precursor of certain types of apophatic thinking transmitted through Cusanus and Jacob Boehme, among others." (Ibid). It buttresses GEM-FS's Third Way of heart and mind rooted in interiority and mercy. Such notions answer to an often undetected, but real spiritual foundation of daily life. Our approach to the histories of Islamic and European thought and to an interiority common to converted Christians and Muslims may be said to be grounded in an apophatic universalism. Lonergan's eight FS help resolve the tensions of the human creative process,[26] calling us to cooperate as we face the innumerable problems affecting humanity. There is at the root of GEM-FS an apophatic universalism in tune with the transcultural base from which *MiT* derives the general and special categories (285). We now turn to explore how the great Islamic mystics addressed such issues in the Middle Ages. We seek to activate interfaith-interdisciplinary bridges potentially *"in-built"* within all humans—a view in tune with Sufism which focuses on the spiritual content of Muhammad's message itself--not on sharia law.

THE ROLE OF SUFISM IN CHRISTIAN-ISLAMIC BRIDGE-BUILDING: AL-GHAZALI, IBN AL-'ARABI AND RUMI

Abu Hamid al-Ghazali (1058-1111 CE) was a noted Sufi, a renewer of the faith, one who, according to tradition, appears once every century to restore the faith of the community. Having begun his career as director of the Nizamiyyah mosque in Baghdad, he restlessly sought to find certitude about our possible knowledge of God--whether through *Kalam* (Islamic theology) or *Falsafa* (philosophy). For him, achieving certitude in faith was through attachment to the teachings of an Imam or through direct spiritual experience of the Divine (Sufism). He wrestled with these possible methods before finally settling on direct religious experience – but only after going through a period of clinical depression. He was dissatisfied with the science and philosophy of his day rooted as they were in observable phenomena. God transcends such phenomena. As did Kant later, al-Ghazali realized that the methods of science and philosophy could not help a believer find certitude in his/her belief. During his period of clinical depression, al-Ghazali resigned his teaching post; he went into a period of a mystical "Dark Night of the Soul." Having affiliated himself with a Sufi community, he began to travel throughout the Middle East.

During this period of reflection and searching, he completed his masterwork, *The Revitalization of the Religious Disciplines*, which deals extensively with human and divine knowledge. It examines *ilm* (secular knowledge) and *ma'rifa* (mystical knowledge) in the Islamic tradition. His short but important work on mystical theology, the *Niche of Lights* (*Mishkat al Anwar*), explains the Sufi experience of *fana* and *fana al fana* (self-annihilation and the annihilation of self-annihilation). *Fana* is an experience of losing oneself completely--being one with Divine Truth. *Fana al fana* expresses a further experience of annihilating "self" in the experience of identity with the One Divine Truth. Still, as is the case with the converted Buddhist Oxherd, a mystic can best return to ordinary life to help others.[27] Al-Ghazali, sees the search for true knowledge as more important than devotion or martyrdom. The science of revelation includes "prophetically mediated beliefs" and religious practices which embrace a profound awareness of the essential states of the heart--the bellwether of one's relationship with God. All humans[28] can know God experientially. This is not to be confused with any rational proofs for God's existence. For al-Ghazali, such "proofs" assume that God is just another being even though infinite and uncaused. Due to him, never again would Muslims make the false assumption that God is a being "like any other, whose existence could be demonstrated scientifically or philosophically."[29] His books, *The Doctrines of the Philosophers* and *The Inchoherence of the Philosophers* were misunderstood in the West.[30] In fact, al-Ghazali does not attack reason; he shows that philosophers' "demonstrations" do not meet their own logical standards. This led to the erroneous view that he rejected Aristotelian teachings. His response to *falsafa* is complex. He adopted many of its teachings but complains in *The Incoherence* that philosophers are convinced that their "demonstrative proofs" are superior to theological knowledge drawn from revelation. This had caused some Muslim philosophers to neglect Islam, its ritual duties and religious law (*sharî'a*). Al-Ghazali wrote *The Incoherence* because the Sufi mystic Mansur al-Hallaj had been crucified (922 AD) in Baghdad for seeming to claim identity with the Divine by saying "I am the Truth" (*ana al Haqq*). His words were interpreted as a claim to being "one" with the Divine[31] and led to his crucifixion. Al-Ghazali's distinction between the "real" oneness of the Divine and an experiential "felt" oneness with the Divine helped stop the kind of retribution meted to al-Hallaj. Al-Ghazali helped save Sufism from attack from legalistic Muslim authorities. Due to him, Sufism could once again flourish during the Middle Ages.

Al-Ghazali knew that Muslims tend to understand the Quran in legalistic, literal-minded, *"exoteric"* ways. For their part, the Sufis, who have been part of Islam religious life since Muhammad's time, tend to understand the Quran in *esoteric* ways, based on their mystical experiences. Al-Ghazali wanted to preserve both tendencies in Islam. He built bridges of understanding between the two. Unfortunately, the sway of Wahhabism during the past three centuries has led to a return of a domineering, literal-minded legalism amongst some politically motivated Muslims in Saudi Arabia.[32] Al-Ghazali is important for his view on the relationship of revelation to the Prophets and on the role of reason in interpreting revelation; he assigns reason a prominent role. This was later challenged by fundamentalists. For him, reason's demonstrative arguments can reach reliable conclusions. "The results of true demonstrations do not conflict with revelation since neither reason nor revelation are false."[33] If demonstration proves that something contradicts the literal meaning of revelation, the scholar needs to interpret (*ta'wîl*) the outward text and read it as a symbol of a deeper truth. There are, for instance, demonstrative arguments proving that God cannot have a "hand" or sit on a "throne." For Al-Ghazali, all humans have a natural affinity to know God through the heart. Heart, for him, is a metaphor for knowledge (*ilm*). *Ilm* consists of more than just intellectual acts; it combines both immanent and transcendent aspects. Aristotle gave us no logical demonstrations for God or for spiritual realities. For Al-Ghazali, faith seeks understanding. He writes in "The Elaboration of the Marvels of the Heart" that all hearts are naturally disposed to experientially know spiritual realities. Humans differ from non-rational animals in that they have a divine "exalted charge," a possible unique nobility. In sec. 33:72, he invokes the Word of God: "We did offer the trust to the heavens, to earth and to the mountains, but they declined to bear it, for they feared it." Humans did accept the offer. This indicates that humans possess a unique characteristic distinguishing them from heaven, earth and mountains. It renders them capable of trusting God. This trust involves experiential knowledge and acknowledging the divine transcendent unity. The heart of every human being is implicitly prepared to trust; any person is inherently capable of it.[34] Al-Ghazali had prepared a way for ibn al-'Arabi and Rumi.

IBN AL-'ARABI: DIVINE AND HUMAN LOVE

Muid ad-Din ibn al-'Arabi (1165-1240), a Spanish Sufi, is the mystic-philosopher who gave the esoteric apophatic-mystical dimension of Islam its first full-fledged kataphatic expression. Traveling through Spain and Morocco, he collected the lives of Sufi saints. At the age of 30, he began to travel further, eventually settling on the Euphrates. His father had been a friend of Ibn Rushd (Averroes) who probably has had more impact on the West than any other Muslim thinker, but he took quite a different direction from Ibn Rushd's. In 1201, he had a vision after meeting Nizam: a young girl, "surrounded by a heavenly aura. He saw her as an incarnation of Sophia,"[35] divine Wisdom. He realized that love of a creature is compatible with Islam: "If you love a being for his beauty, you love none other than God, for he is the Beautiful Being." In his *Futubat al-Makkiyah* he writes: "In all its aspects, the object of love is God alone." (Ibid). His collection of love poems, *The Interpreter of Desires*, expressing his monotheist ideal, is often compared to the *Song of Songs*.[36] An outstanding model for a logic of the heart and mind, he held that each mystic has a unique experience of God. It follows that no one religion can express the whole Divine mystery; there is no objective truth about God to which all need to subscribe. Since God transcends categories of personality, predictions about God's actions or inclinations are impossible. Ibn al-'Arabi viewed religions positively as shown in this counsel: "Do not attach yourself to any particular creed exclusively, so that you may disbelieve all the rest; otherwise you will lose much, nay, you will fail to recognize the real truth of the matter."[37] Such a view can help guide today's movement toward interfaith understanding and dialogue.

EXPERIENCING GOD'S GRANDEUR WITH THE SUFI MYSTIC RUMI AND WITH THE SPANISH MYSTICS

Rumi (1207-1271) is the rare figure who still speaks to the aspirations of Easterners and Westerners. He represents the generation that after Ibn al-'Arabi and Jalal-al-din (from central Asia) helped Islam turn its face from east to west when Sufism "consolidated its organizational aspect. The 13th century saw an institutionalization of mysticism both within Islam and Christianity. Sufism organized itself in lay orders as did the Catholic Franciscan and Dominican orders. The Sufi orders were known as Tariqas. Rumi often travelled throughout central Asia and the Middle East. His burial place in Konya, Turkey, has become a modern day pilgrimage site for Sufis and others attracted to his life and writings. For Rumi, the names of God expressed the theophany of God in Nature.[38] The type of mystical union had by al-Ghazali, Ibn al-'Arabi and Rumi reflects that of other mystics throughout the world. Such mystic commonalities can help us find meeting points in an interfaith language of heart and mind; they offer foundations for religion-secularist bridges. The mystical experiences of the Sufis, of a Teresa of Avila, or a Gulen help us address current dialogues between religion and science as we try to lay transcultural, interreligious, ethical bridges based on universal ways of knowing and doing that transcend self-seeking. They constitute an apophatic apprehension of what the everyday world of kataphatic-secular communication ignores.

The above three Muslim mystics as well as Aquinas are all relevant to a GEM-FS Bridge. Al-Ghazali's method, infused with mystic knowing, anticipated the way Aquinas adapted Aristotelian philosophy. He, Ibn al-'Arabi, Aquinas, Rumi, and Lonergan have provided bridges between seemingly incompatible domains of knowledge which touch on the foundations of both faith and reason. They, as does meditation, all reinforce this book's approach to help bridge religious-secular thinking so as to help ground a global secularity ethics reinforced with love.

COMPARING EASTERN RELIGIONS, THE DEVELOPMENT OF ZEN MEDITATION WITH INSIGHTFUL ISLAMIC VIEWS

While this book's double-pronged GEM-FS strategy focuses on Christian, Muslim and secular views, we do have recourse to some of the insights and teachings of Eastern religions such as Hinduism and Buddhism. With Lonergan, we are interested in the deep structure of both cognitional process and of the spiritual life. Traditionally, Hindus have called the spiritual life's depths *jnani*. *Jnani* (in ways that anticipated Lonergan)[39] is an Indian term meaning insight or wisdom used in contrast to the term *bhakti*, "devotion".[40] *Jnani* is related both conceptually and etymologically to *guarprajna*, (wisdom)--the goal of Buddhist contemplation. We shall not investigate Hinduism's holistic worldview as illustrated, for example, in the Hindu god Shiva, the Lord or King of Dance. Shiva is depicted as the cosmic dancer who performs his divine dance to destroy a weary universe and make preparations for the god Brahma to start the process of creation. "Because You love the Burning-ground, I have made a Burning-ground of my heart - That You, Dark One, hunter of the Burning-ground, May dance Your eternal dance."[41]

As does Catholicism, Buddha's eightfold Path courses between extremes. There are two main traditions in Buddhism. Early Buddhism (*Theravada* or the "teaching of the elders," still practiced in South Asia) gave way in Eastern Asia to Mahayana (Large Vehicle). Nagarjuna (c. 150-220 CE), Mahayana's founder, stressed *anatman* (one's true nature as non-self) rather than Hindu teachings on *Atman* (self). The Sino-Japanese religious tradition of Chan Buddhism,[42] known in the West by its Japanese name Zen, has been met with both praise and skepticism by Westerners. Controversies have arisen regarding the nature of Zen and Western interpretation of it. Zen scholars and Zen practitioners are often at odds with each other regarding the true nature of Zen spirituality. Recent studies have clarified the current controversies around Zen by taking a closer look at our Western self-understanding and relationship to spirituality.[43]

There are parallels in the development of Hindu and Zen forms of meditation. Tai Chi traces Zen's roots back to ancient India through the Buddhist monk, Bodhidharma (known as Ta Mo in China and Daruma in Japan) who is credited for bringing Mahayana Buddhism to the Orient between 525 A.D. and 540 A.D. Actually, "Bodhidharma" was a Dravidian, a member of the black aboriginal population that dominated much of India during his time.[44] Zen riddles (koans) and the ox-herding pictures forego words. As with some other spiritual exercises, they prefer poetic images. Mysticism and art partly operate at the level of affect, symbol, desire. They function first to dislodge us from the loop of habitual discursive thought patterns that commonly fill our consciousness. On this view, art is not a luxury, an extra for those with time and money. It is a basic and essential playful dimension of human living, one that offers the experience of new potentialities able to shake up old habits of mind and feeling. For Lonergan, it is on this artistic, symbolic, experiential level that we live our concrete daily lives. Feelings provide the "mass and momentum" to do so; they motivate new forms of action. Lonergan's deep understanding of art's vital importance in a culture is often overlooked. For example, we wonder how young Islamic terrorists despite many cogent arguments resort to terror. They are ready to die. Arguments often fail to break through deep psychic desires and needs. One must ask how educators might offer an alternative to radicalization. In the Western culture of instrumentalist rationality, we ignore the power of art. Maajid Nawaz, an ex-Islamist jihadi and a founder of Quilliam (which wants to counter Islamist extremism) calls for an emotional sensitivity able to offer alternatives to young people at risk of Islamist radicalization. A root of the problem is that logic cannot immediately reach a young person's depths. Nawaz has inside knowledge of what he is talking about. He speaks from experience.[45] For Lonergan, feelings as well as art require an adverting to the lived experiential level of consciousness at which these operate.[46]

Opening with the challenging query "what might an anthropology of the secular look like?" Talal Asad has explored the concepts, practices, and political formations of secularism, with emphasis on the major historical shifts that have shaped secular sensibilities and attitudes in the modern West and the Middle East. Asad dismantles commonly held assumptions about the secular, arguing that while anthropologists have oriented themselves to the study of the "strangeness of the non-European world" and to what are seen as non-rational dimensions of social life (things like myth, taboo, and religion), modern secularism has not been adequately examined. For him, the secular is not a successor to religion nor is it more rational. It has a multi-layered history, related to the premises of modernity, democracy, the concept of human rights.[47] As does this book, Asad appeals to anthropologists, historians and scholars concerned with modernity. Our own see-judge-act examples focus on GEM-FS efforts to help build a better world. If we want to realize any goals, including building a better and more caring world, we must, once again, begin to appreciate the significance of the value of values in all we do. Without life-affirming values, no strong and lasting foundations can be built and no goals can be realized. Values are the deeply held principles that guide our choices and behaviors and influence our emotions and motivations. (Asad).

The FS and the conversions begin with the data of lived experience. The FS are an interdisciplinary self-correcting process[48] whereby specialists in various fields collaborate. A key GEM-FS pivot is its turning on human consciousness. Each of our four basic operations intends objects; each reveals an intending subject. One is aware of one's intending as one intends an object. At work here is a feedback process: our four basic operations intend objects and we are conscious of the intending. GEM-FS, applicable to the humanities and sciences, helps foster human (interdisciplinary) cooperation. The feedback action can help one sketch theologies of secularization that might integrate mystic insights into the "Ground of Being" with the realities of daily life while also developing needed transcultural, interfaith categories.

ILLUSTRATING HOW MYSTICS INTEGRATE THEIR INSIGHTS INTO DAILY LIFE

Two recently deceased Jesuits, Yves Raguin in Taiwan and Jacques Dupuis in India have explored[49] some of the commonalities of mysticism as understood and practiced in the East and in the West. For Raguin, mysticism in the East *begins with perceiving outer* realities—an account that differs from the type of mysticism practiced in the West. In the West, mystics tend to speak of an inner-to-outer movement, one of solitary interiority as first recounted by St. Anthony and the desert fathers. They "sold everything" and gave it to the poor as counselled by Jesus. Solitary spirituality gradually gave way to the service-oriented spirit of the post-Reformation era as typified in St. Francis de Sales. This means that one's inner self is an integrating *Gestal*t--a unified physical, psychological and symbolic set of configurations that cannot be derived from its parts. Drawing from the East and Teilhard de Chardin, Raguin explored ways to remedy Cartesian dualism. For Christians, an act of love mystically participates in God's depths. Raguin reflected on such depths. Teilhard de Chardin's *Divine Milieu*, helped Raguin peer into the depths of his own being as a way to structure contemplation and to compare Chinese and Western spiritualities. Psychologically, we first become aware of what is outside of ourselves. Although we know that we have "an inside, we do not become aware of it immediately as it is more difficult to penetrate" one's own inside "than to grasp the external world." In negotiating the boundaries between our outside and our inside, what matters is not discovering another world, independent of mine, but being aware of other personalities different from mine. This structure of the world of spiritual experience is intimately connected with a symbolism built deep into our own psychology. Raguin helps reinforce Dupuis' stress on "lived experience" as a basic, common human occurrence--one that has been ideologically sidetracked by postmodernists. The latter tend to prioritize outer, linguistic discourse; failing to proceed to inner self-knowing, they lose sight of foundations. They confuse foundations with fundamentalism. One must avoid the latter while promoting the former. One is to interrelate genuine lived experience, spirituality and ethics through the FS so as to ensure that our expressions of faith be rooted in God.

Nothing that is good, true and beautiful is to be rejected. To understand the nature of faith today we must reflect deeply and plumb the depths of our experience[50] in ways that can help guide our complex lives. The touchstone of a relevant lived experience lies in our ability to bridge "lonely fiefdoms" with the cultural contexts of the world we inhabit. Faith expresses itself in sets of contingent beliefs. All language is subject to the historical contexts in which it is evoked. Too often, language is universalized beyond its applicable realms; it becomes a tool of conflicting dogmas rooted in ethnocentric bias, or self-interest. Each one of us has his/her own life narrative which remains a deeply personal reality but which can also be shared with others despite possibilities of misunderstanding. This applies to our personal experiences as well as that of families, communities and nations. Such experiences occur in cultural situations and historical contexts. It is up to us to mediate our uniquely personal standpoints and limited community perspectives with globally valid spiritual values able to explore and a global secularist ethics.

A global spirituality and a global ethic imply one another but how do secularists and atheists fit in here? How can people of different persuasions cooperate in a globalized world?[51] In the movie, "My Big Fat Greek Wedding" the bride's Greek father is hard put to accept his American son-in-law. In one scene, he says that his family's name in Greek means "orange" and his son-in-law's name, "apple". Oranges and apples! "In the end, we are all fruit." This insight helps him accept the marriage. What keys can help one reach one's deeper self? Zen is one such key that appeals to many. Wise Christians know that one can be both a Zen Buddhist and a Christian but how can we in fact bridge or span seemingly opposed religious traditions? To be sure, our proposed bridge must transcend fundamentalist forms of thought. It is said that young Westerners who have gone to Syria to support ISIS[52] have done so because they had not found the type of structure[53] on which they had vainly sought to build their lives. Secularized countries which no longer teach religion often leave young people confused in a vacuum of relativism-- with no adequate sense of values or virtues. A question we ask is whether secularism, too, can degenerate into intolerant attitudes based on misunderstandings of what faith and religion are. We argue that a global secularity ethics and a global spirituality are complementary. Locally, globally they need one another.

Chapter Six

Sixth Functional Specialty

Policies Based on a Logic of the Heart's Value Judgments

THE ROLES OF MODERNITY AND SECULARITY IN A GLOBALIZED, PLURALISTIC WORLD

While *MiT*'s FS 6 has Christian roots, we adapt FS 6 to help us address a globalized, pluralist world in search of viable policies for bridging divides. Lonergan writes that "Anthropological and historical research has made us aware of the enormous variety of human social arrangements, cultures, mentalities." (*MiT*, 300). Validating GEM-FS as a secular method offers an alternative to Peter Berger's opposing religion to secularism. We now want to assess the role of "modernity" in today's pluralistic world. For us, secularity is a viable alternative to a secularism for it is a state of being separate from religion rather than being opposed to it. In FS 6 we instance some see-judge-act initiatives in various parts of the world illustrating how one can help bridge what on the surface seem to be mutually contradictory religious-vs-secular claims. Having touched on the foundational role of the heart in both personal conversion and in interfaith dialogue, we turn to concrete, lived examples of the see-judge-act method showing the role of the heart in detecting what is wanting in society and "needs fixing." This can be done both on the local level and on the global level. In FS 6, we shall instance several examples of how individuals or groups have implicitly or explicitly engaged in the see-judge-act method—often with a logic of the heart as motivating force. From such examples, we hope to cull some helpful elements that might lead to helpful ecumenical-interfaith policies. Let us first seek contextualizing keys to some large-minded efforts or policies which demand that one critically accept the implications of secularized world.

Chapter 6
NEEDED CONTEXTUALIZING KEYS

A. Critically Accepting the Implications of a Secularized World

Johannes Metz follows Friedrich Gogarten in stressing that secularity is not contrary to Christianity. Rather, Christianity is permanently embedded in the "flesh" of world history. Theology cannot neglect the process of the concrete history of the world, though it has "as it were, a monophysite understanding of salvation history."[1] Its task is to show that the historically irreversible process of secularization means that Christianity has become truly historically effective, not that it is disappearing. There is, however, a constant ambiguity to this process of secularization. It stands beneath the sign of the cross, "which means also under the sign of the constant protest within the world against God" (Ibid, 17). Many reject the holy[2] and God. They assume that God "is no longer a necessary working hypothesis for morality, politics and science. Modern scientific methods (on the immediate pragmatic level) can live with the phrase "God is dead."[3] Christian political theologians would have us experience the absence of God as "eschatological hope" (Moltmann) or see Jesus as the representative of God with whom he is both identical and non-identical (Sölle). A "secularity theology" must be centrally concerned with the methodological principles of interpreting the Christian message and with its fundamental dialogical relation with secularized society. On the other hand, the problem of separating mosque and state does not arise in Islam since mosques are not seen as autonomous institutions. Historically, "mosque and state were one and the same. Muhammad was both a prophet and soldier, prophet and statesman. His career as a statesman was an essential part of his prophetic mission. . ... From its very inception, Islam was associated with the exercise of power. In Classical Arabic there are no pairs of words corresponding to 'lay' and 'spiritual.' Islam knows no distinctions between these realms."[4] Reconciling Christian and Muslim stances on secularization should turn to a sense of mystic reality, a hermeneutic of the relation between theory and praxis and a mediating social ethics.[5] The Zulu ethic Ubuntu motto "I cannot be fully me unless you are fully you" is a model this book adopts in its call for a global merciful secularity.

B. A Sense of the Mystic in Both Christianity and Islam

Meister Eckhart (1260-1327), built on the Greeks, on such Muslim thinkers as Avicenna as well as on Aquinas. For Eckhart, even in the absence of sensory content or of mental objects, the mystic finds the "Ground of Being"; it is an "experience" that lets one unite the profane with the sacred so as to become fully human. As in the time of Eckhart, so Christianity today needs mystics grounded in the reality of God and able to bridge spiritual and earthly realities. Vatican II used valid forms of Christian secularization but rejected a questionable secularism. It went beyond Harvey Cox and John Robinson's trendy ideas of a secularized Christianity--both of whom relied on Tillich's Ground of Being--but without probing into Tillich's debt to the Rhineland mystics. Like Tillich, Pope John Paul II explored Christian alternatives to secularism; having experienced at first hand the evils of Nazism and Communism, he drew upon Christian tradition. His was an implicit theology of secularization partly based on profound mystical insights. If nation-states, religions or persons attempt to substitute themselves for God, the mystic consciousness (of a Rumi, an Eckhart or a Brague) tellingly refutes such hubris. We need to further develop a theology of secularization so as to integrate mystic insights into the "Ground of Being" with the realities of daily life. The goal is that of developing needed transcultural, interfaith categories.

Some Christian and Muslim thinkers have ably addressed secularity's implications—as have Metz and Gogarten on the Christian side, and Orhan Pamuk and Abdolkarim Soroush on the Islamic side. Pamuk recalls how Turkish "literature that confronts representations of the nation-state (*devlet*) with those of Ottoman, Islamic, and Sufi contexts" is treated as "secular blasphemy" in that it would redefine politics.[6] His novel *Snow*, captures a vulnerable sentiment guiding the Muslim world's intelligentsia. It documents how Turkey is convulsed when "Islamists and secularists indulge in ideological fantasies that leave little to no room for a moderate and rationally informed political existence."[7] The novel's main character, Ka, is a mystical poet whose meditations serve as experiments in personal existence amidst ideological rubble. He strives to transcend Islamists and secularists, and to serve as a bridge between Turkey and the West. In contrast, the Iranian philosopher Soroush is inspired by the Sufi writings of Rumi, who experiments with mysticism as a way to transcend Iranian Islamism and Western secularism. "Whereas Ka's mysticism is apophatic, . . . Soroush's mysticism is noetic in that it takes the form of a life of reason reaching out to the divine in a manner not unlike Augustine's account of the soul that stretches toward God."[8] Soroush's Socratic questioning prioritizes dialogue as a central element.

The "breakthrough authors" we have just touched on have realized the need to ever rethink how best address societal and cultural changes--whether they be those of pre-medieval, medieval or modern times. There have been various forms of revolutionary radicalizations which have provoked violent types of terrorism by those who join e. g. ISIS or Boko Haram. We counter with GEM-FS radicalization that seeks to implement the conversions. In our complex world, jargon-filled rhetorics thrive. GEM-FS is moderately radical; it fosters change based on inner conversions that move one to help others.

C. Michel Houellebecq's Inflammatory Rhetoric against Islam in France

Houellebecq published *Submission* at the very time of Muslim terrorists' attack on Charlie-Hebdo in January, 2015. He had already authored in 2001 *The Elementary Particles* which claims that Islam is "the stupidest religion." Sued for inciting racial violence, a court cleared him. His *Submission* prompted more indignation. It is narrated by François,[9] a literature professor at the Sorbonne, "who drifts between casual sex and microwaved, ready-made meals in a state of wry detachment and *ennui*. Then, in an imaginary France of 2022, he is shaken out of his torpor when the two mainstream parties, on the left and the right, are eliminated in the first round of a presidential election. This leaves French voters with the choice between Marine Le Pen's populist National Front—and the Muslim Fraternity, a new party led by Mohammed Ben Abbes. Thanks to an anti-Le Pen front, Mr. Ben Abbes is elected and thus begins Muslim rule with all sorts of "predictable" shocks to heretofore complacent Frenchmen." (Ibid). Since Houellebecq fails to advocate policies based on a logic of the heart, we seek proposals that would do so.

D. See-Judge-Act "Logics of the Heart" that Would Motivate New Policies[10]

This book's effort to foster a better understanding between religious and secular views depends on ethical persons and movements pursuing common policies for the good of all. We might instance the policies developed for bioethics formulated by a Catholic committee (partially inspired by Lonergan) investigating issues in their field. The conditions specified for a fruitful dialogue were: "Participants invited to the colloquium should be willing to collaborate constructively with others. Special care should be taken to involve participants from developing nations and non-Catholic participants. Care should also be taken to avoid a situation where proponents of the extremes of a range of positions are pitted against each other."[11] The said conditions exemplify a GEM-FS application undertaken by persons of good will.

FS 1 to FS 4 pointed to seeming irreconcilable positions among believers and secularists. FS 5 and FS 6 invoke the heart's value judgments needed to help motivate participants to read history correctly and reconsider. This requires a willingness to promote the common good wherever one can. Otherwise, one cannot formulate adequate policies for avoiding conflicts.[12] We turn to evaluate, in section E, see-judge-act examples that have striven to live ethical principles[13] and in section F, some examples that have failed to do so.

Finally, section G lists sectarian views that distort "see-judge-act" in partisan fashion.

E. GEM-FS Subtemplate-Examples that "See-Judge-Act" not Blindly but with Merciful Hearts

1. Opposing Modern Quasi-Religions:
The Example of Frederick Augustus Voigt

Voigt embodies a see-judge-act method in the face of evil. He opposed the totalitarian dictatorships of the 1930's and 1940's. After the Nazis had seized power, "he became disillusioned with the German left, which he believed had ignominiously given up in the face of Nazi pressure. He came to regard the two dominant totalitarian ideologies of Nazism and Communism as being quasi-religions, abiding evils and threats to European civilization of a Christian Europe. These quasi-religions could only be opposed if the Western democracies committed to defend their civilization."[14] Voigt called his readers to look at what had gone so horribly wrong, to make their own judgments as to how one resists tyranny. Lonergan helps his readers distinguish good from evil. We argue that a see-judge-act method is a helpful way to bring the GEM-FS template "down to earth" while not forfeiting the need to interpret the dynamics that have informed Western civilization from the days of the Greek philosophers to the 21st century.

2. The Examples of Pope John Paul II and William Johnston

For Christians, God has entered history with the gift of his love. One accepts God's initiative through faith-- an eye of love emboldening one to act with courage. Pope John Paul II had a "poetico-mystical-see-judge-act ability" that helped him penetrate beneath the surface. In 2002, for example, he invited religious leaders from around the world to pray for peace in Assisi. First, all participants prayed together silently before dispersing to parts of Assisi to pray in their own way. Their silent prayer "was a prayer of union... there was unity in diversity."[15] The diversity came when each group used its own Scriptures.

William Johnston, the late Irish Jesuit spiritual writer, called for a global spirituality on the model of Hans Kung's global ethics.[16] Using the just cited example of Assisi, one might say that beneath the differences in the various claims of world religions, there lies the profounder unitive experience of faith. Faith--the eye of love--responds to God's initiatives and invites cooperation. Notions of cooperation are to be found in religious texts and can be extrapolated to ethical, secularist contexts. Jesus enjoined his believers to first seek the Reign of God. Christians today can engage in Jesus's Reign-of-God mandate by mediating a global spirituality and a global ethics. One need not go into GEM-FS's complexities to do so; one does have to have a "feel" for what needs to be done, in e. g. reaching out to Muslims or secularists. We now turn to two global movements which reflect the broad agenda St. John-Paul II, Kung, William Johnston, and some others have called for. We shall examine how liberation theology and the Islamic movement, Hizmet (Service), have moved in this direction. Their many see-judge actions are founded in deeper philosophies and theologies which in their way are well in tune with a "secularity mentality."

3. Liberation Theology's Influence in Latin America and the Global Repercussions

Until 1984, the English theologian Denys Turner studied the relations between Christianity and political and social theory—including Marxist views. He has since extended his studies to the traditions of Christian mysticism in relation to socio-political commitments. He argues for a post-atheistic theology, which being dispossessed of its language of affirmation, in turn dispossesses atheists of "their language of denial; a theology therefore which joins hands with the radicalism of the *via negativa* and so paradoxically with the theological radicalism of the apophatic traditions of theology."[17] We argue that liberation theologians, as does the Turkish Hizmet movement, has been pursuing for its own faith tradition a vision similar to Turner's. In our view, such a vision reinforces our religion-secularity "bridging proposal" based in part on a "bridge-of-mercy" inspiration as is the case with Pope Francis who has given us reason to try extend liberation theology insights to a Christian-Muslim dialogues.[18] The pope, before his election to the papacy was known as a bishop-leader who used the see-judge-act method in helping foster church policies throughout the South American continent--often inspired by liberation theology.

Cardinal Walter Kasper, in his book *Pope Francis' Revolution of Tenderness and Love* writes that the pope is neither conservative nor liberal but a radical wanting to bring about a revolution of mercy. Kasper describes how in a very short time the new pope managed to bring a fresh wind in the church which has attracted favorable attention worldwide. Most people praise the pope but some criticize him in both open and hidden ways. "A considerable number of people do not trust the new enthusiasm. They are exercising genteel restraint and have adopted a wait and see attitude," writes Kasper. "What for most people seems a new spring, is for them a passing cold spell . . . an intermezzo." Kasper wants to get to the heart of the pope's convictions, treating "the Francis phenomenon theologically."[19] He throws light on the theological content of Francis' pontificate and on the new perspectives it opens up. More than a theologian, Francis is a deeply mystical person. "While the pope's theology cannot be assigned to a particular school of thought, there is no doubt in Kasper's mind that Romano Guardini (1885-1968), a seminal figure in Catholic intellectual life in the 20th century, profoundly influenced Francis after he had studied Guardini's *Attempts at a Philosophy of what is Concrete and Alive* and *The Church and the Catholic* (1922). In *The Church and the Catholic*, Guardini developed the theme of community, addressing a problem troubling the broader Western world: the absence of community. "Modernity had destroyed the bonds of traditional society and marginalized the Church as a source of social unity, leaving in its wake the anarchic individualism of liberal capitalism. Communism offered an alternative to this anarchy, but only at the expense of eliminating individual freedom.[20] Against these two extremes, Guardini held up the Church as the Body of Christ, "an organic union of persons that made possible the full flourishing of the "free personality, the presupposition of all true community." (ibid). Guardini's Catholic message had an influence not only on the Catholic world of his time but also on non-Catholic thinkers and on many architects of Vatican II. As has Fethullah Gulen in Turkey,[21] Pope Francis has embodied an engagement in social problems inspired by an apophatic light.

The helpful mediations of Guardini, liberation theology, Pope Francis and Gulen could well be applied to the phenomemon of mass Muslim immigration in Europe following the devastation of Syria after years of war. Such cities as Homs and Aleppo have been reduced to rubble and are now mostly deserted. Let us recall that formerly, primitive and traditional beliefs protected an individual within the collective. This is because within the collective, individuality as such was not acknowledged. People retained their place within the social order—no further question asked. Islamic traditions in Muslim countries have survived longer than have Christian traditions in Western countries. In the latter, the cult of individualism often leads to people finding themselves isolated, turned upon themselves. Liberation theology and views on the human good have helped Christians reconcile to some extent traditional and modern ideologies. The phenomenon of mass Muslim immigration from northern Africa and the Middle East, on the other hand, has provoked cultural shocks in both Europe and the United States to the extent that these immigrants are still caught within their Islamic culture. Traditionally, Islam has not recognized the equality of the sexes. Due to this, Muslim immigrants, even those fleeing Middle East catastrophes have preyed upon Western women as happened in the 2016 New Year celebrations in several German cities—a happening which has served to change German tolerance to mass Muslim immigration. The tensions[22] between a traditional-minded Islamic collectivity and an individualist-oriented West must be addressed.

4. Differentiating Approaches to "Orientalism" and to Far East Religious such as Zen

A GEM-FS see-judge-act subtemplate can help Westerners and Muslims develop needed policies promoting mutual trust. Let us compare the French historian Edward Said's and Louis Massignon's respective views on Islamic studies. For Said (1933-2005), the term "Orientalism" has created negative images in the West affecting even Western scholars. He rejected Ernest Renan's approach while praising the work of the 19th century scholar Silvestre de Sacy for his pioneering work in oriental studies.[23]

Massignon was 25 when he set out on an archeological mission for the French government in Baghdad in 1908. While doing research on a thesis on al-Hallaj, he experienced an intense encounter with the Divine that he later described as "the Visitation of a Stranger" breaking into his life. It threw him to his knees in a moment of supplication that caused him to cry out in Arabic, "God, help my weakness." Massignon studied Islam reverentially. He is a role model for promoting Christian-Muslim encounters and helping Westerners make informed decisions on important issues affecting Europe's encounters with Islam. He has been described as a "prophetic-mystical" voice in Christian-Islamic relations, even to the point of being called by some an "Islamized Christian." He wanted to understand Islam and the experience of his Muslim friends and colleagues "from the inside out."[24] He held that value judgments are needed in interreligious relations. In an all-too-broken world, we must examine how religious persons and secularists are adapting. Massignon and Said differed in how they evaluated Christian-Muslim relations. Did Said, a Christian Palestinian and a US citizen, help lay a renewed basis for better-informed and mutually-conciliatory Christian-Islam relations[25] as did Massignon? Or, conversely, did his "Orientalism" become a football kicked by both sides of the colonialist and anti-colonialist ideological divides?[26] Said has been exploited by ideologues of both sides, e. g. becoming the darling of those who are critical of the Israel lobby in the US. We try to avoid the extremes of both sides, respecting both Western and Eastern views.

One has to be both conservative and radical in getting to the roots of world religions so as bridge seeming incompatibilities. How, for example, can one infuse Christian freedom into Yoga and Zen on the model of the First Council of Jerusalem? In Christianity's present efforts to spread Jesus' Good News, the term inculturation is used. It refers to adapting the way Church teachings are presented to non-Christian cultures, and to the influence of those cultures on the evolution of these teachings. The churches in Africa and Asia are learning to inculturate. They are learning to implant Gospel values in the light of traditional African and Asian cultures. Colonialism had undermined such a process. Unlike early Jewish Christians who forced their rites upon gentile converts (Galatians, 2:14) or Pope Clement XI who rejected

Chinese Rites in 1704, efforts for Christian inculturation in Asia and Africa ae being made so as to build on all positive elements in any culture. The purgative, illuminative and unitive stages of inculturated prayer help unite seekers of truth; they teach one to beware of New Age naiveté or karmic fate. The effort toward "inculturation" seems to point in the right direction. Still, there are men and women of deep faith in their own traditions who regard ecumenical dialogue as "collaboration with the enemy."

5. Fethullah Gulen's Hizmet (Service) Initiative: An Enlightened Bridge of Mercy and Tolerance

Fethullah Gulen (born in 1941) is a noted exponent of the Sufi tradition who began his teaching mission in Turkey and now lives in the U. S. He founded the global Hizmet renewal movement which has now spread to over 100 countries. He promotes a tolerant Islam which emphasizes altruism, hard work and education, but some question its motives.[27] We argue that Hizmet is one of the most promising Islamic attempts to recover its apophatic tradition[28] as a way to help solve world problems. Gulen originally studied to become a state-appointed religious leader (*Imam*) but also sought to develop a modern understanding of Islam in touch with science and human values. Early inspired by the Kurdish-Turkish scholar Said Nursi's *The Epistles of Light*, he began to delve into the Islamic tradition of *tasawwuf* (the "inwardness of Islam").[29] Since he was also studying such philosophers as Aristotle, Descartes, Kant, Camus and Sartre, he did not follow the usual pattern of Turkish Imams. He set out to work mainly with students so as to help them achieve their education and spiritual goals. His inspirational style led to his becoming well known in Turkey; it also brought him into conflict with the secular Turkish government which fearing his growing popularity, claimed he was a threat to the state.[30] One may get an inkling of the influence of apophatic Sufism and *tasawwuf* on Gulen from a treatise named "A Heart-Based Sufi Mindfulness Spiritual Practice Employing Self-Journeying."[31] It argues that the study and practice of the art and science of the evolution of human consciousness can lead one to discover in one's heart the divine spark that leads to spiritual realization. This is not unlike Doorley's view of the role of the heart in the Christian tradition as we saw above. There we noted that a converted heart is key to possible transvaluations of values in Christianity, Islam and secularity—a point which is at the center of our effort to bridge the three traditions with a "bridge of mercy." For Gulen, a forgiving mercy "is like a spring of pure water in the heart of a desert."[32] He conjoins religious belief and scientific education so as to create a better world. Fusing the two may enable one to better understand the Creator's revelation of Himself to humanity. He writes on his website: "there can be no conflict among the Qur'an," the Universe "and the sciences that examine them." Religion does not oppose or limit scientific work. The two are separate but relatable entities emanating from a same truth. He notes that some have rejected "religion in the name of science (or) denied science in the name of religion, arguing that the two" are in conflict. He counters that since all knowledge belongs to God and religion is from God, the two cannot be in conflict. His efforts in interreligious dialogue are aimed to improve understanding and tolerance among people. Such dialogue should be realistic about scientific materialism's distorted claims. Science and religion rely upon completely independent sources for their claims to facts or of truth. He sees the truths of the Quran and Hadiths as being absolute in nature and unchanging,[33] whereas scientific truths are relative in nature; these can change, based upon new research and investigations into the processes of Nature. The sciences are in constant flux. What "is regarded today as true may appear tomorrow as wrong or, by contrast, what we see today as wrong, may be proved to be true in the future."[34]

Gulen, like Pope Francis and liberation theologians, fits within an "active" GEM-FS paradigm. All of them saw and judged their contemporary situations. They acted to remedy problems so as to prepare for a viable future. We argue that the world's spiritualities and ethics needed today – exemplified by figures like Lonergan and Gulen – must be based on deepening insights into current global realities. This in turn depends on a profound psychological-moral vision. In other words, apophatic spiritualities can help lay a ground for a kataphatic, global secularity ethics. There are many, diverse theological spiritualities of Christian and Muslim origin. Buddhists, however, tend to explain their spiritual worldviews in philosophical rather than theological terms. There is a need to understand the historical evolution of spiritual impulses. An evolutionary understanding of spiritualities, influenced by insights from the frontiers of contemporary science, can assist religious leaders engaged in interreligious dialogue to overcome personal or collective fears in such dialogues. We all need to learn how to prevent cultural conditioning and personal constraints from clouding possible joint local-global ethical strivings.

We address life's ambiguities and conflicting self-interests with a self-transcendent logic of the heart – in so far as may be feasible in a brief book. We aim to encourage generous souls to transcend raw egoism. We believe that a global spirituality and a global ethics imply one another, but we ask: how do secularists and atheists fit in here and how can people of different persuasions cooperate in our complex world? We address the "big picture" while focusing on concrete initiatives. Liberation theology and Hizmet engage in more than local see-judge actions: concerned with global needs, they work out solutions.

The Syrian poet, Adonis, argues that Islam cannot be modernized, that it cannot be adapted to Western societies. "You cannot reform it inasmuch as it would lose its original meaning. . ... If there is no separation between religion and state, there will be no democracy,"[35] no equality for women. Islam is unlikely to change its theocratic system. We believe that Hizmet could provide an alternative way--if given a chance. Let us give an example of Christian-Muslim cooperation in Kenya where Hizmet has shown leadership.

6. See-Judge-Act Encounters in Kenya that Foster Reconciliation

This book seeks to help bridge questionable presuppositions and intolerant attitudes held by persons of different cultural, religious backgrounds. We study some of the structures rejected by many young persons today. Most young Westerners who have turned to a violent Islam are poorly educated. It may be that some of them had sought out meaningful life structures which the West once had but have been eviscerated by postmodernism. They hope to fill a void in their lives— often in vain. Potential bridges between religions and secularism have many fertile sources to explore, but all too often these sources seem to be based on the contradictory claims of Christian, Islamic and secular proponents. One finds Christian dogmas, self-serving Islamic *fatah*, proud secular mentalities. Our attempt to transvalue and "crossfertilize" such seemingly opposed values through a mutual enrichment takes on the riddles of contradictory claims. We align and develop Lonergan's unitive-transformative GEM-FS template with Cardijn's see-judge-act as subtemplate. The latter is a natural "fit" with GEM-FS that simplifies issues.

Gerald Grudzen, president of Global Ministries University (GMU) has joined several Catholic and Muslim leaders in Kenya to conduct since 2013 a series of see-judge-act seminars in Nairobi and Mombasa. The aim is to help Muslims and Christians learn about one another so as to avoid the type of bloodshed[36] that has marked the region. (In nearby Garissa, in 2015, over 140 Christian students were killed by Muslim extremists). The Catholic dioceses in these regions have been using the see-judge-act method, which as we noted, is an *implicit*, hands-on-possible-application of a fully theoretical GEM-FS template. The ongoing project cooperates with the Coast Council of Interfaith Clerics (CICC), with Father Lagho, vicar general of the Mombasa diocese and with representatives of Gulen's Hizmet movement.[37] Put within the context of this book, one may say that GEM-FS see-judge-act subtemplates are not just theory--but also praxis. Theory-praxis complement one another. GMU's Kenya project is an ethical-secularity-in-action. It transcends boundaries by opening up participants' hearts. Christian and Islamic participants learn to live the meaning of dogmas and the principles of secular life. Drawing from interfaith scholars, they partner with local educational organizations brings and teachers from troubled areas. In the face of growing youth radicalization, teachers identify relevant ways to expand interfaith competency in their local areas. GMU's Kenya project promotes interfaith solidarity among Muslims and Christians in the face of frequent harassment by terrorist groups. It brings to mind the example of interfaith cooperation by Emir Abdul Kader who saved the lives of thousands of Christians in Damascus in the 19th century—an example now being used by the Harvard University Religious Pluralism project.

*7. Linda Sarsour, a Young Palestinian Woman from Brooklyn
Who Lives the See-Judge-Act Method*

Our see-judge-act application is clearly embodied in a woman like Linda Sarsour. Perhaps she can be compared to how Malala, being cured of her wounds in England, turned around to inspire the world. Sarsour, director of the Arab American Association of New York, was brought in contact with African-American activists fighting stop and frisk by a biased police and mass incarceration in the United States. She first got involved after watching the images of militarized police cracking down on protesters in Ferguson, Missouri where a policeman in 'August 2014 fatally shot 18-year-old Michael Brown. She helped mobilize Muslims to support actions against questionable police actions.[38] Bridging Christian-Muslim-secular divides is not easy. Since 9/11, immigrant Muslims have been largely on the defensive due to increased suspicion and bias. Sarsour is part of a new generation of social-media-savvy Muslims versed in the new tools of decentralized activism. Such young Muslims assert themselves through multiracial coalitions that challenge parochial approaches based on long-festering prejudices or bias.

*Transition from Successful See-Judge-Act Examples
to the Limits Imposed by the Social Surd*

Lonergan links biases to the "social surd." In fact, such a surd may limit the effect of isolated see-judge-act ethical initiatives due to festering prejudices and lessen GEM's Third-Way dialectic of community (*CWL* 3, 242-55). The social surd, immanent in social facts, is unintelligible, nor can it be abstracted from when one considers the facts as they are. There is the "cumulative deterioration" of social situations (256) such as the terror and political repression[39] afflicting our world today. In anticipating FS 7, systematics, we are examining see-judge-act events. Examples 1 to 7 depicted persons' see-judge-act ability to apply general principles to ethical policies or concrete situations. They pointed to initiatives and policies based on a logic of the heart's value judgments. Examples 8-10 will relate all-too-partisan see-judge-act scenarios inadequate to address the social surd. Some of these touch on questionable Christian or Muslim practices or policies which are "beyond the pale" such as those of ISIS that has beheaded, crucified and burned male captives while passing around women as sex slaves.[40] ISIS lacks mercy. Society needs as-inclusive-as-possible judgments of value that can decipher the root causes of problems while eschewing fundamentalisms rooted in the social surd. This may call for radical policy changes to be made by Christian, Muslim, secularist and mixed societies in the light of a persisting social surd.[41] Example 11 touches on secularist "see-judge-act" intolerance which thereby undermines justice and social progress.

8. A See-Judge-Act Example that Fails to Adopt Ethical Principles Rooted in Merciful Forgiveness

For the evangelist David Noebel, western civilization has embarked on a hazardous journey of rejecting or replacing Christ with mortal men and their ideas. Applying *Collossians* 2:8 to our times, he cautions us to beware lest any educator, politician, rock star, news analysts "take you captive through vain and deceitful philosophy (naturalism, materialism, existentialism, pragmaticism)" along the tradition of Marx, Darwin, Nietzsche, Freud, Dewey, Foucault or "the rudiments of the world (socialism, evolution, higher criticism, humanism, moral relativism, deconstructionism, collectivism), and not after Christ."[42] We note that a view such as Noebel's is a fundamentalist one that almost puts him in a corner with Wahhabism. We presume that since his is a Christo-centric view he should develop it to include ethical principles.

F. Distorting "See-Judge-Act" in Partisan Fashion: The Quran's Ambivalence on Peace and Hegemony

This "global ethical secularity book" attempts to bridge Christianity-Islam-secularism issues. Partisan warfare has occurred since George Bush Jr's tragic invasion of Iraq (2003) and has led to the rise of ISIL terrorism. Let us quote two irreconcilable reactions to ISIL horrors posted on Aljazeera's website:

Abdul-Rahman: "According to prophecy the best way to promote peace in the region at this juncture in the human story is not to get in the way of the black flag types... The leaders of Anbar country have understood this and agreed to help ISIL in their quest to free the region from the yoke of colonialism . . . fake international law." Michael David counters this claim with "Mohammed was just a gangster."[43]

We seek to transcend the dilemma of viewing Islam as a religion of peace with appeals to heartfelt mercy. The "religion of peace" slogan does not occur in the Quran, nor in Muhammad's teachings. It first appeared in 1930 in a book by Ishtiaq Husain Qureshi. Slow to take off, by the 1970s the claim began to appear "frequently in the writings of Muslims for Western audiences." In European languages, peace implies the absence of war, freedom from disturbance. "Islam" derives from the Arabic triconsonantal root sīn-lām-mīm (SLM [س ل م]). Many different words are created from this root word by inserting different vowels between the three root consonants.[44]

Many English speakers wrongly assume that if two Arabic words share the same root word then they are related in meaning. In fact, this is not so. For instance, there are many words derived from the root S-L-M. "One should not equate the word Islam with peace by showing that Islam, meaning 'submission', shares a root word with Salaam, 'peace'.[45]

Beliefs generated by Islamic "experts" who encourage suicide bombings have a totalitarian aspect to them. An Internet site labelling itself, "Islam, a Religion of Peace" claims: "Suicide is against Islam. Martyrdom is not. 'Suicide bomber' is a derogatory term invented in the West to try and describe what in Islam is known as a *Fedayeen* or *Shahid* - a martyr. The point of the bomber isn't suicide - it is to kill infidels in battle. This is not just permitted by Muhammad, but encouraged with liberal promises of earthy rewards in heaven, including food and sex." The site cites Quran (4:74) - "Let those fight in the way of Allah who sell the life of this world for the other. Whoso fighteth in the way of Allah, be he slain or be he victorious, on him We shall bestow a vast reward" and Quran (9:111) - "Allah hath purchased of the believers their persons and their goods; for theirs (in return) is the garden (of Paradise): they fight in His cause, and slay and are slain: a promise binding on Him in truth, through the Law, the Gospel, and the Qur'an" One may note that the site's vague "Gospel" attribution here is baseless, false. In the case of ISIS and other terrorists we are dealing with criminals. In examples 9 to 11 we face ambivalent facts. As in the examples of Turkey and Egypt, GEM-FS radically transcends kataphatic beliefs with apophatic faith. Persons of the caliber of al-Ghazali, Ibn al-'Arabi, Thomas Merton and Massignon have shown a way.

9. Erdogan's Politically-Motivated Actions against the Gulen Movement in Turkey

See-Judge-Act can lead to repressive politics as is the case in Erdogan's Turkey. If Gulen has embodied a strong engagement in social problems inspired by an apophatic light, Erdogan practices a kataphatic self-interest disguised under the label "AKP", the "Justice and Development" Party. The Gulen Movement's exposure of corruption in the AKP (late 2013) led the Erdogan regime to accuse Hizmet of allegedly establishing a "parallel structure" within the state—"a shadow fifth column. Hizmet's network of media entities, charities, business and educational establishments based on Gulen's teachings may have unnerved Erdogan's ambitions. Erdogan's actions against Hizmet led a commentator to write, "Turkey remains a good laboratory proving Islamism and press freedoms can only be an oxymoron." If Hizmet has often emphasized the compatibility of Islam with science, reason and progress, Erdogan's repression of Hizmet and other critics and his attacks on Kemalist secularism defy hopes of such compatibility.[46] His actions mirror what Morsi tried to do in Egypt before being deposed by Sisi. While Sisi uses military might to restore secularism in Egypt,[47] Erdogan has reined in secularity. We argue that secularity-Islamic encounters could help transform systems not ideologically but with realist ideals needed in our world.[48]

10. Islamic Leaders in Egypt and Turkey Would Impose Muslim Views on Others

Germans' generous policy of accepting around one million refugees from the Middle East and wanderers from North Africa was severely tried when, in 2016 New Year celebrations, over 1000 young, drunken, but organized North Africans men attacked and robbed women in front of the Cologne Cathedral. This included the rape of three women. The attacks provoked a change of attitude and policy on the part of the government.[49] Muslim commentators pointed to the Islamic traditions that make relations between young Muslim men and women awkward due to prohibitions such as holding hands. Turkey's top Muslim cleric, Mehmet Gormez, has argued that *some* Islamic schools would not command divorce if a father had lust for his own daughter--if she is over nine. For her part, Professor Suad Saleh, Islamic professor at Cairo's Al-Azhar University, writes that the seizure of "infidel girls and their use as sex slaves is sanctioned in the Qur'an. . . Muslim men can take "captives of the right hand" (Quran, 4:24). According to this verse, any Muslim man may have sex with slave girls "provided that you seek (them) with your property, taking (them) in marriage not committing fornication. Then as to those whom you profit by, give them their dowries as appointed; and there is no blame on you about what you mutually agree after what is appointed." Gormez's view, quickly deleted from the internet, and Saleh's provoking message are questionable.[50] They serve to give excuses to young Muslim immigrants. We cite these reports as questionable use by Muslim authorities of see-judge-act scenarios which might promote strife. At issue here is a viable integration having to take precedence over unilaterally-conceived cultural opinions in a globalized world. A judicious tolerance is needed to offset intolerance based on conflicting premises.

11. Secularist Intolerance that Cannot Serve as a Model to Counter Islamic Intolerance

A GEM-FS bridge calls for tolerant acceptance. It argues that authenticity, a criterion of an ethical secularity, can help undercut rabid secular-atheist emphases. While the religious apophatic is fathomed only by the small minority of humans attuned to God's love. Freud and others pioneered an unusual, effective way to use *implicit apophatic reflection* in our lives. Such an apophatic is the "missing mean" between radically different forms of thought. This book's GEM-FS bridging strategy invokes such a missing mean. We now consider how secularists' forfeiture of apophatic reflection tends to lead to a hapless intolerance, one that matches traditional forms of Muslim intolerance—but from an opposed standpoint. One should be tolerant in a globalized world. More easily said than done. Unlike "secularism" ("*laicite*"), secularity does not dismiss the apophatic. What implications can be drawn from this?

The Front National in France (FN) was founded in 1956 by Jean Marie Le Pen, a former paratrooper in Algeria. By 2011, his daughter who succeeded him as FN leader began to advocate, among many other policy changes, her version of "*laicite*" which sees Islam as a threat to French society. The Far Right in France had always defended France's Catholic foundations, but Marine Le Pen began to play to some of French society's deep anxieties.[51] She changed the focus of *laicite* that had meant the separation of Church and State so that the FN now argues against the building of mosques with public money. It also is against such Muslim customs as having separate hours in swimming pools for women, and against alternative lunch menus in public schools. This has become the FN's tool to "legitimate" French culture as *laïcité*. Islam, not the FN, should be perceived as the major threat to democracy, it says. The FN defends French secular values. Its populism is reflected in parallel developments in other European countries such as Holland where Pim Fortuyn stirred up racial tensions until his assassination.[52] While the dominant self-image of the Dutch in public debate is that of a secular nation, Geert Wilders has campaigned to stop what he views as the "Islamization" of the nation. He has compared the Quran to *Mein Kampf* and has campaigned to have it banned. He believes that all Muslim immigration to the Netherlands should be halted and all settled immigrants should be paid to leave.[53] The FN, Fortuin and Wilders have misinterpreted some of Islam's basic teachings. Any type of intolerance is self-defeating, especially if it ignores Freud's profound insights on how an apophatic can help us transform systems.[54]

Chapter Seven

Seventh Functional Specialty

Adjusting, Transforming Systems

An apophatic-based, tolerant GEM-FS can help transvalue values so as to transform systems as needed. Lonergan studied the issues that arose in the 13th century when Western theologians systematically adopted the Greek-Arabic model of thinking. This meant transposing commonsense thinking in religion to a systematic framework. "One cannot move from commonsense to systematic thinking without creating a crisis. One is introducing a new technical language, a new mode of formulating one's convictions and beliefs, a new mode of intellectual development, a new mode of verification."[1] As in the Middle Ages when Franciscans confronted Dominicans on various issues, so today a globalizing world faces divisive issues. Only experts can engage in the relevant theoretical issues, the result being that large social groups greet "the new movement with incomprehension." (Ibid). Indeed, many Christian, Muslim and secular persons today do not understand one another. Our text is not primarily concerned with fully "resolving" such incomprehensions. That would require a comprehensive FS 7 systematic endeavor. We are concerned, however, with helpful theoretical and practical transformative initiatives.

DISAGREEMENTS LEADING TO CONFLICTS THAT CAN PROVOKE EXTREMIST ACTIONS

Many pressing issues studied by religious ethicists "involve disagreements or conflicts among competing social groups that hold and act upon disparate worldviews and values."[2] Some argue that ethics, while a noble effort with a laudable goal, is a liberal project that tends to exclude religious fundamentalists in both its content and in its ongoing ways of doing.[3] Pleading for a merciful secularity, we apply insights from functional systematics to help address searches for common religious grounds upon which to promote justice and peace. One must first clearly differentiate the tasks involved in such an enterprise. Long before the World Parliament of Religion's Declaration of 1993, Friedrich Heiler had claimed that the history of religions could prepare for the future cooperation of world religions. Many supported Heiler's position; Donald Swearer has criticized it for undermining the objectivity of scholarship on religion. Swearer argues that Heiler did not differentiate clearly between the tasks of history and of systematics—a problem that touches a valid global ethic. We do need both sound history and a sound ethics to counter extremism. With Gabriel Tarde and with Lonergan, we link history and ethics to a systematics able to transvalue values.[4]

We are interested in some of the group dynamics[5] that have motivated extremist actions. Sociologists can help explain the dynamics that reach back into the histories of Christianity and Islam. Such dynamics inform not a few misguided, intransigent Islamic terror groups. This book seeks ways through which moderate Christians, Muslims and secular persons may bridge their differences. We appeal to the distinction between faith and beliefs. Instead of divisive beliefs, we stress human commonalities including faith which can help unite us. Faith bridges authentic religious principles in ways consonant with secularity tenets. We note that in today's democracies, human rights are inviolable, endowed with an authority that transcends the temporal. The pioneer French sociologist Emile Durkheim viewed religion as a unified system of beliefs and practices relative to sacred things.[6] Such a religious system helps unite believers into a single moral community. Gabriel Tarde (born 15 years before Durkheim) criticized Durkheim's somewhat dogmatic views. He proposed a more flexible, adaptive approach; he saw humans' ability to adapt as an unending cycle constituting the process of social history. Tarde also criticized the philosophical problems of resemblance underlying Durkheim's comparative sociology.[7] Tarde's approach is not unlike what FS 7 prescribes for the modern world such as differentiations of consciousness, an ongoing discovery of mind, the need of pluralism and a needed ability to grasp one another's mentalities. (*MiT*, 302-54).

Gustave Le Bon argued that a person's conscious personality in a crowd is submerged in the collectivity. Our see-judge-act template looks beyond collectivities and systems; it appeals to personal freedom and responsibility rather than to intransigent views.[8] The problem in the 13th century, for example, was that of adopting the Greek-Arabic model of systematic thinking in religious issues facing Western Europe. Today, however, there is an urgent problem of transposing commonsense thinking in religion to a systematic framework. This is a task, we argue, that a careful study of GEM-FS could help resolve. In this book we take the more modest approach of citing admirable cases of persons such as Frederick Augustus Voigt who defied Nazism or the courageous Muslim initiatives of Fethullah Gullen and Linda Sarsour and less helpful cases such as David Noebel's too-narrow preoccupation with the collisions of world views.

Chapter Eight

Eighth Functional Specialty

Communicating so as to Overcome Intolerance

FS 8 communication brings us back to where this book began--as it should since it is dedicated to a self-corrective process. As noted, most human communication is "phatic", non-propositional; it seeks to establish relationships rather than merely convey ideas. It keeps open the lines of communication among persons. In going beyond the phatic, GEM-FS's Third Way fosters apophatic communion with God to help deepen human communication. Only in FS 8 does the FS process bear fruit: without communications, "the first seven are in vain, for they fail to mature." (*MiT*, 355). Due to our complex differentiations of consciousness, one must specialize, collaborate. FS 8 helps relate specialists on Buddhist-Christian-Muslim-secularity standpoints through kataphatic communication geared to transform present systems. Since a merciful secularity plays a vital role in this book, our final FS 8 section on communication takes seriously the immanent contexts of both religious and secular experience(s). Lonergan points to the need of interdisciplinary relations among the sciences and humanities; this involves transpositions that would help religion "find access into the minds and hearts of men of all cultures"; it also calls for "adaptations needed to make full and proper use of the diverse media of communication" available to us. (Ibid, 132).

ON THE NEED OF A UNIVERSAL VIEWPOINT AND OF UNIVERSAL VALUES TO HELP BRIDGE HUMAN DIVIDES

Lonergan writes that truth is obscured because meaning is often fragmented, resulting in concomitant shrinkages in the possibilities of human communication. Truth is distorted by individual, group, and general biases. Since common sense is unable to criticize itself, Lonergan appeals to his notion of a universal viewpoint and a "potential totality of genetically and dialectically ordered viewpoints." His "totality" differs from Hegelian dialectic which "is complete apart from matters of fact" (*Insight*, 588). Truth is "potential" as it seeks to order various viewpoints. It is a heuristic structure whose contents are sequences of unknowns. "The relations between the unknowns are determinate not specifically but only generically. . . . There are dialectically opposed formulations with their contrasting invitations to further development and reversal" (589). Lonergan writes of man's profound disillusionment, of "the focal point of his horror" (572). Man "had hoped through knowledge to ensure a development that was always progress and never decline" but the advance of human knowledge is ambivalent. Power does not guarantee truth; myth is the permanent alternative to mystery. An answer to contemporary horrors must be based on the real issue which is that of truth. Lonergan's universal viewpoint can help us bring together the views of spiritual writers from various traditions who focus on faith—not mere beliefs. Our aim in the eight FS has been to study how people and traditions may transcend their limitations; in FS 8 we convey the critical message that our world needs coalitions of willing enablers of an ethical secularity.

THE DECLINE OF FAITH AS A PROBLEM FOR THE RELIGIONS AND SOCIETY – A POSSIBLE GEM-FS SOLUTION

Many people today speak of the decline of faith. Perhaps the decline is in beliefs. In this book, we have outlined some of the roles GEM-FS and its see-judge-act subtemplates could play in promoting faith by deepening forms of communication between religious and non-religious persons. Lonergan would have individual persons in various walks of life ask themselves whether they are true to their tradition. "They might conclude that they are, and they may be correct,"[1] but they might also be incorrect. They may have appropriated some of the ideals demanded by a tradition, but there are other ways in which they have diverged from it. Whether from selective inattention, or a failure to understand, or an undetected rationalization, the divergence exists. What I am is one thing, what a genuine Christian, Muslim or secularist is another. One may be unaware of the difference. "My unawareness is unexpressed. Indeed, I have no language to express what I really am, so I use the language of the tradition I unauthentically appropriate, and thereby I devaluate, distort . . . corrupt that language." (Ibid, 121). Lonergan is here calling us to explore various forms of personal authenticity and to be authentic when engaged in needed transformations of today's complex, globalized societies (as proposed and attempted in this book).[2]

Communications is needed for any type of "action," a lesson not lost on organized criminals or terrorist groups. Some Muslims born in the West commute between ISIS enclaves and the West to attack what they see as Western decadence.[3] They learn how to strike terror. Terrorists' experiences lead them to interpret and judge sacred texts as they see "fit" due to their mistaken cultural beliefs. Such beliefs and violent actions need to be corrected by informed judgments on the course of history. A lack of social acceptance experienced by some Muslims in the West which leaves them jobless is part of the problem. Deeper communication among all parties including a genuine hearing of other persons' possible plight is needed. Europe is now faced with the dilemma of some two million Muslim refugees. Several European countries such as Poland and Hungary refuse to take in such refugees due to fears of Islamization.

LINKING THE PROCESSES OF FS 8 COMMUNICATIONS WITH COMMUNITY LIFE AND THE UNIVERSAL VIEWPOINT

"Community" is one of sociology's oldest concepts—but a most contentious one. It has been suggested that, since the term seems to mean everything and anything, it is less than useful and should be retired from the lexicon. Yet, despite sceptics' views, "community" shows few signs of disappearing. The past few decades have seen a revived interest in "community" in many disciplines. We have touched on "community" and "communities" throughout the text. We now want to briefly link "community life" and communications with the realities of universities in the world and with the notion of a universal viewpoint. All four terms include, pivot on "UNI," signifying a striving for UNIty in the four concepts. The reason that the word "commUNIty" won't go away is that it is at the root of human living. CommUNIties and UNIversities throughout the globe must learn to cooperate more effectively. This will be possible to the extent that UNIversities and commUNIties commUNIcate[4] with a UNIversal viewpoint so that all may foster both local and global interests based on ethical secularity responsive to faith convictions.

We have pleaded for a merciful secularity on the part of all. Radically converted persons are the ones best able to pave roads to mercy—as illustrated in some of our see-judge-act subtemplates which call for tolerance.[5] A foundational element in GEM-FS process is illustrated in the courageous actions of a Malala whose deeds earned her the Nobel Peace Prize. Her example or that of Linda Sarsour in Brooklyn implicitly commUNIcate a GEM reduplicative process as illustrated in FS 6 and based on a logic of the heart's value judgments. Such judgments are what have enabled such young women as Malala and Linda to live authentically. Generalizing from these two women's perceptive and courageous stances, we can go back to FS 1. In FS 1 we collected data on how Christianity, Islam, and an ethical secularity have been interfacing in our world. Malala and Linda have radically lived out in their own way what it means to reach out in transformative ways among conflicting data. In Germany, Chancellor Angela Merkel and Bishop Margot Kässman have both argued that one must defang intolerance based on fear and bias. This book has relied on the deeper aspects of religion, faith, secularity and mercy—depth is needed in trying to UNIfy humans within the parameters of a viable world community.

Conclusion

AN INTERNATIONAL GEM ASSOCIATION (IGEMA) AS KEY TO EFFECTIVELY DEPLOYING GEM-FS

Lonergan was a seminal thinker as can be gauged from his writings even in the field of economics. Our interpretation of his method as GEM-FS invites further reflection as to whether and how a reduplicative eight-step functional specialization--based on the dynamic nature of our four conscious intentional operations—might be applied to the sciences. Scientifically, the human race has made great progress—but is mired in sets of problems we have touched on. The challenge is for GEM-FS exponents to help make up for the many deficiencies in life and academia so as to help relieve humanity's many plights.

Our world has become so complicated in its fragmented divisions of labor that ethics and spirituality risk being left at the margins, falling between the cracks. Ethicists and spiritual writers have to deal with the issues besetting technocratic, bureaucratized societies. We have argued that a GEM-FS template and its see-judge-act subtemplates, its expertise in both the apophatic and the kataphatic, its operational range, its explorations of heart, mind and its division of collaborative tasks rooted in a transcultural base can be helpful in bridging misunderstandings among believers and secularity proponents. We have sought to show how and why secularity trumps both secularism and fundamentalisms. It can help defang the rabid fundamentalisms haunting both Islam and Christianity. Hopefully, secularity and mercy can conjoin to form types of GEM-FS bridges of mind and heart our world needs. Still, we have merely *sketched* how GEM-FS might help.

In our view, GEM-FS can only function in ways advocated in this book if enabled through the formation of an International GEM Association (IGE-

MA). Only an IGEMA, fully able to deploy GEM-FS in detailed fashion, could, for example, help bridge the issues dividing religious-secularist mentalities. For this reason, we conclude this book by calling for an IGEMA that would pioneer a GEM-FS cosmopolis--that is, make operative ideas and inspirations that human biases all too easily overlook or reject. An IGEMA could help overcome biases so as to foster a tolerant love rather than revenge. It would be composed of experts in many fields organized so as to effectively deploy the FS. Humans have an impulse to take an eye for an eye, a tooth for a tooth. Most people know that such an impulse is self-defeating. Love resists hurting others. A well-organized IGEMA would testify to the need and possibility of collaboration across different fields of endeavor. It would respect the secularity option, be open to a transcendent ethical love wanting to forgive and help planners devise solutions based on the actual drivers of progress.[1] Such is the type of path this book has sketched in rather fragmentary, pleading ways.

Short Glossary of Islamic Terms in Relation to This Book's GEM-FS Process

(The terms are primarily selected for their being possible "entry points" for a GEM-FS dialogue).

* *Ijtihad* (Arabic: اجتهاد *ijtihād*, "diligence", "struggle with oneself" through deep thought and "independent reasoning." It includes a decision-making process in sharia through personal effort (*jihad*) completely independent of any school (*madhhab*) of jurisprudence (*fiqh*). It requires a "thorough knowledge of theology, revealed texts and legal theory (*usul al-fiqh*) as well as a thorough knowledge of Arabic." By the beginning of the 10th century, most Sunni jurists argued that all major matters of religious law had been settled, allowing for *taqlid*, "the established legal precedents and traditions," to take priority over *ijtihad*. Shi'a Muslims still recognize human reasoning and intellect as a legal source—thus continuing to acknowledge the importance of *ijtihad*. Some ask whether Muslims can reopen the "Gates of *Ijtihad*." As to GEM-FS dialogue, it is essential that the process of *ijtihad* be restored for transformative possibilities.
* *Sufism is a mystical-ascetic aspect of Islam, but not a sect. Rejected by the Wahhabis and Salafis, many Muslims do consider it as the part of Islamic teaching that deals with the purification of the inner self. It helps believers strive to obtain a direct experience of God. Ibn Taymiyya includes the Sufis among those who belong to the Sunna path,[1] using relevant intuitive and emotional faculties that must be trained.

Tasawwuf (the "inwardness of Islam, the "path of the Sufis, the woollen-clothed ones") is regarded as an orthodox, integral part of Islam by Gulen and even by the Medieval traditionalist Ibn Taymiyya. Both Sufism and Tassawwuf can help ground apophatic foundations for a constructive GEM-FS dialogue.

Ulamā (علماء) or *ulema* are the leaders of Islamic society, including teachers, Imams and judges.

*Umma*h (الأمّة) (literally 'nation') is the global community of all Muslim believers. Both *ulama* and *ummah* refer to constitutive personal, societal elements for encounters with non-Muslim communities.

*Wahhabism: a religious movement stemming from Muhammad ibn Abd al-Wahhab (1703-1792) is puritanical and is accused of being "a source of global terrorism" that has inspired the ideology of the Islamic State of Iraq and the Levant (ISIL). Salafism was imported from Egypt by King Faisal in the 1960's. Puritanical Wahhabism-Salafism indicates a type of fundamentalist mentality much more radical than Christian fundamentalism. Both of them are incompatible with GEM-FS transformative possibilities.

Notes

INTRODUCTION

1. Bronislaw Malinowski, "The problem of meaning in primitive languages" in C.K. Ogden & I.A. Richards, *The Meaning of Meaning.* New York, 1923, 146-52. Language is a mode of action rather than a countersign of thought.

2. "Kata" means "down from" or "down into." "Kataphatic" prayer has content; it uses words, images, symbols, ideas. "Apophatic" prayer has no content. It means emptying the mind of words and ideas and simply resting in the presence of God. Centering prayer is apophatic. Ignatian prayer is mostly kataphatic. D. Hammond, "Interpreting Faith and Reason: Denys Turner and Bernard Lonergan in Conversation", Vol. 35, Issue 02. Fall 2008, 191-202. See www.ignatianspirituality.com/2026/kataphatic-or-apophatic-prayer#sthash.NNQt1Ehi.dpuf That "Allah can be known" has to be qualified by the fact that Wahhabis and others deny this. Susannah Ticciati in *Apophatism Transformed: Augustine and the Redemption of Signs* (Leiden: Brill, 2013) and *A New Apophaticism* (Brill, 2013) draws on Augustine to develop an apophatic theology for the 21st century. Shifting the focus away from the failure of words to say something about God, she suggests that the purpose of God-language is to transform us humans in our relationship with God so as to become better signs of God. For Sara Terreault, the apophatic or mystical is (at least in its pre-modern Christian origins) a theological/linguistic move against idolatry. We are strange, blessed wild creatures of finitude who can think/imagine infinity. Our reach exceeds our grasp. The kataphatic/apophatic is about humans' paradoxical, utterly necessary oscillation between saying and unsaying (chastening our unrestricted desire from thinking in a totalizing grasp). The apophatic challenges conceptualism as well as "experientialism."

3. The urgency is also due to record levels of human suffering worldwide caused by ongoing conflicts--as noted by UN Secretary General Ban Ki-moon at the World Humanitarian Summit held on May 23-24, 2016 in Istanbul.

4. Bernard Lonergan, *Method in Theology* (New York: Herder, 1972), 4.

5. In 1968, Lonergan defined "heart" as "the subject on the fourth, existential level of intentional consciousness and in the dynamic state of being in love": "Horizons" in *CWL*, 17, *Philosophical and Theological Papers, 1965-1980*, 20.

6. Bernard Lonergan, *Insight, A Study in Human Understanding, CWL* 3, ed. Fred Crowe, Robert Doran (U. of Toronto, 1997), 96. The method is generalized because it uses both the data of sense and consciousness (see below).

7. This book was planned by Raymaker. For two months, David Legg joined me as co-writer but had to resign due to other work. Dave's influence remains in not a few parts of the text which has led me to retain the editorial "we".

8. John Savant, *America*, May 2, 2016 notes that the search for mystery and poetry has little utility in today's world. For William James, *Varieties of Religious Experience* (New American Library, 1958) 292-93, while the ineffable is an essential mark of the mystical, it is not clear, whether it is the experience or its alleged object, or both, that are ineffable. For Eric Voegelin, a questioner's language reveals itself as a paradoxical event of the ineffable becoming effable. In reflective distance, the questioner "experiences his speech as the divine silence breaking creatively forth in the imaginative word that will illuminate the quest as the questioner's movement of return to the ineffable silence." See Ellis Sandos, *The Voegelinian Revolution: A Biographical Introduction* (Transaction, 2000), 270.

INTRODUCING THE HEART-MIND INTERDISCIPLINARY ISSUES EXPLORED IN THIS BOOK

1. Lonergan's method is unique in that it gives equal weight to *data of consciousness* as well as to those of sense. Its stand on the virtually unconditioned, objectivity, epistemology and metaphysics in *Insight* and on ethics are also "unique", but not studied in sufficient depth or generally accepted in academia--a lack this book tries to address.

2. Denys Turner, *The Darkness of God: Negativity in Christian Mysticism* (Cambridge University, 1999), 20, 33.

3. Mahayana Buddhism is a philosophical movement that proclaimed the possibility of universal salvation, offering assistance to practitioners in the form of compassionate beings called bodhisattvas. The goal was to open up the possibility of becoming a Buddha to all sentient beings. See http://www.dharmanet.org/traditionsbasicdn.htm

4. That "Allah can be known" has to be qualified by the fact that Wahhabis and others deny this—as we note later. Etymologically, Allah is probably a contraction of the Arabic al-Ilāh, "the God." It is traced back to the earliest Semitic writings in which the word for "god" was *il* or *el* (used in the Hebrew Bible). Allāh is the standard Arabic word for God and is used by Arab Christians as well as by Muslims. See http://www.britannica.com/topic/Allah Allah, says the Qur'ān, "loves those who do good." Two passages in the Quran express a mutual love between him and humanity, but the Jewish and Christian precept to "love God with all thy heart" is nowhere formulated in Islam.

5. *The New Dictionary of Theology*, ed., Komonchak, Collins, Lane, (Liturgical Press, 1997), "Mercy". As with *mu* or *sunya*ta, (nothingness) in Zen, mercy apophatically would turn one to action to remedy mere verbal limitations.

6. See Robert Burns, *Catholic Spirituality and Prayer in the Secular City*, University Press of America, 2008. E. O. Wilson's putdowns of philosophy and religions is based on beliefs rather than faith. His presupposition that "history makes no sense without prehistory or biology" (www.youtube.com/watch?v=lx26k8LTCdI&feature=youtu.be) fits into Lonergan's view that science is compatible with faith, that faith transcends "incompatible" religious claims.

7. In *Insight*, Lonergan developed a generalized empirical method, GEM. This book's Part One applies GEM as a secularist pivot. In Part Two and Three, we develop in various ways *MiT*'s functionally specialized (FS) method. For a sketch of Lonergan's method, see http://lonergan.concordia.ca/reprints/grace-method.htm According to GEM-FS, there is a generalized question as to the beyond, the ultimately worthwhile--a question identifiable with aspects of concrete human consciousness. All established religions and religious institutions are responses to that question.

8. Secular humanism addresses a modern void. Paul Kurtz, one of its leaders, distanced himself from all dogmatisms but promoted a caring, ethical humanism as a key to the good life. http://paulkurtz.net. In ethics (See Tad Dunne, www.iep.utm.edu/lonergan), GEM "clarifies the subject's operations regarding values" relying on a personal appropriation of what occurs when

making value judgments. The innate moral norms of moral consciousness "are expressed in explanatory categories, to be used both for conceptualizing for oneself what occurs regarding value judgments and for expressing to others the actual grounds for one's value positions. GEM is based on a gamble that the odds of genuine moral development are best when the players lay these intellectual, moral and affective cards on the table... This implies a duty to acknowledge the historicity of one's moral views as well as a readiness to admit oversights in one's self-knowledge." Given the many moral issues confronting cultures with their different histories, "it also implies a duty to meet the stranger in a place where this openness" can occur--a "duty" at the core of this book's attempts to bridge hearts-minds. This is in keeping with GEM-FS's critically realist orientation.

9. See Amy Antoninka, *Without Measure: Marion's Apophatic-Virtue Phenomenology of Iconic Love* (on "removing the ego) https://baylor-ir.tdl.org/baylor-ir/bitstream/handle/2104/5519/Amy_Antoninka_phd.pdf?sequence=3. In effect, the profounder aspects of an ethical secularity are reinforced e. g. by Jean-Luc Marion's insights. See also Vernon Gregson, *Lonergan, Spirituality and the Meeting of Religions* (Rowman and Littlefield, 1985).

10. John Courtney Murray clarified the meaning of religious liberty, pluralism and secularity in general in his draft of Vatican II's *Religions Freedom*—despite being opposed by conservative theologians and bishops. Islam leaders will hopefully help clarify the claim that being subject to Sharia law outranks one's responsibility before secular law. See e. g. http://us1.campaign-archive2.com/?u=12857896c3097382b25b80a09&id=33d7068a67&e=ebf203930b

11. There are three levels in ethics: 1) moral rules; 2) the grounds of what makes an action "good" and integrates moral rules into coherent systems; 3) the meta-ethical level that investigates the very presuppositions informing various ethical theories (second level) behind particular patterns of behavior (first level). See W. H. Werkmeister, *Theories of Ethics* (Lincoln, NEB, Johnsen, 1961), 7–8.

12. Lonergan does not conceive culture normatively – the "classicist" mistake. He approaches culture empirically.

13. Many have diagnosed the postmodern condition, religious communities as a whole have hardly devised helpful, creative responses. This is due to impediments lying both outside and within religious domains. Various overlapping Impediments have limited the successes of religiously inspired endeavors. The single most powerful constraint bearing upon the religious ethic is the coercive apparatus of the state, both in its internal and external aspects.

14. Near the end of his *The Antichrist* (1895), Nietzsche argues that the moral framework of Christian civilization is oppressive. His proposed transvaluation of values (*Umwertung aller Werte*) would replace master-slave morality which allows the master to be the judge and creator of values. He sought to avoid the resentment driving a slave morality. In *CWL* 18, ch. 14, "Horizon, History, Philosophy", Lonergan evaluates what needs to be done today.

15. The University College London's Atheist, Secularist and Humanist Society was praised by the secularist Richard Dawkins after it refused requests "to remove an image of Jesus and Muhammad sharing a pint." See http://www.theguardian.com/education/2012/jan/13/muhammad-cartoon-student-atheist-society

16. The West is secularized. Africa and the Islamic world are not. Al Qaeda and ISIS hold such paranoid views as that "Crusaders and Zionists" have been conspiring for centuries to destroy Islam. Paranoia cannot be bridged. Al Qaeda has broad roots going back to Sayyid Qutb, author of *Milestones*--much publicized in 1966 when he was tried and executed in Egypt. For George Soros, www.socialeurope.eu/2016/01/how-to-fight-jihadi-terrorism/, jihadists try to convince "Muslim youth worldwide that there is no alternative to terrorism." The West reacts with resentment.

17. There is a growing openness to mystical religiosity and contemplative styles, witness the popularity of religious self-help books and a fascination with angels (direct emissaries from the divine not requiring ecclesial sanction). On the other hand, many are anaesthetized with the constant distractions of today's technology-oriented life styles.

18. Carlotta Gall, *New York Times*, 22 May, 2016, on how hundreds of Kosovars suicide bombers joined ISIS. They were recruited by extremist clerics and secretive associations

funded by Saudi Arabia and other conservative Arab gulf states using labyrinthine networks of donations from charities, private individuals and government ministries.

19. "Lonergan Responds", *Foundations of Theology*, ed. Philip McShane, (Notre Dame U., 1970, 227). For Lonergan, there are two notions of "the universe": 1) The universe proportionate to the human capacity to know facts through a critical realist epistemology; 2) the concrete universe of absolutely everything apart from which there is nothing. The imaginable universe is the objective of our unrestricted desire to know, what Aristotle called *ousia*/being. For Lonergan, the unconditional universe is the objective of unrestricted questioning—part of the "supreme heuristic" of being. The differentiation of universes grounds the distinction between the natural/ secular and transcendent/divine. In any "secular" discussion there is no need to introduce the notion of the divine, unless the question arises about what is the intelligible ground of absolutely everything. See *CWL* 3, 718-25.

20. In *The Contradictions of Modern Moral Philosophy: Ethics after Wittgenstein* (Routledge, 1999) Paul Johnston argues that many moral philosophers, confused as to the nature of correct moral judgements, cannot make much sense of traditional moral beliefs. They would have us reject ethics as a set of outdated, misguided claims with the result that they are left with finding some ways of preserving moral beliefs. The result is a contradiction at the heart of moral philosophy, it is often impossible to tell whether a contemporary philosopher ultimately rejects or endorses the idea of objective right and wrong. Johnston suggests that the central issues of ethics cannot be resolved by conceptual analysis. Charles Taylor helps resolve the contradictions of contemporary moral theorists.

21. In *The Battle for God: Fundamentalism in Judaism, Christianity and Islam* (Knopf/HarperCollins, 2000) argues that fundamentalism is not a throwback to some ancient form of religion but rather a response to the spiritual crisis of the modern world. The collapse of a piety rooted in myth and cult during the Renaissance forced people of faith to grasp for new ways of being religious--and fundamentalism was born so as to combat modernity.

22. A template is a pattern or guide used in woodworking. A GEM-FS template correlates knowing and knowns.

23. Erich Gamma, Richard Helm, Ralph Johnson, John Vlissides, "Template Method" in *Design Patterns*. (Addison-Wesley), 325–330, 1994. A GEM-FS template radically differs from an objective programming template in that GEM- FS enables us to develop Lonergan's contributions to theoretical and practical aspects of life by using the FS's first phase mediating aspect so as to apply it in the mediated phase in see-judge-act fashion to actual issues that divide religious and secularist views. Closed-source code maintenance is seen by many concerns as a losing battle because the day-to-day work is unremarkable." See Michael O. Church "How do big software companies avoid bad programmers making existing code worse?" at http://www.quora.com/ retrieved May, 20 2015. A GEM-FS template pivots on conversions--not on career planning; its two phases seek to motivate interfaith-secularity cooperation among persons dedicated to addressing societal, intercultural, and community problems.

24. Eric Freeman, Mike Loukides et alii, eds. "Head First Design Patterns" (O'Reilly), 289, 2004. First, a class is created that provides the basic steps of an algorithm design. Subclasses change the abstract methods to implement actions.

25. GEM-FS and computer templates also differ in that GEM-FS requires "moral courage" a virtue rarer "than bravery in battle, yet "it is the one essential vital quality for those who seek to change the world." (Robert F. Kennedy).

26. Practical see-judge-act scenarios are indispensable for concretely bridging seemingly contradictory realities.

Just as scripting languages include a template that can be configured into other web templates, so our proposed simplified see-judge-act *nested* subtemplates can be configured to fit a fully-panoplied GEM-FS template thus vastly expanding GEM-FS' operational range and its global ability to foster spiritual-ethical-secular change. GEM-FS's double secular-religious orientation enables one to try to bridge moderate Christian-Muslim-secular views.

27. In his review of *MiT*, Patrick Kirkwood writes: "This a major work of the 20th century in all areas of human knowledge and wisdom. Lonergan's method can be applied to any field of human endeavor from quantum theory to astro-cosmology. Profound and far-reaching, it is an acute examination of how our minds work. As to the data of consciousness and the apophatic in

GEM, Meredith Secomb, "Soundings from Silence: Insights from the Luminous Core Within", http://aejt.com.au/__data/assets/pdf_file/0011/773345/Soundings_from_Silence_Secomb.pdf

28. Patrick Brown, "Lonergan and Berrigan: Two Radical and Visionary Jesuits" DOI:10.5422/fordham/97808232 39825.003.0012. Lonergan tirelessly promoted cognitive breakthroughs; Berrigan achieved moral breakthroughs.

29. On the various types of biases, Lonergan, *Insight*, *CWL* 3, 214-27, 250-267, passim. GEM-FS bridges persons' internal-conscious operations across cultures, religions and disciplines. It helps us discover and apply universal values (by way of its pivotal ways of ever opening us to new horizons) to current problems so as to overcome bias.

30. Scott Halse, *Functional Specialization and Religious Diversity: Bernard Lonergan's Methodology and the Philosophy of Religion* (McGill U., 2008) explains how Lonergan's FS can play a vital role in the study of religious diversity. Delineating the operations involved in the basic tasks of scholarly enquiry, the FS provide a framework open to collaboration among scholars of diverse philosophical-theological viewpoints. We add the GEM part.

31. Tom McPartland's abstract of Andrew Beards' *Method in Metaphysics: Lonergan and the Future of Analytic Philosophy* (U. of Toronto, 2008, 2nd edition) shows how, despite Habermas' "post-metaphysical age", Lonergan's metaphysics is normative. See U. Quarterly, 79, No. 1, 2010 pp. 406-08| 10.1353/utq.2010.0007.

32. Lonergan, *MiT*, 241-42, uses "sublation" in Rahner's sense. What sublates goes beyond what is sublated, putting everything on a new basis without destroying it. It preserves all proper features, moving toward new realizations. Applied to the conversions and self-transcendence, "moral conversion goes beyond the value, truth, to values generally. It promotes the subject from cognitional moral transcendence. It sets him on a new existential level."

33. Lonergan, *A Third Collection*, (Paulist, 1985), 141. GEM "generalizes the notion of data to include the data of consciousness" as well as the notion of method." It operates on a combination of both these types of data. It does not treat of objects without taking into account the corresponding operations of the subject, it does not treat of the subject's operations without taking into account the corresponding objects." GEM differs from Husserl's correlation of *noesis* (act) and *noema* (object). Husserl integrated the several orders of meaning in "intuited" symbols; he had not thought through the Scotist-Kantian view of the sensible in a priori conditions of knowing. Unlike Kant's *a priori* of transcendental apperception, for Lonergan insight goes beyond a theory of consciousness to the *a priori* conditions of the subject as subject as prior prerequisite to any apperception. On the significance of GEM's emphasis on the dialectics of the human good Matthew Lamb, *History, Method and Theology*, 422-53; *MiT*, 27-55, 235-66. *MiT*'s FS emphasize the dialectics of the human good. Cf. R. Doran, *Subject and Psyche: Ricoeur, Jung and the Search for Foundations* (Washington, D.C.: UPA, 1977) and his "Theological Grounds for a World-Cultural Humanity," M. Lamb, ed., *Creativity and Method: Studies in Honor of Bernard Lonergan* (Marquette Univ., 1980).

34. This transformative notion of praxis includes a hermeneutics of suspicion and of recovery as explained by Paul Ricoeur. See Alison Scott-Baumann, *Ricoeur and the Hermeneutics of Suspicion* (Bloomsbury, 2009).

35. One may ask whether there is a pivot point for *MiT*'s kataphatic first mediating phase transitioning into the mediated phase founded on an apophatic. For affirmative answers, Ian B. Bell, *The Relevance of Bernard Lonergan's Notion of Self-Appropriation to a Mystical-Political Theology Series* (American Univ. Studies, 2008) and Ivana Noble, *The Apophatic Way in Gregory of Nyssa*, http://www.iespraha.cz/node/28 retrieved Nov. 25, 2015.

36. Jim Kanaris, *In Deference to the Other, Lonergan and Contemporary Continental Thought* (SUNY, 2004). Lonergan helps us "surrender all of ourselves to the radically decentering of ourselves" so as to participate in transcendent meaning. Unlike Michel Foucault who questioned the notion of human nature, Noam Chomsky, like Lonergan, held that unless "there is some form of relatively fixed human nature, true scientific understanding is impossible." As does Chomsky, GEM-FS builds on a human creative-foundational potential. Foucault's presuppositions led him to "fish around" in self-defeating circles. See Paul Rabinow, ed., *The Foucault Reader* (Pantheon, 1984), 3.

37. The *Collins English Dictionary - 2012 Digital Edition*, 1979, 2002 defines secularity as being concerned with the secular; "the state of being devoted to the affairs of the world." The definition avoids pejorative secular nuances.

38. Charles Taylor, *A Secular Age*, Boston: Belknap, 2007. Taylor had addressed this topic in his earlier *The Ethics of Authenticity*, (Harvard, 1991) and *Varieties of Religion Today: William James Revisited* (Harvard, 2002). For us, secularity implies the process of secularization and ought not militate against traditional religious beliefs and practices. It respects pluralism. As to trans-cultural bridging, concerned parties mus agree to settle differences. Taylor analyzes secularism. We invoke a GEM-FS secularity's intercultural bridging potential by fitting it within a "secular GEM. "Secularity" implies a differentiated political structures that pragmatically accommodates pluralism.

39. The sciences of nature and the science of man are all empirical. "Science is the resultant of an accumulation of related insights, and scientific insights grasp ideas that are immanent not in what is imagined but in what is given. If the sciences of nature can be led astray by the blunder that the objective is not the verified, but the 'out there', so also can the human sciences." Such a blunder in physics yields no more than the ineptitude of Galileo's primary qualities or Newton's true motion. But "it leads zealous practitioners of scientific method in the human fields to rule out of court a major portion of the data and so deny the empirical principle." Behaviorists and sociologists "may have excuses for barring the data of consciousness" due to the difficulties in determining such data. Scientists cannot allege difficulties as excuses for ignoring them. They must overcome them. Neither objectivity in the sense of verification nor the principle of empiricism" justify the ignoring the data of consciousness." (*Insight*, 260).

40. Frederick Ugwu Ozor, www.encyclopedia.com/topic/Social_constructionism.aspx retrieved May 12, 2015.

41. For Paul Knitter, *Without Buddha I Could Not Be a Christian* (Oneworld, 2009), the Buddhist nun Pema Chödrön's talk of Groundlessness and Karl Rahner's stress on Mystery are two different fingers pointing to the same moon": For both of them, to "feel the Reality of Mystery or *Sunyata* means to let go of self, to trust totally in what both of them call infinite openness . . . to what's going on right now, in the trust that what is going on is what I am a part of and what will sustain and lead me, moment by moment. . .. There are no grand visions promised here. Just a mindful trusting of each moment as it comes, with what it contains, with its confusion or inspiration, with its joy or horror, with its hope or despair. Whatever is there, this suchness right now, is the breath of the Spirit, the power of Mystery, the connectedness of Emptiness. . . . The suchness of each moment is the infinite Mercy of God." 7-8, 20.

42. *MiT*, 28-29, 76-81. Also Carla Streeter, ed. at http://lonergan.concordia.ca/glossary/glossary_m-z.htm

43. Charles Tackney and Imran Shah on "Authenticity / الصحة (*as-sehah*) in Employment Relations: Theology of the Workplace Comparative Analysis of Islam and Roman Catholic Social Teaching," presented to the Management Spirituality and Religion Interest Group at the August 2015 Academy of Management Conference. For Rémi Brague http://press.uchicago.edu/Misc/Chicago/070803.html, presuppositions within Islam's Sunni-Shiite traditions would make "authenticity" much more prone to ideology than Imran Shah implies. There are also tensions within Islam and Christianity, between their respective theological poles which are not negotiated in the same way. Theology (*kalam*) in Islam is institutionalized while philosophy (*falsafa*) is viewed as a private affair—restricted to a few. Islam's great thinkers pursued philosophy during their leisure hours: "Farabi was a musician, Avicenna (who did philosophy at night after a normal workday) a physician and a vizier, Averroes, a judge." See Remi Brague Interview at http://press.uchicago.edu/Misc/Chicago/070803.html. Still dedicated religionists can be wounded healers. See for example, *The Buddha & Jesus: an Anthology* (Jesuit Conference of Asia Pacific, (Sri Lanka, Tulana, 2015) and Richard Kearney, "Psychology of the Other," Harvard/Lesley Universities, October, 2015 (building on the Greeks).

44. Operationally relating modernity to traditions is at the heart of GEM-FS, underlying both its generalized and specialized applications.

For Lonergan, "The difference between essential and effective freedom is the difference between a dynamic structure and its operational range." (*CWL* 3, 643). For Rene Guenon, *The*

Crisis of the Modern World, (Sophia Perennis, 1942) modern secular scientism has lost its connection with the Cosmos' metaphysical unity; the material world is seen as independent of the world of Spirit. This has led to the birth of an exclusively secularist materialism.

45. Christians, Muslims and secularists all depend on cognitive operations such as "seeing, hearing, touching, smelling, tasting, inquiring, imagining, understanding, conceiving, formulating, reflecting, marshalling and weighing the evidence, judging, deliberating, evaluating, deciding, speaking, writing" (*MiT*, 6). For Lonergan, humans have an unrestricted desire to know as evident in and exemplified by these operations. The general and special theological categories adequate for pluralist dialogue presuppose a transcultural base for universal communication. This base has two dimensions. The first is anthropological, that of our dynamic human consciousness. It is not transcultural inasmuch as it refers to specific cultural formulations but only inasmuch as it is based in the realities to which such varied formulations refer. These realities are not cultural products. Rather, they are the very principles engendering a culture's authenticity. The second is the gift of God's love offered to all and manifested in the religious traditions. The gift itself, distinct from its manifestations, is transcultural. The manifestations are not. The theological categories are transcultural only to the extent they refer to the inner core of God's gift of love. (*MIT*, 281-86).

46. GEM-FS, a generalized-specialized method, can have implicit, not-theoretically-worked-out applications which in their own ways can effectively help deploy GEM-FS overall theoretical breakthroughs, e. g. in see-judge-act ways.

47. Alvin Toffler, *Future Shock* (Bantam Book, 1970) 458—referring also to people who want instant gratification. For us, spiritual experience does not imply a flight from reality but rather facing it realistically—not for gratification.

48. *MiT*, 126. Lonergan developed the FS "primarily to meet problems in theology, but he extended the notion of the FS to ethics, the human sciences, etc. by associating doctrines, systematics, and communications with policies, plans and implementations, respectively." The eight FS are not separate university departments. They represent a grouping of the operations of mind and heart by which we can actually do better. They are not a recipe for better living; they are a theoretical explanation of how mind and heart work along with a proposal for collaboration. Each of the eight FS is functionally related to the other seven. Being attentive, intelligent, reasonable, and responsible within the two phases helps us understand the past and plan for the future. We learn about the past by moving upward through research, interpretation, history, and a dialectical evaluation. We move into the future by moving downward through foundational commitments, doctrines, systematic organizations of doctrines, communicating the resulting meanings. See Tad Dunne, www.iep.utm.edu/lonergan/ *Internet Encyclopedia of Philosophy*.

49. The FS can be extended beyond theology as is done in this text. We generalize the FS from their elaboration in *MiT* to a framework for optimizing collaboration among theorists and those who implement theories with needed changes. The FS have a generalized structure which each member of a collaborating team helps modify as needed. Each participant works towards his/her particular contribution to the work of the whole in bringing about change.

50. In the see-judge-act method, one first reviews the concrete situation; second, one forms a judgment on it in the light of these same principles; third, one decides what in the circumstances can and should be done to implement these principles. Phillip A. Egan, *Philosophy and Catholic Theology: A Primer*, (Glazier, 2009), 81 compares Cardijn's and Lonergan's respective notions of praxis against the background of the evolving Catholic notion of praxis which Pope John Paul II embodied. For us, GEM-FS and its "secularity" is a "universal human method" accessible by any human being, secular or religious, because it expresses the basic cognitive operations of human consciousness. The "see-judge-act" subtemplates we use simplify this process but are consonant with the GEM-FS template itself.

51. "Complementarity" plays a central role in the GEM-FS such as the complementarity of classical and statistical methods (*Insight*, 126-61) or between GEM's levels of consciousness which are at the root of the FS process, that is between *MiT*'s two mediating-mediated phases. The eight FS, involving many types of operations, are dynamically and functionally related to one another. GEM-FS helps us integrate such complementarities in ways that can reinforce efforts to combat pressing problems and to relate the scientific method to the religious and the spiritual.

52. Karen Armstrong, *Fields of Blood: Religion and the History of Violence* (Bodley Head, 2014) on the impulse toward violence in the world's religions from prehistoric times to the present. Daniel Pipes "The Danger of Partial No-go Zones to Europe," www.danielpipes.org/16322/muslim-no-go-zones-in-europe. For us, religions are not inherently violent--if people come to realize how their deeper self can *correct* urges toward violence. In our troubled times, people risk making decisions based on fatal lacks of understanding by the proponents of religion and of secularism.

53. For Lonergan, building on Aquinas, schemes of recurrence mercy can help heal human situations on both local and global levels. See Evaristus Ekwueme, "Bernard Lonergan notion of Emergent Probability"

54. See *Summa Theologica*, Question 30, "Mercy" at http://www.newadvent.org/summa/3030.htm

55. Paul Berman, *Terror and Liberalism*, (Norton, 2004) writes that the Enlightenment had promoted a liberal society that encourages individual freedom keeping religion and government in separate corners. Such societies would be liberal in the philosophical sense, based on liberty. "But in the aftermath of WWI as a reaction to the successes and failures of liberal civilization, there arose in Europe paranoid, apocalyptic mythologies" of world events obsessed with purity but "ultimately nihilist promoting mass mobilizations for unattainable aims." (xiii). Liberal society and habits of mind also aroused revulsion among such Islamic extremists as Sayyid Qutb who drew heavily on the Europeans' writings but repudiated secular societies with Quran-derived notions of what a good society might be.

56. There is a burgeoning women's rights movement in Muslim-majority societies today. From Pakistan to North Africa, each country has a network of activists, writers and academics struggling to bring women's rights to their countries and overthrow centuries of patriarchal oppression. Networking on the internet and on social media enables them to stay in contact with one another, making the movement a transnational one." See http://www.clarionproject.org/understanding-islamism/muslim-womens-rights-activists

57. "Modern sociocultural systems originated in post Feudal Europe in the commercial and industrial revolutions when centers of economic production gradually shifted from the countryside to burgeoning cities. Separate pre-modern communities began to form broader integrated market systems." Charles L. Harper and Bryan F. Lebeau, "Social Change and Religion in America" http://are.as.wvu.edu/sochange.htm The world may now be on the verge of another depression such as Lonergan witnessed in 1929, which led him to write two books on business cycles.

58. Lonergan, *MiT*, 305-6, notes that in humanity's ongoing discovery of mind, metaphor and symbol are important.

59. James Marsh, *Lonergan in the World: Self-Appropriation and Justice* (Univ. of Toronto, 2014) critiques those who fall prey to a pre-critical realism which claims that knowing of the real world should be immediate, thus distorting the meaning and role of justice. Self-appropriation, whereby one becomes more conscious of one's operations, their relations and intended values, is socially and culturally conditioned and is preliminary to a striving for justice.

60. More on overdoing the theme "Islamophobia."www.meforum.org/6014/islamophobia-coming-to-college-near-you

61. Cited by Antony Valentini in "Quantum Mechanics and Reality", The 1927 Solvay Conference p. 8. See https://www.friendsofimperial.org.uk/Media/Slides/QuantumMechanics-Valentini.pdf

62. Some critics see in the "Cardijn method" an implied relativism as if truth can be manufactured by consensus employing the see-judge-act process. Yet the Latin American bishops in 1968 and in 2007 were doing nothing more than following a course that Pope John XXIII had outlined for them in his 1961 encyclical, *Mater et Magistra* (no. 236) where he describes "See Judge Act" as a method for putting "social principles into practice." One first reviews a concrete situation, judges on it and then decides what should be done in the light of the relevant social principles.

63. *MiT*, 137. The Mandela Foundation states its mission is one of Dialogue and Advocacy: "the art of speaking and listening to others." The mission is not unlike that of GEM-FS in that both explore areas of effective collaboration.

64. Cf Phillip A. Egan, *Philosophy and Catholic Theology: A Primer*, (Glazier, 2009) 81.

65. As pioneered in St. Ignatius of Loyola's *Spiritual Exercises*, we seek a response of the heart, then of the mind.

66. The see-judge-act method involves common sense; the "see" is insufficient epistemologically--an issue Lonergan raises in *Insight*. Beyond this epistemological insufficiency, there are many social injustice issues that must be addressed. As archbishop-cardinal, Pope Francis was a strong force in the Church's social revolution in Latin America. He and his colleagues were practicing the see-judge-act method. GEM-FS is a bit too convoluted to be readily applied (as such) in the successful ways the Latin American bishops applied it. While our "see-judge-act" method skirts epistemological issues such as nominalism, conceptualism and dualism, it does offer a viable (if not the best available) application of what GEM-FS should not omit, namely working out at least an implicitly thought-out way to address blatant issues of inequality such as the struggling 99% vs the 1% getting ever richer etc.

67. See for instance, John Raymaker, Gerald Grudzen, Joe Holland *Spiritual Paths to an Ethical & Ecological Global Civilization: Reading the Signs of the Times with Buddhists, Christians, & Muslims*, (Pacem in Terris, January, 2014).

68. Most of the see-judge-act examples in FS 6 are implicitly informed by apophatic strivings for human authenticity.

69. ISIS is only a part of a much larger problem. When talking both with those fighting ISIS and with those who sympathize with it, one notes the stark differences in perception between the Middle Eastern view of ISIS and the Western media's presentation of it. The latter presents ISIS as dreadfully evil, the natural enemy of all mainstream forces in the Middle East. "In fact, ISIS is not a unique organization; it is one of the most extreme points along a continuum of movements committed to Sunni political Islam. The inchoate mass of Sunni Islamist groups is engaged in a region-wide struggle against a more centralized bloc of states" and movements organized around the Islamic Republic of Iran and its Shia version of political Islam. ISIS has the same ideological roots and similar practices as other Salafi jihadi groups in Syria. ISIS treats non-Muslims brutally in the areas it controls; it adheres to a rigid and fanatical ideology based on a literalist interpretation and application of religious texts. This description also applies to Jabhat al-Nusra, the al-Qaeda franchise in Syria. Nusra opposes ISIS, and is part of a rebel alliance supported by Saudi Arabia, Qatar, and Turkey. In March 2015, when Nusra captured Idleb City in north Syria, the city's 150 Christian families were forced to flee to Turkey. "The alliance Nusra was a part of also included Muslim such Brotherhood-oriented groups, as the Faylaq al-Sham militia, which . . . had no problem operating alongside the jihadis." Jonathan Spyer Jan 19, 2016 www.meforum.org/5801/isis-is-not-the-main-problem-in-mideast

70. Tad Dunne, *Internet Encyclopedia of Philosophy* at http://www.iep.utm.edu/lonergan/ "There is an experiential component of objectivity in the sheer givenness of data. In commonsense discourse, we imagine that what we experience through our five senses is really 'out there.' But we also may refer to what we think is true or good as really "out there." Unfortunately, such talk stifles curiosity about the criteria we use to come to this knowledge. Knowing reality is easily reduced to a mental look. Similarly, the notion of moral objectivity collapses into a property of objects, detached from occurrences in subjects, so that we deem certain acts or people as "objectively evil" or "objectively good," where "objectively" means "out there for anyone to see." This *naiveté* condenses the criteria regarding an act's morality to what we picture, overlooking the meanings that the actors attach to the act.

71. Daniel C. Dennett, *Breaking the Spell: Religion as a Natural Phenomenon* (Penguin, 2006) argues that religious beliefs "derived literally and selectively from religious texts, can lead to behavior that is dubiously moral according to more universal principles of right and wrong. The killing of innocents in the name of holy war is only the most obvious instance. . . . Dennett extends a conciliatory hand to believers so long as they are willing to subject any purportedly God-given moral edict 'to the full light of reason, using all the evidence at our command.' See https://archive.org/stream/christianity_201401/Dennett_%20Daniel%20-%20Breaking%20the%20Spell_djvu.txt GEM-FS does accept "the full light of reason" even in spiritual apophatic domains Dennett or Harris deny exist.

72. This summary is partly based on the introduction to GEM given in Raymaker, Durrani, *Empowering Climate-Change Strategies with Bernard Lonergan's Method* (Lanham, MD: American University Press, 2014), 4-9, 117-20.

73. See Dunstan Robidoux, "Form" http://lonergan.org/wp-content/uploads/2013/01/Form1.pdf. Lonergan notes that St Augustine (a former neo-Platonist), in his *Confessions* narrates his Christian conversion as being an insight that truth (*veritas*) is the existential component of the Christianity; he did understand St John's Prologue (1, 14).

74. Husserl first referred to his notion of conscious intentionality and intentional content as "act-matter", then later as intentional "*noema*". "To speak of the 'intentional content' of a thought is to speak of the mode or way in which a thought is about an object. Different thoughts present objects in different ways (from different perspectives or under different descriptions)." They have "different intentional contents." See www.iep.utm.edu/huss-int/

75. Husserl's method suspends or brackets away the "natural attitude" so as to have philosophy become a rigorous distinctive science; he focused more on consciousness than of empirical things. The crucial difference between phenomenology and Lonergan's method is that the former would integrate the several orders of meaning in symbols (somehow intuited) thus reflecting the Scotist or Kantian grasp of the sensible in a priori conditions of knowing. See John Raymaker, *The Theory-Praxis of Social Ethics: The Complementarity between Bernard Lonergan's and Gibson Winter's Theological Foundations* (Marquette Univ, 1977, 291); Lonergan, *Insight*, 357-59.

76. Matthew C. Ogilvie: *Faith Seeking Understanding, The Functional Specialty, "Systematics," in Bernard Lonergan's Method in Theology*, Marquette Univ., 2011, 39-41, 48-53, notes that for Lonergan and many of his commentators, Kant's "Copernican Revolution" was incomplete; this incomplete turn to the subject resulted in relativism. Kant did succeed in bringing the subject into a technically prominent position in philosophy; many philosophers now focus on thinking subjects. For Lonergan, after the changes effected by absolute idealism, the subject was helpfully addressed in Kierkegaard's stand on faith, Newman's position on conscience, Nietzsche's will to power. . . Blondel's philosophy of action and Scheler's views on feeling. (*MiT*, 264). These authors differed in emphasis but were united in the belief that "pure reason" does not exist. One must consider how persons' minds operate. This means that authenticity cannot be taken for granted; human activity is never "pure." A struggle between authenticity and inauthenticity ensues. We argue with Lonergan that authenticity is achieved through self-transcendent values.

77. For Lonergan, one's insights enrich, illuminate a sensible image and make it intelligible thus linking the concrete level of presentations via direct and reflective insights with the abstractive, universalized world of concepts. The illuminating role of an insight is pivotal for it anticipates intelligibility and then erects heuristic structures in its grasp of significant ideas. The abstractive procedures of classical method are complemented by the inverse insights that yield statistical methods. Further practical and speculative insights yield the heuristic structures of dialectic and genetic methods. (*Verbum*, 34; *CWL* 3, 30, 38-40, 87-88, passim. "Insight arises with respect to an appropriate image: without the insight, the image is a coincidental manifold; by the insight the elements of the image become intelligibly united and related; moreover, accumulations of insights unify and relate ever greater and more diversified ranges of images, and what remains merely coincidental from a lower viewpoint becomes systematic from the accumulation of insights in a higher viewpoint." (Ibid, sec. 7.5, 506). Questions anticipate further insights.

78. All operations of a subject are directed towards, intend, an object. A subject is aware of these operations. For Lonergan, introspection, sheds light on a subject does when objectifying the contents of consciousness: just as we move from the data of sense through inquiry, insight, reflection, judgment, to statements about sensible things, so too we move from the data of consciousness through inquiry, understanding, reflection, judgment, to statements about conscious subjects and their operations. (*MiT*, 8). Lonergan distinguishes his meaning of introspection from the mistaken notion of it based on "ocular vision." Consciousness is not a mere inward inspection. (Ibid.).

79. The transcendental precepts: "be attentive, intelligent, reasonable, responsible-loving" are connected with attention to data and ensuing questions: What is it? (be intelligent), is it so?

(be reasonable); is it worthwhile (to be responsible); is it ultimately worthwhile? (be loving). This covers the gamut of human thinking applied to living. Lonergan examines basic issues in ways that complement Aquinas so as to establish the foundations of knowledge.

80. The cognitional theory and the theory of human freedom Lonergan retrieved from Aquinas on the procession of the inner word and on freedom of the will under the action of grace, informs Lonergan's conception of existential ethics. www.researchgate.net/publication/254599457_The_ethics_of_Lonergan%27s_existential_intellectualism

81. In empirical-related situations, the epistemological theorem and intellectual conversion require that one provide evidence for the right relationship between knowledge and reality. Since we are dealing with what we think is "real", epistemology and intellectual conversion underpin a full understanding /affirmation of both the moral and spiritual life-- providing the basis for understanding authenticity and motivating a faith-driven life. Lonergan uses operations and outcomes to methodically explain how we come to factual knowledge in science. In philosophy, however, one uses precepts that embody the method, e. g. such as when one gains insights into insight.

82. Lonergan, *MiT*, 25. Tad Dunne, http://www.iep.utm.edu/lonergan/ stresses a fourth basic question: "What therefore should we do?" The question lays out a framework for collaboration, based on the answers to the first three questions as well as a basis for *MiT* and this book. Michael Vertin, "Intention, Intentionality," in *The New Dictionary of Catholic Spirituality*, Michael Downey, ed. (Collegeville, MN: Liturgical Press) 2000: 542-43.

83. Lonergan, "Metaphysics as Horizon," *Collection*, 211. A question does not yet have conceptual or symbolic content. It is identified with the attitude of the inquiring and critical mind whether religious or not. However, conservatives tend to take this fact out of context. They think that you have to be religious to be patriotic. But one may follow Jesus' more secular teachings (being charitable, loving one another, treating strangers with kindness) as did the founders of the U. S. For Samuel Adams, "In regard to religion, mutual toleration in the different professions thereof is what all good and candid minds in all ages have ever practiced, and both by precept and example inculcated on mankind." On the rights of the colonists, see https://history.hanover.edu/texts/adamss.html

84. Development involves increasing explanatory differentiation (*Insight*, 478), "a major flexibility that consists in a shift or modification of the ultimate objective" (479), of the various roles of cells (480), psychic integration (483). This is followed by a study of genetic method, a world-view of generalized emergent probability (487). Genetic intelligibility is what we expect to grasp when we ask how new things emerge. Here, the notion of potency is important for ethics. Potency covers all the possibilities latent in given realities to become intelligible elements of higher systems. Creative thinkers expect that nature brings about improvements as when floating clouds of interstellar dust congeal into circulating planets or when damaged brains develop alternate circuits around scar tissue. See Tad Dunne www.iep.utm.edu/lonergan/ . Lonergan's metaphysics is based on a generalized heuristics.

85. Lonergan notes the differences of method that commonly lead scientists to find philosophy baffling, repellent, or absurd. "The basic difference is that scientific method is prior to scientific work and independent of particular scientific results, but philosophic method is coincident with philosophic work and so stands or falls with the with the success or failure of a particular philosophy. This difference leads the scientist to conclude that it is nonsense to talk about a philosophic method and that the plain fact is that philosophy has no method at all." (*CWL* 3, 450).

86. After *Insight*, Lonergan forged links between self-appropriation and mediation. An authentic self "performs within a self-assembling structure of cognitive and moral operations underpinned by the basic intentionality of unrestricted questioning. The self is "located" between lower, material manifolds and the beyond correlative to the unrestricted sweep of questioning." This creates a tripolar tension of the below, the above, and of limitation and transcendence. See Thomas McPartland, http://voegelinview.com/self-appropriation. Lonergan had entered Eric Voegelin's territory. Lonergan's threefold tension is the equivalent of Voegelin's in-between participatory reality. Negotiating one's psychic depths is analogous to Voegelin's portrait of consciousness opening to the unfathomable psychic reaches below, as depicted in Plato's *Timaeus*. One touches on the centrality of divine-human encounters.

87. "Durkheimian sociology and behaviorist psychology may have excuses for barring the data of consciousness, for there exist notable difficulties in determining such data; but the business of the scientist is not to allege difficulties as excuses but to overcome them, and neither objectivity in the sense of verification nor the principle of empiricism can be advanced as reasons for ignoring the data of consciousness." Lonergan, *Insight*, 260.

88. In *History, Ethics, and Emergent Probability* (1999), Kenneth Melchin outlines a heuristic structure for sociology, history and ethics: "Prior to a theory. .. stands a heuristic -- a way of asking questions" which pre-organizes the data, a signpost indicating where the data will lie." Lonergan's heuristic structure of emergent probability reinforces the context of interdisciplinary ethics" (xi-xii). Emergent probability draws upon the complementarity of classical and statistical heuristic structures and integrates them into a model that is dynamic in space and time.

89. While operators are a key notion-procedure in the entire "GEM-FS" enterprise, Lonergan's students seldom address them systematically. The notion of operator first appears in *Insight*, ch. 15; in the general case, it "is the upwardly directed dynamism of proportionate being that we have named finality . . . Operators form a flexible series along which the organism advances from the generic functioning of the initial cell to the flexible circle of ranges of schemes of the mature type. (490-91). The difficulty in studying the operators lies in the complexity of its data. "There is the subject as he is functioning more or less successfully in a flexible circle of ranges of schemes of recurrence. On the other hand, there is the subject as a higher system on the move. One and the same reality is both integrator and operator; but the operator is relentless in transforming the integrator" (501). As opposed to this general notion of operator, *MiT* (249-50) develops a notion of operator which can help us change the future. In dialectic, operators develop positions and reverse counter-positions. For Phil McShane, this operator is one of "discovering operatively." It is a "serious forward speaking. . . a direct speaking. We cannot just remain with the givens of our operations; we have to get into the givens of applied operators in various fields--which is one of Lonergan's use of data both sense and of consciousness. For McShane, "An old style of . . . discussion would have people express their positions to each other and then entering into dialogue. Such a procedure has all the flaws Lonergan identifies in *Insight*, ch 17, sec. 3. A transition is needed, that is, we cannot restrict ourselves to the top of *MiT*, 250 for it is too compact as a scientific intimation. Hiding behind it is the scientific heuristics of *Insight*, 17.3. At issue is that investigators operate from within different horizons—not uniformly. The conversions etc. are needed. See http://sgeme.org/BlogEngine/post/2011/11/11/Seminar-4-Dialectic-by-John-Raymaker.aspx).

90. Tad Dunne "Bernard Lonergan" http://www.iep.utm.edu/lonergan/ *Internet Encyclopedia of Philosophy*

91. Nikolas Kompridis, review of Akeel Bilgrami, *Secularism, Identity, and Enchantment* (Harvard, 2015). See https://ndpr.nd.edu/news/57311-secularism-identity-and-enchantment/ 04/27/2015. Using M. H. Abrams' classic *Natural Supernaturalism*, Bilgrami creates the conceptual space for rethinking the relation between natural and supernatural, so that besides denoting a contrast between what is natural and what is sacred and between what is immanent and what is transcendent, it also comes to represent a contrast between "the idea of the natural as what the natural sciences study and the supernatural as what falls outside of the coverage of the natural sciences" (182). With this third distinction we gain clearer access to the secular repertoire of re-enchantment that romanticism bears and transmits: "not only the words on our pages and on our lips and not only the images on our canvases, but objects and things in the world, including in nature, are filled with properties of value and meaning" (183).

92. Benedict Smith, review of Mario De Caro and David Macarthur (eds.), *Naturalism and Normativity*, Columbia Univ Press, 2010. See https://ndpr.nd.edu/news/24614-naturalism-and-normativity/

93. *Caring about Meaning*, ed. P. Lambert, C. Tansey, C. Going (Montreal, Thomas More Inst., 1982), 53. "Kant's *Verstehen* is the faculty of judgment. You can get along without understanding and judgment on that basis."

94. Liddy. "Changing Our Minds. See http://works.bepress.com/richard_liddy, 3. Lonergan (*CWL*, 3, 417) defines an integral heuristic structure as "the ordered set of all heuristic notions." Among the eight illustrations he gives, p. 418, he clarifies the relations between GEM meta-

physics, science and common sense in the light of what in fact is. See also Tad Dunne, http://www.iep.utm.edu/lonergan/ on distortions of meanings and values today.

95. Eric Voegelin and Lonergan shared the conviction that reason could be properly understood only if taken as motivated by a questioning that had an ultimately transcendental thrust such as the transcendental notions. See Eugene Webb, "Differentiations of Consciousness" at http://faculty.washington.edu/ewebb/EVitaly.pdf

96. GEM-FS (and Lonergan's *opus*) stands or falls with a "feedback" notion of the data of consciousness interacting with sense data and the two forms of data being capable of interaction within an individual but also communally.

Inquiry and insight are into both types of data. Data appealing to the contents of experience (as color to sight) are necessary to establish laws that verify the data of experience. GEM-FS (as a transcultural base) leads us to religious questions asked by all in various ways. It does not begin with the doctrines of religion; rather, it is an empirical base for the questions that underpin religious doctrines as it guides subjects experientially, intelligently, rationally, morally. The formulations of a law contain two types of terms: experiential and explanatory conjugates. The latter are correlatives defined implicitly by empirical established correlations or functions. Lonergan, *CWL* 3, 95-99; 337.

97. The base of GEM-FS general categories is the transcultural reality to which it refers. There are historically conditioned formulations of it-- subject to corrections and modifications. The gift of God's love as transcultural is not "universalist" in the classicist sense but rather in the context of special theological categories. Not conditioned by human knowledge, "it is the cause that leads man to seek knowledge of God." Unlike ordinary love which must first be known to be loved, God's love is pure gift. This gives it a transcultural aspect "manifested more or less authentically in the many and diverse religions of mankind." (*MiT*, 282-83). For those who reject religious meaning, the general categories rooted remain transcultural to them regardless of the state of their religious foundations.

98. For Michael H. McCarthy, *Authenticity as Self-Transcendence: The Enduring Insights of Bernard Lonergan*, (Notre Dame U., 2015), Lonergan's achievement is helping us meet the intellectual challenges of our time. Lonergan critically appropriated our cultural heritage within the problematics created by Descartes, Kant, Hegel, Darwin, Nietzsche, etc. His analysis of human subjectivity helps us remedy the paradoxes at the heart of a nihilist culture.

99. Religions and secular societies all teach moral standards but from conflicting viewpoints. "The fundamental conflict lies not between religious and secular interests but rather between opposed meanings of 'good.' Some mean just 'what benefits me or my group,' and others mean 'what is objectively better, without regard for who benefits.' The first is a self-absorbed morality; the second is a self-transcending morality. These two moral stances are entirely opposed." Tad Dunne, http://users.wowway.com/~tdunne5273/Ethics%20&%20Religion.pdf

100. Pat Byrne, "Ecology, Economy and Redemption as Dynamic," http://www3.nd.edu/~ecoltheo/text_byrne.htm

101. Lonergan, *MiT*, 41, notes why he speaks of contemporary values and self-transcendence as well as to the more ancient Aristotle-Aquinas emphases on virtue. The two latter men did not have the modern notion of "values".

102. GEM-FS is a heuristic model of development, decline, and change. GEM-FS represents an early model of complexity that can be translated as the qualitative vision of emergent probability and studied as a viable network computer study. *Insight* sees the task of constructing a cohesive body of explanatory knowledge as a convoluted building process of recurrent schemes that act as foundational elements to further growth. Lonergan's recurrent "schemes are composed of the cognitional dynamics surrounding insight, but other examples of recurrent growth schemes abound in nature: resource cycles, motor skills, biological routines, autocatalytic processes, etc. The corresponding growing generic World Process can alternatively be thought of as chemical, environmental, evolutionary, social. . ., economical, psychological, or ethical and its generality might be of particular interest to complex systems researchers." See Mike Bretz, http://arxiv.org/ftp/cond-mat/papers/0207/0207241.pdf

103. William A. Mathews, *Lonergan's Quest: A Study of Desire in the Authoring of Insight* (U. of Toronto, 2005) notes that mind and heart, at their core "constituted by a restless desire for truth and value", (vi) are central to GEM-FS.

104. Formerly, faith and belief were the same. "In acknowledging religious beliefs we are acknowledging" what was also termed faith. In acknowledging a faith grounding belief we are acknowledging infused wisdom." (*MiT*, 123).

105. "Just as the conjugate form 'mass was reached by Newton inasmuch as he reduced Kepler's planetary scheme of recurrence to his abstract laws of motion and gravitation", one discovers the "conjugate forms of the organism, the psyche, and intelligence by proceeding from the schemes of organic, psychic, and intellectual recurrence to the underlying correlations." One discerns a regularity of events then advances to abstract relations. *Insight*, 485.

106. Frederick Crowe, *Developing the Lonergan Legacy: Historical, Theoretical, and Existential Themes*, 2004, 358.

107. There is an urgent need to deal with bias since insights that can solve a problem may be available--but the insights will not be grasped and implemented by biased minds. Among the biases "there is the bias of neurosis, fertile in evasion of insight, there is the bias of the individual egoist by which someone exploits each new situation to his own personal advantage, there is the bias of group egoism blind to the fact. . .that in one way or another blocks development and impedes progress." Lonergan, *Microeconomic Dynamics: An Essay in Circulation Analysis*, 102.

108. Tad Dunne, "Bernard Lonergan," *Internet Encyclopedia of Philosophy*, http://www.iep.utm.edu/lonergan/

109. Our view that GEM-FS is at its base secular with an opening to faith helps us bridge secular-religious divides. Buddhism originated with a discovery of the immanent nature of the secular process. Early on, it did not use the word "God". It became a religion only later. Both GEM and Buddhism are "secular processes" open to mystery. The GEM-Buddhist rootedness in the dynamic nature of secular process can be a help in mediating religious-secularist divides. The history and realities of East-West encounters include a coming to terms with the differences between and the interpenetration of the immanent and the transcendent in our lives. When this is not grasped, problems will arise as both the Buddha and Jesus taught us. Since Buddhist philosophy does not refer to "God", it can be seen as atheistic/ secular. It does have a strong this-worldly orientation seeking inner peace. Its seeming atheistic bent is in contrast to Christianity and Islam for whom God should be at the center of a life of faith and thought. Many people think of Buddhism as a religion partly because of its ritualistic aspects. In fact, "all" humans have their rituals, if not religious ones: for example, such rituals as those of sport, television, politics etc. The Islamic community is both religious and political, business and prayer, as the Quran is said to be both human and divine.

110. Giovanni Sala, *Theological Aspects of Bernard Lonergan's Method in Theology*, tr. Donald E. Buzzelli www.lonergan.org/dialogue_partners/Sala/theological_aspects_of_bern ard_l.htm For Lonergan, there is an inversion in the way conversion would ordinarily occur. Logically, "religious conversion should come last, since it is the culmination of the human spirit's natural movement of self-transcendence. But in the real order God . . . takes the initiative". It leads to religious conversion, then "expands in different ways into all of human life—into free and responsible choices, and finally into the reordering of one's explicit criterion for knowledge and truth."

111. Lonergan, "Theology in Its New Context," *A Second Collection*, ed. William F.J. Ryan and Bernard J. Tyrrell, Univ. of Toronto, 1996, 67. For David Tracy, FS "foundations" lacks critical justification. Lonergan, (*Foundations of Theology*, 230f) counters that a theologian's choice of one horizon in preference to others is illuminated by a sufficiently broad comprehension of the truth and the errors, the values and the disvalues, informing a horizon. The resources for this comprehension are supplied by the first four FS. If a theologian is both enlightened and virtuous, then along with a "good conscience" he/she will make correct judgments of values. Foundations occurs at the existential level since it is "a fully conscious decision about one's horizon . . ., one's world-view." It deliberately selects the framework for doctrines to take on meaning, be systematized, reconciled and communicated. (233).

112. For Peter Berger, "Secularization Falsified", (www.firstthings.com/article/2008/02/002-secularization-falsified) there is "a confusion of categories." Modernity is not necessarily secularizing but "it is necessarily pluralizing." It is characterized by an increasing plurality, within the same society, of different beliefs, values, and worldviews." Plurality poses "a challenge to all religious traditions" in that there are "all these others," both far and near with which they must "cope". This challenge, however, is not the one assumed by secularization theory." (Ibid). Berger has changed his mind on this issue by stressing pluralism: see Gregor Thuswladner, "A Conversation with Peter L. Berger: How my Views Have Changed" Sep. 12, 2013, http://thecresset.org/2014/Lent/Thuswaldner_L14.html

113. Ibid. Freud could not explain why such highly religious figures as Jesus, Lincoln or Gandhi had such influence in transforming existing social and cultural systems or why their opponents resorted to making martyrs of them.

114. Brian Braman, *Meaning and Authenticity: Bernard Lonergan and Charles Taylor on the Drama of Authentic Human Existence*, Univ. of Toronto, 2008, studies the two men's responses to the secularity question. Focusing on "authenticity," Braman discovers a *telos* proper to classical philosophy: searching for what is true and good, and doing so in such a way as to appropriate what we discover. Being authentic is "a way of living one's life in a new dimension" (98). "Taylor and Lonergan agree with Augustine in holding the priority of love [over] knowledge" (99).

115. Taylor's *A Secular Age* begins with Bede Griffith's description of a religious experience he had as a school-boy: trees are blossoming, birds are singing, the author has the sensation that angels are present and that God is looking down on him. Much of the rest of the book explores why it has become increasingly rare and difficult in our secular age to live these kinds of experiences. See also Kristina Stoeckl at http://blogs.ssrc.org/tif/tag/charles-taylor/. Philip Rieff, *My Life Among the Deathworks* (Univ. of Virginia, 2006) argued that the cultural elite have been producing "deathworks." Instead of enriching the culture, they lead to its death; they define social order without reference to sacred order. He focused on the deathworks of artists and writers and also of Supreme Court justices and medical professionals who do not respect life. Their approaches differ, but the deleterious effects on society are the same.

116. Since the 17th century, the "Western world" has been seen less as a geographical area than as a movement in the world's cultures and minds. Differentiations of mind and secularism (as in political orders) each brings about its own sets of problems. Conservative reactions against secularism provoke organized forms of resistance. There are both authentic and inauthentic responses to differentiated consciousness. "Partly-converted" religious believers overlook the faith-belief disjunction, causing them to miss the breadth of faith-conversion. Interreligious dialogue (as in the World Parliament of Religions or among ecumenists) are helpful. Secularism is anti-religious; we advocate secularity because it fosters tolerance in politics and free religious institutions in the world's distinct cultures.

117. Charles Blattberg, "What's wrong with hypergoods" http://psc.sagepub.com/content/33/7/802.abstract. For Charles Taylor, 'hypergoods' are "the architechtonic goods that serve as the basis of our moral frameworks"; they "are a moral culture-driver helping us solve our dilemmas in the face of the plurality of human goods ... They orchestrate the arrangement and hierarchy of other goods, interpreting their priority and their moral play. They "can raise or lower their priority... even eliminate certain goods from moral play altogether. Hypergoods, "are incomparably more important than the others" providing the standpoint from which other goods must be "judged, decided about." (1989, 63). For Blattberg, "freedom is not to be reduced to a mere matter of the will alone, to naked individual choice. Taylor fails to clearly distinguish between ethical conflicts and those relating to the religio-aesthetic domain. A proper identification of hypergoods as aesthetic... requires us to revise his accounts of ordinary life, of evil and of the controversy over university curricula." Lonergan's human-good views need no such revision.

118. "Genuine objectivity is the fruit of authentic subjectivity. To seek and employ some alternative prop or crutch invariably leads to reductionism. (*MiT* 262-65). Hans-Georg Gadamer, *Wahrheit und Methode*, (Tübingen: Mohr, 1961) contends that there are no satisfactory methodical criteria that prescind from the criteria of truth.

119. Taylor is here using the late Wittgenstein's imagery in *On Certainty*—unorganized notes he took on matters related to knowledge, doubt, skepticism, and certainty: several themes and preoccupations recur throughout.

120. The split between religion and science began during the Enlightenment. Jean-Luc Marion, *Being Given: Toward a Phenomenology of Givenness*, tr. Jeffrey L. Kosky, (Stanford, 2002) rehabilitates the phenomenological project by beginning with the radical primacy in it of *givenness*. Marion's unique "theme is the givenness that is required before phenomena can show themselves in consciousness. What shows itself first gives itself." (5). Christian De Quincey, *Radical Nature: The Soul of Matter* (Invisible Cities, 2002) also calls for new radical approaches.

121. Charles Taylor, *The Sources of the Self: The Making of the Modern Identity* (Harvard Univ., 1989), 3. Augustine's theories--the central doctrines throughout Christian civilization for a millennium, were far removed from the more radical inwardness of enlightenment philosophers such as Descartes and Locke. Following Descartes, Locke argued that our minds' understanding involved a radical disengagement from the world. Unlike Descartes, whose understanding of the mental depended on an autonomous inward reasoning not affected by the surrounding world, Locke rejected "innate ideas". For Locke, understanding the world and mankind's place in it depended on our sense impressions. Experience of the world was constituted by simple ideas resulting from these impressions. Reflection combined these ideas into more complex ideas. Understanding of the world was no more than the combination of sense impressions. The mind was seen as a mechanism that constructed and organized understandings through the building blocks of simple ideas. Whereas Plato saw reasoning as inherent in a vision of a meaningful world, Locke saw reasoning as a mechanistic procedure able to make sense both of the surrounding world and of the mind itself. Taylor refers to the radical reflexivity that allows the mind to objectify the mind as a "punctual self". The person can now look at his own reasoning, will and desires as though these were extrinsic and, according to Locke, manipulatable objects. The self that looks upon his/her mind is extensionless, "it is nowhere but in this power to fix things as objects." (*Sources*, 171, 72). See commentary: www.sunypress.edu/pdf/60558.pdf

122. For Taylor, accounting for the moral sources orienting our lives should include the strong evaluations "we make about particular modes of life as we seek to identify the constitutive good of our lives. By constitutive good, Taylor refers to a good "the love of which empowers us to do and be good". (*Sources*, 93). The constitutive good, whether it be a belief in reason over desire, the inherent benevolence of the natural world, or the intuitively benign nature of human sentiment—orients us towards the evaluations that we make and the goods we aspire towards."

123. Sam Harris, *The End of Faith: Religion, Terror and the Future of Reason* (Norton, 2004).

124. This "central role" is moot in the way Islam imposed a *jizya* tax on conquered people who refused to convert. *Jizya* appears in Quran 9:29, "Fight those among who do not believe in Allah nor the Last Day, nor forbid what Allah and his Messenger have forbidden, nor embrace the religion of truth, until they pay the *jizya* ... and feel themselves subdued." *Jizya* was first imposed on Jews and Christians in the Arabian Peninsula, North Africa and Spain, then on Hindus. Some Muslim jurists tolerated humiliating rituals when subjugated Christians and Jews paid the *jizya*; they received a smart smack on the nape of the neck or forehead from the collector. *Jizya* had vanished in modern times until ISIS reinstated it. See Raymond Abrahim http://humanevents.com/2015/05/29/islamic-jizya-fact-vs-fiction/

125. *Loss of transcendence* recalls Heidegger's pointing to our loss of the question of being: "transcendence" appeals to some religious communities, but not to scientists focused on "empirical method."

126. GEM-FS is a doing, an apophatic-inspired-kataphatic reflection on how to take needed and possible action.

127. Benjamin Straumann, argues that the Peace of Westphalia (1648) was a secular constitution which "successfully solved the problem of deep religious disagreement by imposing protoliberal religious liberties on the estates of the Holy Roman Empire" leaving the subjects with exclusively secular duties towards their authorities. It addressed "the issue of compliance with

its religious provisions by establishing a secular procedure to adjudicate religious disputes that excluded religious reasoning from the courts." It had "important implications for any view of sovereignty." The Treaty "established a secular order by taking sovereignty over religious affairs away from the discretion of territorial princes and by establishing a proto-liberal legal distinction between private and public affairs." The Treaty must thus be seen as a successful constitutional experiment in dealing with deep religious disagreements." There arose an "institutional arrangement for organizing political life that is based on two principles: territoriality and the exclusion of external actors from domestic authority structures." See Institute for International Law and Justice, New York Univ., "IILJ Working Paper 2007/7". The situation in the Islamic world has been quite different.

128. Pope Francis' Year of Mercy 2015-2016 recalls Pope John XXIII's call for the "medicine of mercy."

129. Peter Kreeft, "What Christians Can Learn from Muslims?" http://www.catholiceducation.org/en/religion-and-philosophy/other-religions/between-allah-and-jesus-what-christians-can-learn-from-muslims.html His Muslim-friendly Christian site notes: "Please ask yourself whether you would like others to judge Christianity based on the picture of it now being presented in the modern Western media. Then please remember the Golden Rule, and apply this to the picture of Islam presented by the same source." He continues "I am a Catholic Christian. I write to other Christians. Muslims are invited to listen and talk back and correct what I may have gotten wrong about them. But where am I coming from? Neither left nor right, neither liberal (or modernist) Christianity nor fundamentalism. And that includes my take on Islam, which is neither the naive, limp 'Why can't we all just get along?' nor the blind demonization of 'Enemies!' As a Christian, I say Islam crucially lacks the Cross, and Christ, and his radical love. But as a Christian I also say Islam has great and deep resources of morality and sanctity that should inspire us."

130. Kreeft, *Between Allah and Jesus* (Nottingham, England: IVP Books, 2010), "uses the figure of 'Isa, a devout Muslim, to highlight the commonalities between Islamic and Catholic piety. Through 'Isa (Arabic form of Jesus) Kreeft argues that terrorism and a jihad trying to subjugate "unbelievers" ... are not germane to the Muslims' religious lives. They are perversions of Islam's true spirit, as witch-burnings... and religious wars were distortions of Christian faith." Bassam Michael Madany, www.unashamedofthegospel.org/kreeft-on-islam.cfm faults Kreeft for being "unacquainted with the tremendous changes that have occurred" in Islamdom since the end of colonialism. Tom Pyszczynski, "What are we so afraid of? A terror management theory perspective on the politics of fear" in *Social Research*, (Winter, 2004) on why, when stressed, people defend their cultural worldviews more vigorously.

131. Hiiran Online, www.hiiraan.com/news4/2015/Apr/99167/what_ayaan_hirsi_ali_doesn_t_get_about_islam.aspx

132. See Joby Warrick, *Black Flags: The Rise of ISIS* (Doubleday, 2015). In a May 2004 video, Zarqawi was shown "slaughtering" Nick Berg, an American radio repairman. It gave him the "confidence" to help launch ISIS as a super-state. Robert Spencer argues that the West has underestimated Islam's goal of global supremacy. *In The Complete Infidel's Guide to ISIS* (Regnery, 2015), he details ISIS' inner workings, its financing, the ideology driving it. On Christian-Islamic misunderstandings of *Tawhid* or divine simplicity, Poh Sen Tan, www.academia.edu/6211315/AL-GHAZALI_AND_THOMAS_AQUINAS_ON_THE_DOCTRINE_OF_DIVINE_SIMPLICITY_TAWHID

133. *Leaving Islam: Apostates Speak Out*, Ibn Warraq, ed. 8 (Prometheus Books, 2003).

134. As to the unity of human consciousness being disputed by some, Lonergan writes that the conflict lies "between human reality and human thought about human reality." It is between that reality and giving an account of that reality. Consciousness "is not some inward look but a quality of cognitional acts, a quality that differs on the different levels of cognitional process, a quality that concretely is the identity immanent in the diversity and the multiplicity of the process. However, one cannot insist too strongly that such an account of consciousness is not itself consciousness. The account supposes consciousness as its data for inquiry, for insight, for formulation, for reflection, for grasp of the unconditioned, for judgment. But giving the account is the formulating and the judging, while the account itself is what is formulated and affirmed.

Consciousness as given is neither formulated nor affirmed. Consciousness is given independently of its being formulated or affirmed." (*CWL* 3, 350).

135. Field specialization divides and subdivides the field of data; subject specialization arranges and divides the results of its investigations. The FS are developmental, as is consciousness. With each new differentiation and formalization of a field and/or subject, the dynamism of the FS re-emerges: from data to results, going through the different FS cyclically. There are highly disparate emphases, e.g., research fields and subjects are quite different from communications; still, all engage in the process of distinguishing and separating successive stages in the process from data to results. (MiT, 125-27).

136. Traditional analytical models are inadequate to understand today's conflicts; religious insights are also needed. GEM is a systems approach that correlates the subject's operations of knowing and choosing to their corresponding objects. It understands objectivity as a correlation between the subject's intentionality and the realities and values intended, See Tad Dunne, "B. Lonergan" http://www.iep.utm.edu/lonergan/ *Internet Encyclopedia of Philosophy*

137. A *fatwa* is an Islamic legal pronouncement issued by a religious law expert (*mufti*), pertaining to a specific issue.

Some Muslims have bemoaned the misuse of core teachings of the Quran and hadiths by extremists and unilateral "uses" of such hadiths as Sunan Abu Dawud, Book 32 - Clothing (Kitab Al–Libas, no. 4092) by refugees initially welcomed in Germany. They sexually attack European, non-Islamic women for not covering their bodies more!

138. Raymond Ibrahim, http://www.meforum.org/5423/us-oath-of-allegiance-shariah, Aug. 6, 2015, relates why new Muslim citizens in the US are exempt from US military service. This is based in part on *Quran* 3:28: "Let believers not take for friends and allies infidels rather than believers: and whoever does this shall have no relationship left with Allah...." Nidal Hasan, a Muslim serving in the U.S. Army, convicted of murder for killing two American soldiers and wounding fourteen, attacked the men for he was concerned U.S. troops would kill fellow Muslims in Iraq." See also www.latimes.com/nation/nationnow/la-na-nn-fort-hood-shooter-islamic-state-20140830-story.html

139. "Where knowing is a structure, *knowing knowing* must be a reduplication of the structure", *Collection*, 224. All humans in whatever culture come to know through this reduplicative structural process. On the basis of this, all disciplines can engage in FS transcultural, transformative bridges in an age of constant change. One appropriates one's operations through schemes of recurrence and reduplicatively applies the operations to schemes of nature.

140. One attains cognitional self-transcendence when one attends, inquires then judges through direct-reflective understanding. One reaches moral and religious self-transcendence by deciding for the truly good and loving the truly lovable. To the extent that one achieves cognitional, moral and religious self-transcendence, one is authentic. One is unauthentic when not open to data, one scoffs at understanding, refuses to reflect and judge, rejects the love of the truly lovable. The data, a mixture of authenticity and inauthenticity, and the investigation of the data may be affected by an investigator's low level of authenticity. One must presume neither a speculative intellect, nor a pure reason drawing necessary truths from self-evident principles. Analytic propositions, too, must be submitted to the process of GEM-FS critical verification which is in large part concerned with knowing subjects.

141. The human family, increasingly linked by globalization, stands before the great mystery of the Cosmos that has brought us from the utter chaos of the first instant of creation to our present civilizations bound together by communication systems, economic interdependence, and our need to solve global problems of poverty, climate change, and sustainability of ecosystems. Our text seeks to promote a global understanding of universal values.

142. GEM-FS's eight-step collaborative method helps participants adapt issues so as integrate their helpful points while discarding aberrations. GEM-FS is more than a "tool"; it is a transformative template. In our case, we seek to detect within secularization processes what is to be changed or eliminated so as to infuse it with a secularity ethic.

143. Human adults "operate on the mediating operations" but "the mystic withdraws into the *ultima solitudo* whereby "he drops the constructs of culture and the whole complicated mass of mediating operations to return to a new, mediated immediacy of his subjectivity reaching for God." (*MiT*, 29).

SKETCHING A GEM-FS BRIDGE'S MEDIATING PHASE AS OUTLINED IN *MIT*'S FIRST FOUR SPECIALTIES : PROBING INTO BUDDHIST-CHRISTIAN-MUSLIM TEACHINGS SO AS TO BEST BROACH A GLOBAL SECULARITY ETHICS

1. The first mediating phase's proper function is that of reaching its results by an appeal to the data (*MiT*, 143). This book's mediated phase includes see-judge-act subtemplates as well as the underlying GEM-FS template itself.
2. Lonergan's focus on the conversions can help bridge our divides as to intra- and extra-Church issues. It can serve as a key to bridging divisive issues. Its global spirituality underpins and complements a global secularity ethics.
3. Arvind Sharma, "Mahatma Gandhi as a Mystic", https://www.highbeam.com/doc/1G1-81137817.html

1. FIRST FUNCTIONAL SPECIALTY

1. Sean McNelis, *Making Progress in Housing* (Routledge, 2014) reviews methods operating within FS 1, research which has the limited role of contributing empirical evidence to find valid answers to "what-is-it-questions", i.e. to help develop explanatory theories in FS 2, interpretation. Research also helps interpreters generate theories.
2. The leftist critic Andre Vltchek in his "Who Should Be Blamed for Muslim Terrorism?" Jan. 9, 2015, squarely puts the blame on Western governments who e. g. in the 1960's undermined leftist Muslim leaders such as Sukarno, while failing to appreciate Islam's great cultural contributions. He counsels reading Edward Said's memoirs. http://www.counterpunch.org/2015/01/09/who-should-be-blamed-for-muslim-terrorism/
3. Unlike 'deconstructionists' who focus on the separateness of lived experience, Buddha's teaching that all things are 'empty' (devoid-of-individual-essence-but-interrelated-in-dependent-origination) can help provoke conversion. One's true nature is that of a non-self. See Raymaker, Grudzen and Holland, *Spiritual Paths*, 123, 213. As opposed to Eastern holistic views, scientists are today exposed to a cartesianism with its ironic tendency of being at once overly-subjective and overly-objective. They are over-subjective in that they get trapped by language's limits. If scientists see "reality" in terms of interpreted phenomena to be verified through experiments, the question still arises as to the underlying cognitional procedures which guarantee a verification to be true and objective.
4. See Maurits G. T. Kwee, "Relational Buddhism," National Academy of Psychology (NAOP) India 2011.
5. Kung, *Islam, Past, Present, Future*, tr. by John Bowden (Oxford: Oneworld, 2007), 95-97.
6. Nick Bostrom, "Transhumanist Values", *Review of Contemporary Philosophy*, Vol. 4, May (2005)] [pdf]. On hypermodernism, Charlene Spretnak, *States of Grace: The Recovery of Meaning in the Postmodern Age* (Harper, 1993). Spretnak argues persuasively on the relevance of spiritual issues in creatively renewing modern life.
7. See David Cook "Paul Virilio: The Politics of 'Real Time' at http://ctheory.net/articles.aspx?id=360 and Jacques Derrida, *Edmund Husserl's The Origin of Geometry*, tr by John P. Leavey, Stony Brook, N.Y.: Hays, 1978, 169.
8. A reigning ideology "from above" can, in fact, permeate all aspects of life—as epitomized e. g. in Saudi Arabia.

2. SECOND FUNCTIONAL SPECIALTY

1. www.independent.co.uk/news/world/asia/pakistan-blasphemy-laws-increasingly-misused-to-settle-petty-disputes-against-christians-a6768546.html In Pakistan, blasphemy laws can punish the insulting of Islam with death. Some see the laws as being a means to persecute minority faiths and settle petty grievances.

2. Leo D. Lefebure, *True and Holy: Christian Scripture and Other Religions* (Orbis, 2013) writes of the possible deadly consequences when believers read the sacred texts of other religions through a "hermeneutic of hostility." Christians, too, have erred in this respect but in recent decades, many Christians have radically refashioned their approaches to other faiths. The "new 'hermeneutics of generosity' seeks to uncover what we can learn from other holy texts and the communities treasuring them. It seeks to find common ground on important issues such as human rights and religious liberty. Lefebure offers Christian readings of Jewish, Muslim, Hindu, and Buddhist holy texts that suggest new bases for friendly understanding. Noting the tensions in the relationship between Christians and these four other religious communities," he examines issues involved in interpreting the Bible in interreligious dialogue. See a review at http://www.amazon.com/True-Holy-Christian-Scripture-Religions-ebook/dp/B00JJWCZKI

3. Sharia law is cast from the actions and words of Muhammad (the "Sunnah") and the Quran. Sharia law cannot be altered, but interpreting the sharia (*fiqh*) by imams is tolerated. Many new interpretations are needed today. Traditionally, sharia as "law of God" has counterbalanced state tyranny. Each person is responsible to God alone. The Medina Charter allowed Muhammad, a former outsider, to take charge of the community (Kung, *Islam*, 106).

As to possible later accretions to the Medina Charter, see Sean William White, "Medina Charter of Prophet Muhammad and Pluralism," www.islamicity.org/5685/medina-charter-of-prophet-muhammad-and-pluralism.

4. GEM-FS gets us beyond Western or sharia legal formulations by stressing our cognitional operations as well as the terms and *relations* of implicit definitions and higher viewpoints (*CWL* 3, 37). It avoids *relativism* (Ibid, 366-71).

5. See Rudolph Peters, "Revivalist Movements in Islam from the Eighteenth to the Twentieth Century and the Role of Islam in Modern History" in *Islam in the World Today*, ed. by Werner Ende and Udo Steinbach, Cornell U., 2010, 100, on how Atatürk and others helped lay foundations to reinterpret Islam so as to "reform Islamic society."

6. We are here indebted to Catherine King. See also Jayandra Soni and John Raymaker ed. "Toward Sharing Values across Cultures and Religions" in *Journal of Religious Ethics*, Vol. 39, May, 2011.

7. For Hendrik Vroom, *No Other Gods: Christian Belief in Dialogue with Buddhism, Hinduism, and Islam*. (Grand Rapids, MI, Eerdmans, 1996), "true tolerance requires understanding of religious "others" in one's midst", 268. "A critical exchange through dialogue is of paramount importance. "The alternative to clashes and conflicts between religious groups is an open, sensitive, yet critical discussion." In doing so, we can use categories such as good, evil, transcendence to compare concepts, "as long as we realize that we are grouping very different entities." (Ibid, 275). On Buddhism and religious pluralism, see "The Pluralism Project" http://pluralism.org/religions/buddhism/

8. Umar F. Abd-Allah, "The Perceptible and the Unseen: the Qur'anic Conception of Man's Relationship to God and Realities Beyond Human Perception," *RSC*, 209-264. He argues that the notion of the Unseen was to some extent a carryover from pre-Islamic belief in Arabia: "The world of the Unseen [encompasses] the realm of God (Allah), the lesser gods [pre-Islamic], the angels (*al-mala'ika*), and the spirits (*al-jinn*)." For Abd-Allah, there is a strong element of continuity linking religious practices of the pre-Islamic Arabs and those of the ancient Near East, just as fundamental parallels appear between Zarathustra, the biblical prophets, and Muhammad. Quoted by Dan Lee, *Mystics, Messiahs and the Authentication of Belief*, unpublished PhD thesis, Mahidol Univ. Thailand, 2015, 116; see rsc.byu.edu/archived/selected-articles/perceptible-and-unseen-quranic-conception-mans-relationship-god-and

9. Cardinal Ratzinger, "The Religion According to Reason" see http://www.zenit.org/en/articles/cardinal-ratzinger-on-europe-s-crisis-of-culture-part-4 "It is necessary that both sides

engage in self-reflection and be willing to correct themselves." Christianity must not forget that it is the religion of the *Logos*....faith in the ... Creator Spirit, from which proceeds everything that exists. Today, this should be precisely its philosophical strength, in so far as the problem is whether the world comes from the irrational, and reason is not, therefore, other than a "subproduct," on occasion even harmful of its development -- or whether the world comes from reason, and is, as a consequence, its criterion and goal." (ibid). Lonergan, "Emerging Religious Consciousness of our Time" *Third Collection*, 63-65, on a second enlightenment whose significance may be that of "offering hope and providing leadership to the masses alienated by large establishments under bureaucratic management."

10. By using both the Quran and valid Hadith as sources, the scholar relied on analogical reasoning to find a solution to legal problems; it was a religious duty for those qualified to conduct it. One was recognized as a scholar when competent to interpret sharia by *ijtihad*. Sunnis but not Shiites have vastly curtailed the role of *ijtihad*—causing a crisis within Islam. The role of the apophatic is now distorted as in Wahhabism's rejection of Sufism. See Harold Rhode, "Can Muslims Reopen the Gates of *Ijtihad*?" www.gatestoneinstitute.org/3114/muslims-ijtihad

11. Robert R. Reilly, *The Closing of the Muslim Mind: How Intellectual Suicide Created the Modern Islamist Crisis* (ISI Books, 2011). Kung, *Islam,* 384, on the traditionalist Ash'arites' victory in Iraq—which led to the sharia being preeminent over free philosophical discussion. Here lies the germ of much Islamic intolerance. It was "the victory of traditionalism and of al-Mawardi (born 974). Ibn Taymiyyah (born 1263) reinforced the rejection of philosophy's role in favor of legal science (*fiqh*). Were al-Mawardi and Taymiyyah "bridge-destroyers" rather than bridge-builders. Can one reconcile their approach to *fiqh* with that of bridge-building Sufis such as Arabi, al-Ghazali and Rumi? Aquinas' synthesis helped lay a metaphysical foundations of modern science; sharia laid barriers in Islam. For Stanley Jaki and Stacy Trasancos, "The Stillbirth of Science in Arabia," www.strangenotions.com/tag/fr-stanley-jaki/ modern science was stillborn in Islam after what seemed to have been its real start with Avicenna and Averroes.

12. Shiites tend to believe that the Quran is created while the Sunnis see it as uncreated. (See Kung, *Islam,* 291-93).

13. Shia, a term stemming s from *shi'atu Ali*, Arabic for "partisans of Ali," believe that Ali and his descendants are part of a divine order. Sunnis follow the *sunna* (verbally transmitted records of Muhammad's teachings and deeds). Due to their being persecuted by Sunnis, Shiites resorted to forms of deception such as *taqiyya* (related to the Arabic word for "piety" and its root meaning of "protect" and the Quran verses advocating it (3:28 and 16:106). In early Islamic history, Muslims deceived non-Muslims not to escape persecution but in order to make Islam supreme as occurred with Mas'ud who became a Muslim and betrayed his community in at the Battle of the Trench, 627. Today's Sunni-Shiite struggles have fed a Syrian civil war that threatens to transform the map of the Middle East, have spurred violence that is fracturing Iraq, and has widened fissures in a number of tense Gulf countries. Growing sectarian clashes have also sparked a revival of transnational *jihadi* networks that pose a threat beyond the region.

14. Sunnis use the term "*imam*" for the men who lead prayers in mosques. This is not to be confused with *imam* denoting a believer's faith in the six articles of faith, nor with *imam* as used in law theology, nor with the Shiite propensity to call leaders of a community "*imam*" referred to in the text—or as attributed to Khomeini in Iran.

15. For Martin Rhonheimer, the Islamic State ISIS is not un-Islamic, its "model is Muhammad himself". He rejects the media view that Islam and Islamism differ as night and day. "Islamic State's legitimation finds its basis in the Quran and the Sharia." See http://www.jihadwatch.org/2014/10/professor-at-pontifical-university-of-the-holy-cross-in-rome-islamic-state-not-un-islamic-model-is-muhammad-himself "You do not hear many official Muslim voices condemning the Islamic State." When some do, they tend "to condemn the bestiality because it harms Islam's reputation." The Islamic State is no heresy, but "a recurring pattern in the history of violent expansion." For him, moderate Islam has its advocates (mainly professors at Western universities such as Anver Emon) who when confronted with Islamic violence today, cannot but return to Islam's origin, its warlike expansion from Medina, the legitimacy of killing for Allah's honor and a violent Muhammad." Ibid. Rhonheimer goes through the suras

in the Quran that prescribe what should happen to the conquered Christians and Jews, pointing out that the Islamic State strictly adheres to these regulations. Islam would like to influence the state and society in details.... Islam is more than a religion. It is a cult with political and social rules... (that) unite religion, political and social order in one." (Ibid). Our appeal to the conversions seeks to bridge not Islamic militarism but the hearts of Muslims open to the entirety of the GEM-FS conversions process. Implied in our project is a notion of a piously critical Islam. Open questions are how familiar with the Western tradition is Emon, how would he handle arguments of the not-so ecumenical Rhonheimer or the very ecumenical Kung--who nevertheless draws a line (Kung, *Islam*, 522-555). See also Tarek Fatah, http://www.meforum.org/4931/muslims-must-save-islam-from-islamists Dec. 16, 2014.

16. Legal systems serve to keep societies together and avoid crime; they also provide loopholes to get around the law or to refuse heartfelt interfaith encounters. See Gerald Grudzen, John Raymaker, *Steps to Vatican III*, 109--13, on the need of inter- and intra-religious dialogue so that understanding and relationships can blossom. This can happen to the extent that people---regardless of their religion--- are able to deepen their consciousness so as to experience spiritual enlightenment. One is moved beyond 'things' and is grasped by Ultimate Mind.

17. See Thomas McPartland, "Philosophy of history and a second Axial Age: Bernard Lonergan and the Differentiation of interiority" Philosophical Research Online http://philpapers.org/rec/MCPPOH. For David Oyler, Lonergan's third stage of meaning (*MiT*, 99) helps us understand technology's role in the emergence of social media. It provides a potency for developing the "socialization of interiority" and differentiations of consciousness.

18. "Natural Law" at http://encyclopedia2.thefreedictionary.com/Natural+Law+Theory based on J. Maritain, *The Rights of Man and Natural Law* (Gordian,1971); see A. Battaglia, *Toward a Reformulation of Natural Law* (1981). Natural law became the basis for Hugo Grotius' development of the theory of international law. For Spinoza and Leibniz, natural law is the basis of morality. Rousseau made natural law a basis for democratic principles but its influence declined in the 19th century under the impact of positivism and materialism. In the 20th century, Maritain saw in natural law a foundation to oppose totalitarianism. For him, "there is a single natural law governing all beings with a human nature. The first principles of this law are known connaturally, not rationally or through concepts — by an activity that Maritain, following Aquinas, called 'synderesis' (an innate principle in each one's moral consciousness, directing one to good but restraining him/her from evil). Thus, 'natural 'law' is 'natural' because it not only reflects human nature, but is known naturally." See http://plato.stanford.edu/entries/maritain/

Natural Law was seen as a "universal moral code (having) a validity for every culture and government. It is the proper and just standard for governmental law, functioning as a criterion for evaluating civil law. The content of Natural Law and revealed law is basically the same, but Natural Law operates by reason based on natural principles. Natural Law and natural rights intersect; the two underly the U. S Declaration of Independence. Today, postmodern morality and social constructivism lead to moral relativism (let a culture imply or dictate what is right or wrong).

See "Natural Law" http://ccnmtl.columbia.edu/projects/mmt/udhr/concepts/384.html, retrieved March, 2016.

19. Reacting "to the penetration of Western capitalist modernity into all aspects of Muslim society from the Arab world to Southeast Asia," some 19th century Muslim intellectuals such as Sir Sayyid Ahmad Khan (1817-1898) outlined a project for an 'Islamic modernism', seeking to reach a medium between adaptation and rejection. See http://social-epistemology.com/2015/06/15/sir-sayyid-ahmad-khan-1817-1898-on-taqlid-ijtihad-and-science-religion-compatibility-tauseef-ahmad-parray/ and John L. Esposito, "Contemporary Islam: Reformation or Revolution?" *The Oxford History of Islam*, (Oxford Univ., 1999), 644-45 on *ijtihad* or independent reasoning.

In his *The Future of Islam* (Oxford Univ, 2010), Esposito suggests that the future of Islam and the effectiveness of its hoped-for reforms will depend both on Muslim reformers and on the potential role of Western nations now struggling with Muslim migrations. Active Muslim moderates and enlightened Western policies are both needed to offset present impasses. We need a rethinking of Islam based on the history of reforms within Islam itself. (93-98).

20. Univ. of Toronto, Law Faculty, http://religion.utoronto.ca/people/cross-appointed-faculty/anver-emon/

21. Russel Powell "Toward Reconciliation in the Middle East: A Framework for Christian-Muslim Dialogue Using Natural Law Tradition," *Social Science Research*, http://papers.ssrn.com/sol3/papers.cfm?abstract_id=1031269

22. Harper and Lebau, "Social Change" write: "Early modernity carried the seeds of its own transformation. Large scale transformations" are gradual and continuous with the past, not "discontinuous, sudden... or revolutionary." They prefer Giddens' term "late" modernity to "postmodernity" since there have been ongoing, large-scale sociocultural transformations. See Giddens, *The Consequences of Modernity* (Stanford U, 1990). They add that "If differentiation was a hallmark of *early modernity, in later modernity* the process in some senses has reversed." At elite levels, "the global system is being extended by bureaucrats, technologists, . . . strategic planners, scientists, INGO mobilizers, and notable 'public citizens' such as, Jimmy Carter or Mikhail Gorbachev "who share common outlooks and strategic network connections--almost irrespective of nationality or professional training."

23. For an exception: http://ordinary-gentlemen.com/blog/2014/05/08/a-postmodernist-defends-natural-law/

24. Tom Heneghan, "Spread of the French *Malaise*", *The Tablet*, June, 25 2015.

25. Olivier Roy, *Holy Ignorance. When Religion and Culture Part Ways* (Columbia Univ., 2010). As to Lonergan's intercultural theology see Andrew Beards, *Insight and Analysis* (2010) chapter 8, "Christianity, Interculturality and Salvation." Beards reinforces our arguments as to the roles of relativism and indifferentism haunting our culture and GEM-FS's way of dealing with such issues. Contrasting Lonergan's view with Ratzinger's and Rahner's, Beards argues that Lonergan holds that any authentic project aimed at intercultural, interreligious "bridging of divided worlds" requires a prior orientation in those cultures (and persons involved) to be open to whatever is true and good...from any source. The authenticity of any culture is gauged precisely in terms of its openness to the true and the good from whatever source this may come." Failing such a needed prior orientation then any authentic attempt at "bridging" will be doomed. The opposite of intercultural authenticity is fanatical violent confrontation.

26. A majority of Americans continue to believe in supernatural forces, and identify themselves in religious terms. See Harper, Lebeau, "Social Change and Religion in America" http://are.as.wvu.edu/sochange.htm

27. Marxist materialism, which views law as a reflection of the economic order and political structures, dispenses with natural law as a precondition "for the existence and validity of existing law. In society there may be only one system of law, which is established by the state. . . In its law-making activities the state is bound by the principles of a given social system...determined not by the 'nature of man' but by the socioeconomic order and the means of production......Marxism does not consider false everything that stands behind the concept of natural law" for it attaches "great significance to the inalienable rights of man" It assigns important roles to ideals, values and justice which are however, socially conditioned, "class-bound, and historically changing, not a priori categories." See http://encyclopedia2.thefreedictionary.com/Natural+Law+Theory

28. Phil McShane notes that as a radically new idea with enormous institutional and cultural implications, the FS require "a cultural change, out of feudal order and classicist culture, into contemporary dynamic thinking." Cultural changes of the magnitude Lonergan envisioned" do not come easily. See Boston College Workshop, June 17, 1976.

29. Friedrich Nietzsche, *Thus spoke Zarathustra*, Walter Kaufmann tr., 130. Other ideas relevant to postmodernism are expressed in Nietzsche's *The Genealogy* (tr. Walter Kaufman & R.J. Hollingdale; Vintage Press, 1989): "values" are relative to time and cultures; they are "created" by society's "masters"; Christianity's "slave morality" of the weak seeks to gain concessions from the strong by causing them guilt and shame. This requires a "sublimation" of natural passions. Christianity's "illusion" of other-worldliness, is based upon "resentment" of this world.

30. Norman Lund, "General Revelation and Natural Law in a Postmodern Context", a review of Sydney Ahlstrom, *A Religious History of the American People* (Image Books, 1975), vol. 1, 21. See http://www.shuv.org/naturallaw.html. Lund adds that Christian thinkers in high-

er education today are "painfully aware of the absence of any mainstream morality that adequately engages the intellectual and artistic expressions of secular society. Of the various disasters that litter the three decades between 1960 and 1990, none was more deleterious in its effects than the social reliance upon technique to solve all our problems for us." Even the most perfect structures cannot long endure if their inhabitants do not have virtuous habits, attitudes and behavior. Lund notes that scientific pioneers such as Johann Kepler and Francis Bacon stressed the religious motif of science: they understood "God's handiwork."

31. Michel Foucault, *Madness and Civilization: A History of Insanity in the Age of Reason* (Vintage, 1965). Other French postmodernists have also questioned the very existence of truth--denying the objectivity of reason. For Jean-Francois Lyotard, *The Postmodern Condition* (U. Minnesota, 1984), universal truth is impossible because meta- narratives are no longer credible or "communicable." The earlier Jacques Derrida, in *Writing and Difference* (U. Chicago, 1978), discusses whether language is ultimately subjective--incapable of communicating objective truth.

32. Alasdair MacIntyre, *After Virtue*, (Notre Dame U., 1984). Louis Roy, "Development and Faith: A Few Suggestions from Bernard Lonergan" http://www.lonergan.org/dialogue_partners/roy/Moral_Development_and_Faith.htm

Johann Georg Hamann (1730-1788), initially a devotee of secular Enlightenment, became its stern critic. His change in world-view coincided with his reading of Berkeley and Hume. He saw "the idealism of the former and the skepticism of the latter as constituting a *reductio ad absurdum* of Enlightenment thought: Scientific reason leads us either to doubt or to deny the reality of the world around us." He began to emphasize the importance of aesthetic experience and the intuiting of nature. See www.iep.utm.edu/hamann/. Herder's *Besonnenheit* (reflective discernment) was influenced by Hamann's critique of Kant. He had a great impact on Goethe. See Isaiah Berlin, *Three Critics of the Enlightenment* (Pimlico, 2013). In the writings of Vico, Hamann and Herder, Berlin finds good critics of the Enlightenment, but he identifies much that is misguided in their rejection of universal values, rationalism, and science. Berlin traces much of the next centuries' irrationalism and suffering to the historicism and particularism they advocated. Today, also, Enlightenment beliefs are being challenged by academics, nationalists and powerful fundamentalists. See Internet *Encyclopedia of Philosophy* http://www.iep.utm.edu/hamann/

33. Reynold Price's review of Robert Coles, *Temporal Salvation* (Princeton Univ., 1999). Coles once asked Paul Tillich to expand on his notion of "the secular mind." Tillich explained that, in effect, he wanted to describe the difference between "Man the thinking materialist and Man the anxiously aspiring creature who bows his head and prays." Dorothy Day, the Catholic exponent of social mercy and justice told Coles: "Some people say to me, 'The secular mind is your enemy.' I say no, no; I say the secular mind is God's huge gift to us, for us to use for the sake of one another." (Ibid). Day, the mystic activist, had put her finger on a "bridge of mercy" in actual life--one that many admire but do not emulate. https://www.nytimes.com/books/99/07/25/reviews/990725.25pric.html

34. Jean Piaget, *The Moral Judgment of the Child* (Free Press, 1965), studied how children across the world mediate their own incipient world. He asked how they learn new skills or use acquired skills to adjust to new situations. They do so by developing their differentiated operations--mentally and physically return to their starting points to master skills. In the process, they become self-aware, deepen their differentiations of consciousness and acquire new patterns of experience. They also begin to develop a sense of community open to the sacred. See *MiT*, 27-29.

35. Confusing faith and beliefs, the apophatic with the kataphatic is endemic to secularism. Lonergan's expertise in the apophatic-kataphatic, helps us reconnect with reality as concerned citizens intent on implementing GEM-FS. Scientists have no choice but to believe that mathematical axioms or previous experiments which they cannot themselves repeat are true. To live religiously is not merely to live in the presence of symbols; it means to be involved with them so that one is led beyond the symbols which demand the totality of a person's response. Wilfred Cantwell Smith called such a total involvement faith. Language and beliefs are often universalized beyond their proper realms of application; they become tools of conflicting dogmas or ideologies stemming from bias. The faith-belief distinction we use differs from New Age

eclecticism of the late 1970's. New Age roots go back to such earlier movements as that of occultism and theosophy. It was motivated by a suspicion of traditional Western values. It attempted to semi-spiritually quasi-bridge our societies' divides. Perhaps, partly due to some Catholics' uncritical New Age views the Church became polarized after Vatican II. In contrast to such naivite, some spiritual writers have reached deeply to find mystic commonalities between Christian, Buddhist and Islamic spiritualities.

36. Is the operational range of our human knowing-doing operations curtailed in e. g. the Morsi-Sisi confrontations in Egypt, in Muslims' and Christians' attacks upon one another, in Erdogan's Turkey? Lonergan's way of the heart and mind evaluates historical realities; this will lead us in FS 5, foundations, to the role of Sufis, Christian mystics and Zen Buddhists as embodying an implicit unity within human yearnings all over the planet—a yearning that tends to be swept under the rug due the frenetic pace of modern life. For Denys Turner, *The Darkness of God* (20), theology's kataphatic mode is "a kind of verbal riot, an anarchy of discourse in which anything goes. . . When we have said that much, narrowly about the formal language of theology, we have only begun: for that is to say nothing about the extensive non-verbal vocabulary of theology, its liturgical...action, its music, its architecture, its dance and gesture, all of which are intrinsic to its character as an expressive discourse, a discourse of theological articulation." Zen meditation is one possible foundational ground. *MiT* extends I*nsight*'s GEM. Zen is a type of conversion without words, beyond words.... Zen and GEM-FS reinforce one another. In invoking radicality as part of the GEM-FS achievement, this book stresses that there are several types of mutually contradictory "radicalities". While strongly rejecting ISIS's extreme, mindless radicality; we promote the radicality of GEM-FS conversions.

37. Richard Rorty, *Philosophy and the Mirror of Nature* (Princeton, 1979). In his *Objectivity, Relativism and Truth* (Cambridge U., 1991), Rorty ridicules claims of objectivity as fictional "sky hooks." He advocates abandoning "the search for Truth" (13, 21). Adopting the postmodern stance of "weak thought" that rejects a transcendental structure of reason, G. Vattimo in Gianni Vattimo and Richard Rorty, *The Future of Religion*, ed. by Santiago Zabala (NY: Columbia U., 2005), notes that Modernism claimed to be based on "objective truth." Rorty grants that privatized religion may be a source of consolation for some. Unlike postmodernists, Catholicism accepts valid forms of transcendentalism as an immanent "entry" into the world of the transcendent. On this view, a "transcendent God" (completely outside of and beyond the world) has revealed Self in various ways such as in Scripture. "Nothingness" in Buddhism reinforces Vattimo's interpretation of Nietzchean "nihilism." For Vattimo, nihilism does not imply the negation of all values; rather, it removes value and truth from a supposedly ahistorical status.

38. Alister McGrath, *A Passion for Truth: The Intellectual Coherence of Evangelicalism* (InterVarsity, 1996). 180.

39. Editorial "The Atheist Delusion" in *The Irish Times*, March 20, 2008. Hitchens was no philosopher. This did not stop him from claiming that Mother Teresa "was no more exempt from the realization that religion is a human fabrication than any other person" or that her professions of faith deepened the pit that she had dug for herself." See *Catholic League*, 2007 http://www.catholicleague.org/mother-teresas-faith-hitchens-still-doesnt-get-it/

40. For Dwight Garner, Dawkins' memoir *Brief Candle in the Dark* (Bantam, 2015) lacks intimacy. It runs "for mayor of our brains." See http://topics.nytimes.com/top/reference/timestopics/people/g/dwight_garner/index.html

As a notion, used to differentiate between the religious-transcendent and political-temporal spheres, "secular" can function rationally as the recognition that different spheres have their own intelligible discourse. Aquinas acknowledged this with his notion of "secondary causes." When "secular" is used to deny, or block assent to, the reality of the transcendent, then it functions like any other domineering ideology; it lacks intellectual integrity.

Some Christians are amazed at how secular society tries to twist "mercy into blinking, happy-go-lucky acceptance of every behavior one can imagine. This warped and sinister reasoning follows a...distortion of logic and Church teaching." Gabriel Garnica, http://www.catholicstand.com/modern-secularisms-triple-distortion-of-divine-mercy/

Mercy, one of the bases of Buddhist, Christian and Muslim teachings, is open to differentiated, heartfelt nuances.

41. Sara Terreault, Catherine King: https://groups.google.com/forum/#!topic/lonergan_l/a-3sVa99n2M Gerald Walmsley, *Lonergan on Philosophic Pluralism: The Polymorphism of Consciousness as the Key to Philosophy* (U. of Toronto, 2010). Our four cognitional operations are intentional and conscious on four levels; the conscious intentionality differs from level to level; within each level the... operations involve further differences." (*MiT*, 9).

42. The sociologist Dick Moodey pursues the metaphorical aspect of bridging misunderstandings among groups.

The kinds of persons required are those who strive to go beyond what Lonergan calls the "minor authenticity" of obeying written rules. One needs the major authenticity able to go beyond the ideological tenets of Christians, Muslims or secularists. Mohammed Arkoun interprets the Quran's symbols in the light of Ricoeur and Levinas. See Carool Kersten, "From Braudel to Derrida: Mohammed Arkoun's Rethinking of Islam and Religion", *Middle East Journal of Culture and Communication*, Vol. 4, 2011, 23-43. Arkoun has sought new ways of engaging with Islam by combining intimate familiarity with the Islamic civilizational heritage (*turath*) with a solid knowledge of the West.

43. GEM's strategy for resolving differences among principles occurs in FS 5 to reveal their true source; one does not prove one's principles or disprove another's. We tap one another's experience of a desire for authenticity. Those with secure intellectual, moral and affective horizons will "by laying bare the roots" of differences, attract, guide" those with less secure horizons. Tad Dunne, "Bernard Lonergan", http://www.iep.utm.edu/lonergan/

44. Tad Dunne, "Bernard Lonergan" www.iep.utm.edu/lonergan notes that in GEM, the basic meaning of duty is found in an originating set of "oughts", in the impulses to be attentive, intelligent, reasonable, responsible, and in the overriding "ought" to maintain consistency between what one knows and how one acts. The oughts issued by conscience provide all the norms expressed in written rules and also issue more commands and prohibitions than do parents, police, or public policies. This inner duty helps one break from a minor authenticity that obeys the written rule so as to exercise a major authenticity that may expose a written rule as illegitimate.

45. *Reimagining the Sacred: Richard Kearney debates God with James Wood, Catherine Keller, Charles Taylor, Julia Kristeva, Gianni Vattimo: Studies in Religion, Politics, and Culture*, R. Kearney, J. Zimmermann, editors (Columbia U., 2015) explores the intersection of secularism, politics, and religion. Refusing to paper over religious differences, the book locates "the sacred within secular society and affirms a positive role" for religion today. It develops a basic gesture of hospitality for approaching the question of God by the best-known voices in continental philosophy and their views on spiritually-minded individuals and skeptics: how to reconcile God's goodness with human evil, how to believe in both God and natural science, how to talk about God... and how to balance God's sovereignty with God's love?" It offers rich insights into the place of the sacred in the world after the supposed 'death of God'. Kearney leads discussions exploring not just the clash between atheism and theism but the traces of the divine, termed 'anatheism'. Today the debate between religion and culture is framed by two reductive definitions of secularity. In one, multiple faiths and nonfaiths coexist free from a dominant belief in God. In the other, we deny the sacred altogether and exclude religion from rational thought and behavior. Kearney pioneers a third way for those hoping to rediscover the sacred in a skeptical society: What kind of faith do we proclaim after the ravages of terrorists?" See www.amazon.com/Reimagining-Sacred-Catherine-Kristeva-Religion/dp/0231161034

46. Dick Moodey, https://groups.google.com/forum/#!topic/lonergan_l/PMMEaRbn3h8. Individuals can disagree about some things, and remain members in good standing, but disagreement about some other things may result in "excommunication." The paths followed by persons striving for personal authenticity are very different, but there are commonalities. The cost of staying on one's is quest is that it will put one at odds with ideologues from all traditions. For Moodey, an "ideologue" is a person who does not seek to know truly and to act conscientiously, who does not seek to struggle against his individual, group, or general biases. The ideologies such persons create or embrace serve as legitimations for their biased beliefs and actions." Moodey relies on Alisdair MacIntyre's view in *Whose Justice? Which Rationality?* (Notre Dame U., 1988) that traditions are maintained by internal and external arguments. See

also David Trenery, *Alasdair MacIntyre, George Lindbeck, and the Nature of Tradition* (Pickwick, 2014). FS-GEM coasts between the the kataphatic and the apophatic. The former suggests there is much we can say about God. For the latter, there is far more that we cannot say; we can only be silent. Both succumb to a tendency to see itself as the only way. Yet, the artificial boundary between the two is porous. Richard Kearney, *Anatheism: Returning to God After God* (Columbia Univ., 2009) explores the porousness. For him, "anatheism is not an end but a means to overcome the theism-atheism extremes, while resisting a teleology of ineluctable progress. Unlike the Hegelian dialectic, it does not subsume singular persons or events under some Absolute. Kataphatic theology is inclined towards decisive statements about God with varying degrees of certainty. Apophatic theology is equally swayed towards resolute denials that are also held with differing intensities of certainty. Kearney's anxiety about a purely negative theology is that it can too easily go to a drastic, dangerous extreme of radical apophasis (ultimately, a "mystical atheism" where one comes to the edge of a precipice at which the Divine and Abyss, Good and Evil, the Stranger who brings life and the Stranger who kills, all become indistinguishable from one another). Kearney addresses the 'anti-God squad' of the Dawkins sort, but is more interested in modest atheists not carrying out an (anti-) Holy War; he draws on Ricoeur's treatment of the three masters of suspicion: Marx, Nietzsche, and Freud. Ricoeur's pioneering anatheistic appropriation of atheism is "corrective surgery." See Kearney, "Ricoeur and Biblical Hermeneutics: On Post-Religious Faith" in Ricoeur, *Across the Disciplines*, ed. by Scott Davidson, (NY: Continuum, 2010), 30-43). Ricoeur's thought and faith both ask 'What comes after God?' Ricoeur's *"ana-theos"* is a *post-religious faith*. https://godaftergod.wordpress.com/2012/12/09/the-apophatic-way-part-2-of-the-anaphatic-way/

47. https://catholicsensibility.wordpress.com/2006/02/07/113935137530363615

48. Merton would end his letters with "I Jerry Ryan". "The Mystical Vision of Louis Massignon," *National Catholic Reporter*, 12/17/04 counsels us to remain wary if lurid images of a "battle against Islam" seem to attract us. Our fascination with conflict is deep-rooted" but poisonous. "The ecstatic glow that makes us in war feel as one people" is real, but part of war's intoxication." For Merton, "friendship is an enlightening blessing from God."

49. https://catholicsensibility.wordpress.com/2006/02/07/113935137530363615/   Merton did add that some ways to God are more perfect, more complete than others. Thomas A. Carlson, *Indiscretion: Finitude and the Naming of God* (Oxford Univ., 2000) on religion, postmodernism, and the ineffable interpreted by Christian mystics --the rhetoric of "darkness" or "unknowing," Carlson appraises the influence of Nietzsche and Derrida among others.

50. GEM-FS radicality is based on the apophatic, on converted responses to the good. Grounded in interiority, it is directly opposed to terrorists' beliefs whose radicality is reinforced by both ideology and ignorant fundamentalism.

51. David Steindl-Rast, "Recollections of Thomas Merton's Last Days in the West," 1969, *Monastic Studies* 7:10. Kenneth Bragan, *The Making of a Saint* (Writers Literary & Publishing Services, 2011) writes that at the root of Merton's engagement with people different from himself was the sense of "original unity," which he recognized bound all people together as children of God. He understood that he could not have an authentic conversation about faith with others if he did not have a firm commitment and deep love for his own tradition." Christians can no longer rely as much as they had on dogmas and buildings. There is now required a total inner transformation.

52. M. and J. Batchelor, "The Agnostic Buddhist" www.stephenbatchelor.org/index.php/en/the-agnostic-buddhist.

Buddha was mostly reticent about the question of theism/atheism because he was primarily focused on teaching people how to alleviate suffering in their everyday life in a concrete, immediate, direct and practical way.

53. In 1993, at the Chicago meeting of the Parliament of the World's Religions, Hans Kung drafted the "Declaration toward a Global Ethic." It addresses the issues of ecology, poverty and social injustice. Religious leaders must help shape a better global order. The Declaration commits members to a culture of non-violence and respect for life, to a culture of solidarity and a just economic order, to tolerance and truthfulness, and a partnership between men and women. We must collaborate to solve the huge challenges facing the entire human community.

54. Reda Benkirane, "The Origin of the Clash of Civilizations" www.wafin.com/clash.phtml argues that Huntington borrowed his Clash of Civilizations thesis from Mahdi Elmandjra who in 1991 referred to the Gulf war as a "post-colonial" situation while stigmatizing Western fears of Islam. For Benkirane, "Religions, civilizations and cultures should not be reduced to political confrontations." Instead of "policing civilizations, the world needs to 'civilize politics'" which fail to comprehend our world's complexity. We need a better grasp of the cultural and religious.

55. For Mike Albertson, Lonergan's view of faith, Girard's theory of mimetic scapegoating, and Voegelin's gnostic pneumopathology can help us respond to modern violence. http://orthosphere.org/2012/03/07/liberalism-as-cultural-atavism-voegelins-theory-of-gnostic-modernity-and-girards-theory-of-sacrifice-3/ for a similar view.

56. Daniel Pipes, http://www.meforum.org/5628/paris-massacre-impact. Thomas Beronneau, March 7, 2012, laments the "mutation of classical liberalism into today's politically correct totalitarianism...Liberalism began as the cautious younger sibling of the revolutionary spirit that found its emblem in the destruction of the Bourbons and its articulation in the slogan-like promotion of equality, fraternity, and liberty" Left-radical activity implies "hostility to custom and habit." The republican-type nation-states that followed the French model arose "through the violent disestablishment of the smaller, ethnic polities that characterized the long period of feudalism in Europe." (Ibid). The incompatibility of customs is also illustrated in Islam's condoning of child marriage practiced by Muhammad himself who wrote a marriage contract "with Aisha while she was six years old and consummated his marriage with her when she was nine years old. She remained with him for nine years (i.e. till his death)" (Bukhari 7.62.88). Our reliance on faith to resolve problems with incompatible beliefs and customs presupposes local adaptations.

3. THIRD FUNCTIONAL SPECIALTY

1. On GEM-FS judgments of value based on an integral ethics and global, cooperative communities working for the future of humanity, see Brian Cronin, www.lonergan.org/wp-content/uploads/2010/12/Total-Book.pdf. Cronin offers an integral, methodical, critical ethics to forge a global community based on a common vision and values.

2. Franklin's plan for the Seal was to illustrate the inner life and the outer life of hard work. "The outcome of his outer life was the founding of a club composed of workers ... the 'Junto,'" allied to the Rosicrucians and interested in moral life. See http://rosicrucian.50webs.com/various/scribe-benjamin-franklins-rosicrucian-affiliations.htm

By endorsing the phrase "time is money", Franklin reflected the Calvinist ethic: people engage in work in the secular world, develop their own enterprises and engage in trade. They accumulate wealth so as to invest it.

3. Gerald Grudzen, *Medical Theory about the Body and the Soul in the Middle Ages: The First Western Medical Curriculum at Monte Cassino* (The Edwin Mellen Press, 2007) documents the historical relationship of the rise of western medical science with the transfer of knowledge from the Arabic world in the 11th century at the Monte Cassino. It examines this cross-cultural transmission between Jewish, Christian and Muslim communities. Attention is given to the debates over the relationship of the body and soul—still a central concern of contemporary thought. Aquinas studied at Monte Cassino from age five to thirteen. His integration of faith-reason is still relevant today.

4. Abdullah Al-Arian, *Between Terror and Tyranny: Political Islam in the Shadow of the Arab Uprisings*, 2015 shows his sympathies for the Muslim Brotherhood—unlike Sisi. See Tom Perry, "Egypt's Sisi turns Islam on the Islamists", May, 2014 www.reuters.com/article/2014/05/09/us-egypt-sisi-religion-idUSBREA480G820140509 The question is whether Egypt can finds its way between Sisi's military autocracy as opposed to the terrorism represented by ISIS.

5. Small peaceful protests started on 26 January 2011 in Syria and escalated to an ongoing internal conflict when residents of the small southern town of Dara'a took to the streets to

protest the torture of students who had put up anti-government graffiti. Spreading protests demanded reforms, the ouster of President Bashar al-Assad, equal rights for Kurds, and broad freedom for the press, speech and assembly. The government did make some trivial concessions. On 21 April, it repealed an emergency law in place since 1963 allowing the government to suspend constitutional rights but it soon launched a series of crackdowns, opening fire on demonstrators, etc. Water and electricity were shut off and security forces began confiscating flour and food in particularly restive areas. The conflict is complicated by Syria's ethnic divisions. The Assads and much of the military belong to the Alawite sect (Nuşayrī), a small minority in a majority Sunni country. http://guides.library.cornell.edu/c.php?g=31688&p=200753

6. Reza Aslan, *Zealot: The Life and Times of Jesus of Nazareth* (Random House, 2013) asks what does Jesus stand for? Who has the authority to determine what a figure of massive religious and cultural importance really taught? Aslan asserts that he is a Muslim not because he believes Islam is more correct or true than other religions, "but because the symbols and metaphors that Islam uses to talk about God and humanity . . . are the symbols and metaphors that work best for me." See www.theatlantic.com/entertainment/archive/2013/08/the-book-that-changed-reza-aslans-mind-about-jesus/278410/. On the other hand, the ex-Muslim, Rumy Hasan, criticizes Muslims' "psychiatric detachment" from mainstream British culture which in turns leads to a "social detachment" where minority communities do not mix with wider society. www.breitbart.com/london/2016/01/13/muslim-prof-rape-gangs-inevitable-muslim-men-live-in-britain-as-if-it-was-pakistan/

7. Hayan Hirshi Ali, www.facebook.com/permalink.php?id=493044800809216&story_fbid=733896463390714

8. Tarek Fatah is the author of *Chasing a Mirage: The Tragic Illusion of an Islamic State* (Wiley, 2008).

9. A bridge of mercy is partly rooted in an apophatic rejected by many. Frederick G. McLeod: "Apophatic or Kataphatic Prayer?" http://opcentral.org/resources/2015/01/13/frederick-g-mcleod-apophatic-or-kataphatic-prayer/ writes on *The Cloud of Unknowing*'s still wide influence today. "It provides a clear, concise and convincing statement on what is 'apophatic' prayer and how one can enter into it . . . In the state of union, one becomes totally self-forgetful, yet paradoxically finding one's true self in a fuller way." One realizes what one is thirsting for at one's deepest level. The heart "knows on a level beyond our conscious awareness and control for what state and for whom it has been made and when this has been attained." One also glimpses how mercy is rooted in the heart.

10. Mark Doorley, *The Place of the Heart in Lonergan's* Ethics (Lanham, MD: UPA, 1996). Catherine King, *Finding the Mind*, (UPA, 2011), 42, writing on our dynamic consciousness from a GEM-FS standpoint notes: "Our feelings underpin all forms of language... (They) may become more remote to our discursive expression" but are a key to efforts to transvalue values. For Charles Taylor, *Sources of the Self*, 428, "The moral or spiritual order of things must come to us indexed to a personal vision.... Moral evaluations have become mediated by the imagination." For R. J. Snell and Steven Cone, *Authentic Cosmopolitanism: Love, Sin, and Grace in the Christian University* (Pickwick, 2013), humans are lovers. Still, much of pedagogical theory "assumes an anthropology at odds with human nature, fixed in a model of humans as 'thinking things.'" Augustine, Aquinas, Lonergan and Taylor provide normative visions for Christian higher education. "A phenomenological re-appropriation of human subjectivity reveals an authentic order to love, even when damaged by sin." A loving grace, allows morally, intellectually and religiously converted persons to attain an integral unity. Understanding the integral relation between love and a fulfilled human life "overcomes the split between intellectual and moral formation, allowing transformed subjects to live, seek, and work towards the values of a certain kind of cosmopolitanism." See http://wipfandstock.com/authentic-cosmopolitanism.html

11. Lonergan's doctoral thesis on grace (1940) argues that from the 16th century onwards, commentators on Aquinas lacked historical consciousness, thus obfuscating the issues. Lonergan retrieved Aquinas' actual position on grace, anticipating contemporary theologians who now agree on the need for a historical method. Lonergan discovered in St. Thomas a mind in constant development, displaying radical shifts on fundamental questions.

12. One must advert to our desires and fears, our hopes or despair, our joys and sorrows. (*MiT*, 31) "The important thing to note about these feelings is that they arise in the subject following the apprehension of some object, either real or imagined. One may wake up experiencing a non-intentional dread that becomes real intentional fear when acing a difficult task. "One may experience non-intentional hunger, but also experience an intentional desire" for some rare tuna. Intentional responses respond to the specific content of the apprehension. This means that these responses follow knowledge. One cannot respond with joy at a friend's arrival unless one first knows of his arrival. (Doorley, 53). With von Hildebrand, Lonergan distinguishes between feelings as non-intentional states or trends like fatigue, hunger and anxiety, all of which occur independently of perception and/or apprehension, and intentional states or trends which occur in "answer to what is intended, apprehended, represented" (*MiT*, 30). Intentional feelings relate a human subject to an object such as an apple, rather than a goal like relieving hunger (as with non-intentional feelings). Rather than being moments in the formation of a viewpoint, as are insights, intentional responses have the capacity to become vectors in the flow of consciousness (Doorley, 54). Since the Enlightenment, much of ethical philosophy has presumed that rational persons must set aside their emotions when seeking to make sound moral decisions. Robert J. Fitterer, *Love and Objectivity in Virtue Ethics* (U. of Toronto, 2008) argues that compassion and love are powerful aids in the complex process of attaining objective moral truths in decisions and actions. We can "take a conscious process and turn it into a self-aware, self-critical method" (53).

13. Marion's *The Idol and the Distance* "mirrors the path of Martin Heidegger's metaphysical critique, insofar as he "begins with Nietzsche, enters into the 'fled gods' of Hölderlin, and concludes with a gesture toward invisible appearance and the giving that withdrawals." This suggests a profound linking of the holy and apophatic. See www. academia.edu/12234875/Apophatic_Sacramentality_The_Gift_of_Holy_Mediation_in_Heidegger_and_Marion for article by Ashley Gay, "Apophatic Sacramentality: The Gift of Holy Mediation in Heidegger and Marion." Remi Brague's views on Islamic and Christian mysticisms would tend to reinforce Marion's stand as interpreted by Gay.

4. FOURTH FUNCTIONAL SPECIALTY

1. FS 4 seeks to clarify contentious topics; it advocates change without resorting to any exclusions. Our cognitional-volitional acts, prior to our giving an account of them, constitute Lonergan's transcultural base but formulations of it are prone to counterpositional oversights—leading to core philosophical problems. "Fixing" such oversights requires FS 4 dialectics. Phil McShane refers to the following key *Insight* passage: "The explanatory differentiation of the protean notion of being involves three elements. First, there is the genetic sequence in which insights gradually are accumulated by man. Secondly, there are the dialectic alternatives in which accumulated insights are formulated, with positions inviting further development and counterpositions shifting their ground to avoid the reversal they demand. Thirdly, with the advance of culture and effective education, there arises the possibility of the differentiation and specialization of modes of expression, and since this development conditions not only the exact communication of insights but also the discoverer's own grasp of his discovery, since such grasp and its exact communication intimately are connected with the advance of positions and the reversal of counterpositions, the three elements in the explanatory differentiation of the protean notion of being fuse into a single explanation." (609-10). McShane comments: "This is a massively complex point that regards the paradoxical inclusion of the full cyclic heuristic in the revisable genetic structure of the seventh functional specialty. But the simple point of *Insight* survives right through the mutiplicities of Lonergan's paradigm shift" to a genetic ordering that lifts the scattered "ramblings of pre-scientific interpretation into a science yielding cumulative and progressive results." (*MiT*, 5)

McShane goes on to explain how this passage points to the core of the cyclic collaboration as effected in *MiT*'s FS. It is precisely due to this important linkage, pointed out by McShane, that our text speaks of a "GEM-FS" process.

2. Sunni fundamentalism emerged after the modernization of Egypt leading to the creation of the Muslim Brotherhood by Hasan al-Banna and incited by Sayyid Qutb. Ayatollah Khomeini fostered Shia fundamentalism.

3. In his *Capital in the Twenty-First Century*, 2014, Thomas Piketty argues that the rate of return capitals "r" will persistently exceed "g," the growth in total output. For a contrary view see Robert P. Murphy at http://rare.us/story/thomas-piketty-wants-to-keep-billions-of-people-poor-to-stop-a-few-from-becoming-rich/

4. The Marrakesh Declaration January 2016, calls for religious freedom for non-Muslims in Muslim-majority countries. Karen Armstrong, *Fundamentalism in Judaism, Christianity and Islam* (HarperCollins, 2000) argues that, in fact, a militant piety has characterized the three religions of the book and shaped the course of world history.

5. Jeremy Wilkins, Review of Matthew Lamb, *Eternity, Time, and the Life of Wisdom* (Naples, FL: Sapientia, 2007) at www.academia.edu/9472029/Review_of_Matthew_Lamb_Eternity_Time_and_the_Life_of_Wisdom

6. In a letter to the United Baptist Chamber of Virginia (1789), George Washington wrote: "Question with boldness even the existence of a God; because, if there be one, he must more approve of the homage of reason, than that of blindfolded fear." "If I could conceive that the general government might ever be so administered as to render the liberty of conscience insecure, I beg you will be persuaded, that no one would be more zealous than myself to establish effectual barriers against the horrors of spiritual tyranny, and every species of religious persecution."

7. Maria Hornung, *Encountering Other Faiths* (New Jersey: Paulist Press, 2007), 65. *Interfaith Dialogue at the Grassroot*s (Temple Univ., 2009), edited by Rebecca Kratz Mays, speaks of possibly intense encounters in interfaith meetings. It can be awkward, even violent, but creating a dialogue can help reconcile differences. In a world full of division, injustice, and exploitation, we must work "to unite people of faith and goodwill to help confront the ills so present in our world….We must cultivate harmony among religious and spiritual communities and work with organizations, institutions, and movements for the interrelated causes of peace, justice, and sustainability. www. Parliament of religions.org/civicrm/contribute/transact?reset=1&id=1&mc_cid=ae08d349cf&mc_eid=74dd357e34

8. Leonard Swidler, Paul Mojzes, *The Study of Religion in an Age of Global Dialo*gue (Temple Univ., 2000), 41.

9. The meeting was held at the initiative of Jean Maher, president of the Franco-Egyptian Association for Human Rights and of Whalon. The Union of Experts, founded in Dec. 2014, comprises 500 Muslim dignitaries from around the world – Sunnis, Shiites, and Sufis. Without ties to any organization or government, it aims to promote peace between peoples and religions. It calls for reforms within their own traditions. See Maher, http://episcopaldigitalnetwork.com/ens/2015/11/19/europe-convocation-hosts-interfaith-evening-for-peace-and-dialogue/ This initiative is also an example of a GEM-FS see-judge-act subtemplate which we will study in FS 6. A GEM-FS bridge avoids Episcopalian bishop John S. Spong's efforts to completely revise or do away with dogmas.

10. "The Believers were intended to be an *ummah* (community) that serves as a model for others, as one reads in the Qur'an: "We have made you (*ummatan wasata*) a median community / a people of moderation in order that you may be a model for humanity." [Qur'an 2:143]. It is the absence of the balance provided by *wasatiyyah* (moderation) that extremism creeps in. *Wasatiyyah* is an antidote to *ghuluww* (excessiveness), t*anattu'* (harshness), *tashaddud* (severity), *tatarruf* (extremism). See "Intolerance Whence? How is it then that some Muslims are so intolerant of other faiths, involved in atrocious and heinous acts of violence and senseless killing?"   www.islamicity.org/6258/the-call-of-islam-peace-and-moderation-not-intolerance-and-extremism/

11. Lonergan recognized the need to separate tasks in the eight FS but also to interrelate them. GEM-FS enables "the converted" to show and interrelate the generalized, specialized complementarities in collaborative fashion. We intentionally deploy a part of FS's mediated phase in see-judge-act fashion, invoking Cardijn's method used in Liberation Theology. Pope Francis as archbishop used it in South America to oppose flagrant injustices. Lonergan is

proposing a normative, faith-based method which can bridge Christian-Muslims-Buddhist-secularist differences.

12. Catholic sacramental doctrine has lost much of its credibility. Baptized people leave the church, adolescents stop attending shortly after they are confirmed, supposedly indissoluble marriages are regularly dissolved, few go to confession, and many do not believe in transubstantiation. Drawing upon his decades-long study of the sacraments Joe Martos, *The Sacraments: An Interdisciplinary and Interactive Study* (Glazier, 2009) shows how teachings that seemed rooted in the scriptures and Catholic life have become unmoored from the contexts in which they arose, and why seemingly eternal truths are actually historically relative. Martos goes back to Catholic teaching from the church's own documents, then deconstructs it by demonstrating how biblical passages were misconstrued by patristic authors and how patristic writings were misunderstood by medieval scholastics. Such misinterpretations culminated in the dogmatic pronouncements of the Council of Trent, which continue to influence Catholic thinking. For Martos, spiritual realities symbolized in the sacraments can be reapplied to help transform today's cultures.

13. Taylor's "secularity 3" arose along with the possibility of exclusive humanism, which for the first time widened the range of possible options, ending the era of 'naïve' religious faith." Exclusive humanism arose through the intermediate form of Providential Deism. Both Deism and humanism were "made possible by earlier developments within orthodox Christianity. Once this humanism is on the scene, the new plural, non-naïve predicament allows for multiplying the options beyond the original gamut. But the crucial transforming move in the process is the coming of exclusive humanism." (Ibid, 78). For Rita Gross, "Excuse me, but What's the Question?" Isn't Religious Diversity Normal?", *The Myth of Religious Superiority: A Multifaith Exploration* in Paul F. Knitter, Orbis, 2005, 77. Arguing that religious diversity is a "problem" comes from traditions "that historically have made exclusive truth-claims."

14. It is in part "open" because of the apophatic deep within converted hearts but inaccessible to the kataphatic.

15. Our use of the visual metaphor ("see") for the act of understanding risks using the language of the counter-position. Our see-judge-act method does not omit experiencing or deciding—two essential but tacit personal acts.

16. Sarah Gordon on O'Connor (07/10/2002), www.georgiaencyclopedia.org/articles/arts-culture/flannery-oconnor-1925-1964. On the grace and mercy experienced by saints, see Judith Schneider, "Filial Relationship, Mercy and limitation in Thérèse of Lisieux" (Notre Dame U., Australia, 2012, 326-64); Lonergan, "The Redemption", *CWL 6, Philosophical Papers 1958-1964*, 3-28. Pat Byrne, "Ecology, Economy and Redemption as Dynamic," www3.nd.edu/~ecoltheo/text_byrne.htm. For Lonergan, human innovations and self-correction correspond to the emergence, growth, development, and decline in the natural order. Unlike the latter, the possibilities of genuine social and economic development are distorted by the biases. Grace can help heal some of the distorted dynamics.

17. Michiko Kakutani, May 2, 201, quoting Prince Bandar, former Saudi ambassador in Washington; see http://artsbeat.blogs.nytimes.com/2011/05/02/a-survey-of-books-about-osama-bin-laden-and-al-qaeda/?_r=0

18. Steve Coll, *Ghost Wars* (Penguin: 2001), explores the CIA's role in the anti-Soviet *jihad* in Afghanistan in the 1980s. America's abandonment of that country after the Soviet withdrawal left behind a chaotic land with heavily armed, feuding warlords: conditions that created a perfect environment for the rise of the Taliban and Al Qaeda."

19. This is another way of saying that our GEM-FS approach implicitly deploys the subjective and objective aspects of human living. See-judge-act subtemplates involve a commitment to the good that respects the various notions of meaning Lonergan develops in *MiT*. Such subtemplates are also GEM-FS praxis in the good sense.

20. Kung, *Islam*, 369-86. With Kung, we call for a global ethic to foster common values and attitudes—not as an ideological superstructure but as a help to reinforce traditional ethical convictions. See also Küng, Josef van Ess, Heinrich von Stietencron, and Heinz Bechert, *Christianity and the World Religions, Paths to Dialogue*, (New York: Orbis, 1993). Richard Morgan notes in "Peace among Religions" (*Forum on Public Policy*, Oxford Univ., 2007) that the history of religious wars, conquests, schisms and inquisitions has been a scandalous, self-

contradictory factor in the decision of many people to reject the message of hope held out by the religions. A false witness to the power of religion is partly responsible for angry neo-atheist authors writing about the "delusions" of a religious world view.

21. For differences in the role of grace in Christianity and Islam, www.answering-islam.de/Intro/comparison.html

22. Taylor explains the rise of secularity with an alternative, more complex narrative than the traditional subtraction stories. In the Middle Ages, the world was seen as an enchanted cosmos, which involved a social embeddedness and an acceptance of the order of things. The self was embedded within a social and cosmic order. Gradually, this enchanted cosmos became 'disenchanted'. Crucial to disenchantment was a 'great disembedding': the world came to be seen as constituted by individuals. As a result, the porous, socially-oriented self in an enchanted cosmos gave way to a universe of buffered selves and bounded 'minds', which have thoughts and feelings situated within them. With Descartes, mind or subject (*res cogitans*) and world or object (*res extensa*) became separate domains.

23. For Wayne Proudfoot, *Religious Experience*, (Univ. of California 1985, xiii) the term 'religious experience' originated early in 19th century due to an interest in "freeing religious doctrine and practice from dependence on ecclesiastical beliefs." Daniel Dennett in *Breaking the Spell: Religion as a Natural Phenomenon* (Viking, 2006) argues that religion is a natural phenomenon in need of scientific analysis so that we may better understand its nature.

24. Akeel Bilgrami, *Secularism, Identity, and Enchantment* (Harvard, 2014) distances himself from Taylor's view of secularization, arguing that the "transformation of the human subject to an object or, to put it more elaborately, an increasing detachment of the wrong kind in one's relation to the world, including one's relations to others" (130) must be better contextualized. For him, Taylor's conception of secularism is too state-neutralist, too equidistant from the different religions within a pluralist society, and so not sufficiently clear about the stance towards religion that secularism must minimally (but not always inflexibly) take. Bilgrami offers a minimalist definition of secularism. He asks a more general question as to subjectivity which he divides into a series of quite specific questions: 1) how and when did we transform the concept of nature into the concept of natural resources? 2) How and when did we transform the concept of human beings into the concept of citizens? 3) How and when did we transform the concept of people into the concept of populations? 4) How and when did we transform the concept of knowledge to live by into the concept of expertise to rule by?" (133): he calls for more human "enchantment".

25. Gabriela Baczynska, "Poland's cross wars revive debate on role of church", Aug. 2010. The Cross has become a polarizing symbol in Poland. See http://www.reuters.com/article/us-poland-church-idUSTRE67H2HN20100818

26. Five terrorists, posing as refugees, were arrested as they attempted to cross the Bulgarian-Macedonian border with ISIS decapitation videos on their phones, see www.breibart.com/national-security/ 2015/ 09/01-posing-as-refugees/. ISIS terrorists first attracted attention when tipping the scales in favor of rebels in Aleppo who had spent nearly two years attempting to conquer the seemingly impenetrable Menagh Airbase.summer (2013). ISIS chief, Abu Omar al-Shishani, had been trained by the U.S as part of an elite Georgian army unit from 2006 to 2013.

27. Nicos Mouzelis, "Exploring post-traditional Orders" in Martin O'Brien, Sue Penna, Colin Hay, ed. *Theorizing Modernity: Reflexivity, Environment & Identity in Giddens' Social Theory* (Routledge, 1998), chapter 4.

28. In *Contextuality and Intercontextuality in Public Theology*, Heinrich Bedford-Strohm, ed. (Lit Verlag, 2013), 321.

29. A. Forti, "History of the concept of the individual and individuality in Western society", Feb. 2010. See www.worldacademy.org/forum/history-concept-individual-and-individuality-western-society

30. Todd Weir "A clash of secularisms?" notes secularists' various claims. At one extreme, U.S. secularists portray their cause as a "beleaguered defense of the separation of church and state… Faith in naturalistic worldviews often bubbles up" in fuzzy definitions" underlying their advocacy. "At the other extreme, political and critical theorists use the term as shorthand for a master theory of global modernity." See Weir's blog, http://blogs.ssrc.org/tif/

31. Rugged individualism, Herbert Hoover's famous phrase, embodies much of the American spirit that led to the Great Depression and is now again a threat. Lonergan's GEM-FS calls individualists to be converted to a larger agenda: caring for neighbor and for the indispensable needs of the global community and of the environment.

32. J. A. B. Van Buitenen, "Dharma and Moksa", *Philosophy East and West*, Volume 7, Number 1/2 (Apr. - Jul., 1957).

33. Operative grace is conversion, the replacement of the heart of stone by a heart of flesh. Cooperative grace is the heart of flesh becoming effective in good works. It is what makes conversion "effective" through a gradual movement towards a full and complete transformation of the whole of one's living and feeling.... Religious loving is without conditions, qualifications, reservations; it is with all one's heart and all one's soul and all one's mind and all one's strength. See *The Lonergan Reader*, Mark and Elizabeth Morelli, editors (U. of Toronto, 1997, 524-25).

SKETCHING A GEM-FS BRIDGE'S MEDIATED PHASE AS OUTLINED IN *MIT*'S LAST FOUR SPECIALTIES: TOWARD ENABLING NEEDED TRANSFORMATIVE CHANGES AMONG THE RELIGIONS AND SECULARITY

1. Futurists such as James Canton are enthralled with ever new game-changing trends in technology, the economy and the environment, but one must also discern what is really beneficial to the planet and humankind. To thrive in the future, we must be predictive, adaptive, and agile, but also understand the past, including religious traditions.

5. FIFTH FUNCTIONAL SPECIALTY

1. We ask how can the foundations for a GEM-FS bridge answer the concerns of those unfamiliar with Lonergan?

2. See Seventh Annual Globalization for the Common Good: An Inter-Faith Perspective Conference: "From the Middle East to Asia Pacific: Arc of Conflict or Dialogue of Cultures and Religions?" held at Trinity College, University of Melbourne, Australia (June 30–July 4, 2008) organized by the economist-turned ethicist Kamran Mofid.

3. "The immanent source of transcendence in man is his detached, disinterested, unrestricted desire to know. As it is the origin of all his questions, it is the origin of the radical further questions that take him beyond the defined limits of particular issues." (*Insight*, 659). Self-appropriation is, in principle available to every person, is rather rare.

4. Dupre's "mysticism of negation" was inspired by Simone Weil. See his *Spiritual Life in a Secular Age* (Daedalus (1982), p. 25; Dupre speaks of the "true significance of the believer's current urge towards a spiritual life. From it emerges an intensive revelation of the infinite and a revitalization of his religion." (27). Denys Turner argues that after the 16th century, theological metaphors such as "darkness, mystical" etc. were used to express faith in the God who is not only beyond words, images, etc but also beyond human experience. They were then evacuated of that meaning and refilled with its exact opposite: the "mystical" came to designate not the truly transcendent but rather an *experience* of some *thing* labeled "darkness", "apophatic," "mystical." This implies the idolatry of experience, the individualist-expressivist interiority of the modern subject, the dropping away of community as indispensable complement to individual spirituality. Augustine, Dionysius, and Bonaventure are sources for the Christian apophatic. Meister Eckhart, *The Cloud of Unknowing* and John of the Cross pioneered the theology/ spirituality of the apophatic. Turner has a point, but we speak of religious experience in Louis Roy's Lonerganian sense: www.lonerganresearch.org/site/assets/files/1230/religious_experience_lecture_at_lri.pdf. See also Heather McAdam Erb, "*Pati Divina*": Mystical

Union in Aquinas, https://maritain.nd.edu/ama/Faith/faith104.pdf: "Dupre's reply to a world which has lost its sense of divine presence is an apophatic model of mystical experience where spiritual emptiness, transfigured in the night of divine absence, becomes a space of transcendence." (73).

5. Brague traces "the trajectory of apophatic tradition from its ancient origins to its postmodern avatars in his *On What Cannot Be Said: Apophatic Discourses in Philosophy, Religion, Literature, and the Arts* (Notre Dame U., 2007).

6. Hsing Yun, *Four Insights for Finding Fulfillment: A Practical Guide to the Buddha's Diamond Sūtra* (2012), 87. "All conditioned phenomena are like a dream, an illusion, ... When you understand the Buddhadharma you know that everything is empty .... realized from a conflux of conditions which only seem to be real." If you do not understand, you are like the fool who considers everything to be real. ... People who do not understand the Buddhadharma think that being wealthy is real and think that official positions actually exist." In fact, all is one. "A person is the same whether he is rich or impoverished. If you understand that everything is empty and illusory, then you.... will not become attached to unreal states. Bubbles are also basically unreal, and quickly disappear to show their emptiness. Shadows follow people around. When there is form, then there is a shadow. The form is an actual substance, the shadow is empty, unreal." (Ibid). www.drbachinese.org/vbs/publish/452/vbs452p025.pdf

7. See Raymaker, *Buddhist-Christian Logic of the Heart* (UPA, 2002) on *kokoro* (heart in Japanese), 49, 88, *passim*. For Toyohiko Kagawa, *kokoro* and consciousness typify humans' unique ability to act on idealist motivations.

8. Fritz Williams, *Wisdom Quotes*, http://www.wisdomquotes.com/quote/fritz-williams-1.html

9. With the help of Meister Eckhart, Dorothee Soelle, *The Silent Cry: Mysticism and Resistance*, rehabilitates Martha's active role in the story of Bethany (Luke 10:38-42). By not separating Martha's service from Mary's contemplative devotion but, rather, conceiving of Mary in Martha, Eckhart rejects the false separation of the active and contemplative life. In the perspective of mysticism, such a hierarchy is untenable. Cited by Carl McColman, http://www.patheos.com/blogs/carlmccolman/2012/06/mary-martha-and-meister-eckhart/ June, 2012.

10. Andreas Grünschloß, *Religionswissenschaft als Welt-Theologie: Wilfred Cantwell Smiths interreligiöse Hermeneutik* (Göttingen: Vandenhoeck & Ruprecht, 1994) analyzes Smith's contribution to Islamic studies. Starting with the studies on modern Islam in India, a major epistemological shift in his thinking can be identified: from the socio-historical perspective on religio-political developments to an empathetic understanding of Muslims' inner faith. Most of his informants identified with a modernist Islam dissatisfied with traditional legal orthodoxy and wanting to reform their own tradition in the light of modern values. wwwuser.gwdg.de/~agruens/summ_wcs.html

Influenced by Islamic mysticism, Smith traces Islamic stratifications to their primal function based on personal faith.

11. In a personal message, Sara Terreault writes: "When I see my students, young 20-somethings at a large comprehensive university in an ultra-pluralistic and a highly secularized society, I lament their loss of aesthetic sensibility (attunement to what Alexander Baumgarten called *veritas aesthetica*) which he distinguishes from *veritas logica*-- *aesthetica* being an important" register for religious meaning and one that religious praxis can cultivate in us. Aesthetic tone-deafness is a modernist tendency, shared by believers and non-believers alike. However, there is a flip-side to these young folks and their general lack of religious formation: they have not totally been absorbed by modernist religion's fundamentalist tendencies. They often can be encouraged to *hear* the register of "faith" (πίστις) of the New Testament, that is belief (trust) in person(s), not assent to a proposition. My students are mostly non-believers in the latter sense, but in their very humanness, they can "get" it in the former sense, intersubjectively, by pursuing truth. For Lonergan, 'we must acknowledge the existence of an older and more authoritative tradition in which faith and beliefs are identified' (*MIT*, 123). Still, faith itself is mysterious. I have no doubt that it comes in *forms* that do not necessarily conform to the speech-forms of tradition. These students may well be (perhaps radically) 'departing, not from the older doctrine, but from the old manner of speech.' (Ibid). They give me cause for

great hope. I think of Simone Weil's sense that one needs to give oneself over to truth. One gives oneself over to God ... God finds the way from there. (He's good at that ... trust him!)" One can never wrestle enough with God if one does so out of pure regard for the truth. Christ likes us to prefer truth to him because, before being Christ, he is truth. By turning from him toward the truth, one falls into his arms.

12. The *Dialogue of Saint Catherine of Siena*, tr. by Algar Thorold www.ewtn.com/library/SOURCES/CATHDIAL.HTM

Also, Robert Stackpole, "The Bridge of Mercy", Jan, 2006. www.thedivinemercy.org/library/article.php?NID=2241

13. "*Siraat*" is the path of knowledge. "Knowing" Allah consists of two Siraats, one in this world and the other in the next. *Siraat* is not mentioned in the Quran; some verses speak of "the right and straight path of guidance in this world that, if followed, will "remain in the hereafter. "A hadith narrated from Imam Sadiq reinforces the claim. See "Crossing the Bridge of Siraat" www.islamicinsights.com/religion/crossing-the-bridge-of-siraat.html One must ask which hadiths are fabricated. Some hadiths, attributed to Muhammad, were formulated long after his death.

14. Read more: http://www.onmarkproductions.com/html/kannon.shtml

15. James Finley, *Jesus and Buddha: Paths to Awakening*, (Center for Action and Contemplation, July, 2013).

16. William FitzGerald, *Spiritual Modalities: Prayer as Rhetoric and Performance* (Pennsylvania State U, 2012), 81, on habitual attitudes of prayer (such as reverence) which are habits of the heart partially known even to secularists.

17. Religion and religious doctrine are ongoing processes. FS 5 is concerned "largely with origins, the genesis, the present state, the possible developments and adaptations of the categories in which Christians understand themselves, communicate with one another, and preach the gospel to all nations." (*MiT*, 293). Islam, too, is concerned with developments and adaptations. Dealing with such adaptation is one key to this book's procedure.

18. For Scott Kelley, "Formal existential ethics in the thought of Bernard Lonergan and Ignatius of Loyola" UMI (2006), "spiritual experience is normative for ethics: one's elected worldview orders feeling-values according to an appropriated scale of preference." Kelley analyzes the normative influence of spirituality on feeling-values by defining the term spirituality as a framework for identifying a particular form of ethics. Lonergan's account of subjectivity helps us understand the normative function of spiritual experience. The normative component "is not a property of objects; it is a property of subjects. We speak of it when we say, 'You're not being objective' or 'Objectively speaking'. It guards us against wishful thinking and against politicizing what should be an impartial inquiry. Still, while this view incorporates the subject in moral assessments, some philosophers tend to collapse other aspects of objectivity into this subjective normativity. For them, thorough analysis, strict logic, and internal coherence are sufficient for objectivity. They propose their structural analyses not as hypotheses that may help us understand concrete experience correctly but as complete explanations of concrete realities. The morality of an act is determined by its coherence with implacable theory, suppressing further questions about actual cases that fall outside their conceptual schemes. Beyond the experiential, normative components of objectivity, there is an absolute component, by which all inquiry bows to reality as it is." See Tad Dunne, www.iep.utm.edu/lonergan.

Dorothy Day's *The Long Loneliness* illustrates how spiritual experience is normative for moral-decision making.

19. Overspecialization has led to a loss of wholeness that must be recaptured. Rituals can help connect humans to one another and to nature. Ancient societies felt connected to the cosmos through many types of rituals marking the change of seasons. Today, basic spiritual communities which treat persons as persons can be an effective means of recapturing a sense of unity within the human family, the earth community and the cosmos.

20. An ethics whose field covers universal potentials traces how morality is about allowing better. "It means allowing not only the potentials of nature to reveal themselves but also a maximum freedom to the innate human imperative to do better." One thinks of any moral option as a choice between preventing or allowing "the exercise *of a pure desire for the better*." Dunne http://www.iep.utm.edu/lonergan/ *Internet Encyclopedia of Philosophy*.

21. Authenticity is "an opposition within the human reality of individuals and of groups" (*MiT*, 111).

22. For atheists who have rejected all religious meaning, a claim of God's love as transcultural is simply dismissed. In his "stages of meaning" Lonergan concludes with the need "to speak effectively to undifferentiated consciousness. (*MiT*, 99). One must incrementally evaluate the stages as perceived today by well-educated persons. Hans Joas, *Faith as an Option* (Stanford Univ. 2014) is concerned with debunking two myths: "First, the idea that modernization—advances in technology and the sciences—renders religious belief obsolete; second, the argument that secularization leads to moral decay." Joas knows that criticisms of these claims are not new. Scholars are much less keen to establish a law "connecting modernization and secularization" since there is "little or no correlation between societies with higher rates of atheism and moral decline." Joas provides some explanations for why these views captured the imaginations of so many for so long. See http://blogs.ssrc.org/tif/author/steinmetzjenkinsd/

23. Rémi Brague, "The Impossibility of Secular Society Without a transcendent horizon, society cannot endure" in *First Things* at http://www.firstthings.com/article/2013/10/the-impossibility-of-secular-society Oct., 2013. As does Lonergan, Brague insists on "moral precepts." The debate as to how the word secularism was coined is a false one. "Advocates of secularism assume they are proposing a novel possibility, which is that moral precepts can be known without any particular revelation by God. Yet this is precisely what Christianity has taught, explicitly since Paul's *Epistle to the Romans* and, implicitly, since Jesus himself. This was lost sight of in the modern era, when many Christians defended religion against skeptical and rationalist attacks by arguing that it is necessary for ensuring the moral basis of society. Men without religion, it was argued, could not be trusted to behave in an upright fashion. So advocates of secularism were drawn into the false debate." For Lonergan, moral and affective orientations rely on intelligent and reasonable analyses of situations to produce moral precepts. This contrasts with ethics that look chiefly to virtue and good will for practical guidance. See Lonergan, *Collection*, "Finality, Love, Marriage", 16-53.

24. Brague, ("Impossibility") adds: Mill used "secular" because "he was eager to avoid 'atheistic', which is the more fitting term to describe the opposite of religious. But atheism was hardly the thing in Victorian Britain, and the word was felt to be rude." For his part, T. E. Huxley coined "agnosticism" during a discussion at the Metaphysical Society in 1869. "In present-day Britain, a third word, humanism, is often used with the same meaning and with the same intention: to evoke the possibility of a nonreligious basis for a morally animated society."

25. For William Franke, "The New Apophatic Universalism: Deconstructive Critical Theories and Open Togetherness in the European Tradition," *Parrhesia*, 21, 2014, 86-100, the Quran assimilated Judeao-Christian traditions, claiming "to correct the original source texts and to reveal a religious truth" held as corrupt. It appropriated these traditions but erased their alterity. However, Europe "remained obsessed with its sources as permanently external and other to itself." It enshrined mythic, mystic moments of preternatural creativity and even divine revelation in relation to which its own transmission remained always secondary. Christian Europe never seriously considering itself to be its own source. Hegel's idea of System closed by Absolute Knowing through the concept "provoked the rebellion of many highly influential thinkers, notably in France in the second half of the 20th century, giving rise to postmodern styles of thinking." For Rudolf Siebert, Adorno discussed religion within "the framework of Western Marxism, which had reactivated the philosophical aspects of Marx's work but at "the high price of regression into Hegelian idealism." While Hegel did not discuss dissonances in religious reality in the context of the Western Civilization" and in his philosophy of religion, he "sought to reconcile religion and reason, revelation and enlightenment...Adorno sought to differentiate them." http://journal.telospress.com/content/1983/58/108.abstract.

26. Creative artists feel an apophatic deep within self which they cannot but try to "universalize" as best they can. Further horizons open up for them which "run-of-the-mill," practical people cannot fathom (cf a van Gogh or a Poe—still, a Da Vinci or a Shakespeare are so great that they just leap-frog across the universalizing dilemma). Otto Rank's view of authenticity was inspired by Nietzsche's creative *Übermensch* mode that focuses "on the awful freedom of choice". Edward W. L. Smith, *The Psychology of Artists and the* Arts (McFarland, 2012, 107). As to physics, Frank Wilczek: *A Beautiful Question* (NY: Penguin, 2015) meditates on the deep

laws of the universe. This Nobel laureate (for the discovery of asymptotic freedom in the theory of the strong interaction, 2004) is inspired by the universe's beauty. Pythagoras and Plato had anticipated the harmony embedded deep in nature. As a young man of 23, Wilczek had implicitly felt nature's harmonies. This has remained his guiding inspiration in his work.

27. At this level of mystical awareness words fail to communicate on a literal level; one's life reveals deeper roots. Cf. A. Belyaeva on Wittgenstein's *Tractatus* and his "saying-showing" distinction, http://journal.iph.ras.ru/node/122 and Martin Pulido, "The Place of Saying and Showing In Wittgenstein's *Tractatus* and Some Later Works", *Aporia*, 19 no. 2—2009, http://aporia.byu.edu/pdfs/pulido-saying_and_showing_in_wittgenstein.pdf

28. John Renard and Ahmet Karamustafa, *Knowledge of God in Classical Sufism*, (Paulist, 2004), 46-47. Mystics seek to verbalize ineffable experiences. Sufis' esoteric interpretations proceed from the written to ineffable experiences.

29. Karen Armstrong, *A History of God* (New York, Ballantine) 191. Al-Ghazali explored revelation and Greek philosophy. Claims such as the eternity of the world and philosophical determinism seemed to contradict revelation. Wanting to harmonize the two, al-Ghazali asked: how can humans arrive at a knowledge of God?

30. During the 12th and 13th centuries *the Logica et Philosophia Algazelis* was a principal source for Latin authors on the teachings of the Arabic philosophers (Alonso 1958). Al-Ghazali's identification as one of them is attributed to the limited knowledge of Latin scholars. They assumed that the *Doctrines of the Philosophers* is not merely a *report* on the teachings of the *falsafa* but rather represents al-Ghazâlî's genuine positions in philosophy. This false view is not limited to the Latin tradition. *Stanford Encyclopedia of Philosophy* (Online: "Al-Ghazali" 1959a, 18 = 2000b, 61).

31. The apo-kataphatic distinction occurs in Sufism as the difference between the exoteric and esoteric meanings of Quranic texts. Historically this exoteric-esoteric distinction was developed to deal with problems Muslim mystics encountered because "The Truth" (*al Haqq*) is one of the names for Allah. This book uses *GEM-FS's operational range to correlate the mystic elements of Christianity and Islam with secularity*. As with the Sufi experience of *fana* and *fana al fana* (self-annihilation and the annihilation of self-annihilation), Turner (*Darkness*, 20) notes that 'apophatic theology' is simply "that speech about God which is the failure of speech." Kataphatic and apophatic theologies converge through mutual self-subversion: "they 'undo' each other and then 'undo' themselves resulting in 'disorder.'" (22). If the kataphatic says, 'God is Three,' the apophatic responds, 'God is not Three.' The "negation of the negation" that comes after "is not some intelligible synthesis of affirmation and negation," such as 'God is Three and One.' Cooperation of these two modes of theology results in "the collapse of our affirmation and denials into disorder ...[expressed]...in bits of collapsed, disordered language." An atheistic *via negativa* ('hermeneutic of suspicion') calls into question all that is sacred. It tries to destroy religion. In fact, the two seemingly opposed paths of theism and atheism both rely on negations. Atheism is a negative "a-theology." Jacques Derrida, *On the Name*, (Stanford, U. 1995) argues that embedded within any negative theology is a proclivity for atheism: "apophasis...at times so resembles a profession of atheism as to be mistaken for it" due to its push to "speak of God as being nothing or beyond being" (36). Meister Eckhart *seems* "a-theistic" for he sought to empty himself of "God.

32. Al-Ghazali helped overcome divides in Medieval Islam. Today, secularity and Islamic literalism confront one another. A Christian-secular GEM-FS is caught in the middle. The secular world's positions on religion are based on political expediency. GEM-FS openness can help solve many such problems often caused by misunderstandings.

33. N. Heer, "The Priority of Reason in the Interpretation of Scripture: Ibn Taymiyah and the Mutakallinum" in *The Literary Heritage of Classical Islam*, M. Mir, ed. (Davin Press, 181-95). For Frank Griffel, "Al-Ghazali", *The Stanford Encyclopedia of Philosophy)*, the charge that al-Ghazali led to the devolution of reason within Islam errs. The clearest break between revelation and reason including the Sufis' tolerance of diverse views came with Ibn Taymiyya (1263-1328) who questioned the Sufi orders' orthodoxy and the role of philosophy. He wanted to completely separate the Islamic faith from any Christian connection, feeling that Sufis shrines that lauded Sufi "saints" deviated from Islam. In his "On the Necessity of the Straight Path," he preached that the beginning of Muslim life was the point at which "a perfect dissimi-

larity with the non-Muslims has been achieved." He opposed celebrating Muhammad's birthday or the construction of mosques around the tombs of Sufi saints saying: "Many Muslims do not even know of the Christian origins of these." See Muhammad Umar Memon, *Ibn Taymiyya's Struggle against Popular Religion, with an annotated translation of Kitab Iqitada*, (The Hague, 1976), 78, 210.

34. See Renard and Karamustafa, *Knowledge of God in Classical Sufism*, 394.
35. Armstrong, *A History of God*, 234.
36. "O Marvel! a garden amidst the flames.
My heart has become capable of every form:
it is a pasture for gazelles and a convent for Christian monks,
and a temple for idols and the pilgrim's Kaa'ba,
and the tables of the Torah and the book of the Quran.
I follow the religion of Love: whatever way Love's camels take,
that is my religion and my faith." *Tarjuman al-Ashwaq*. Poem XI. (Theosophical Publishing House, 1911).

See also Henri Corbin, *Creative Imagination in the Sufism of Ibn Arabi*, (Princeton U, 1970), 138. *Meccan Revelations* (*Futubat al-Makkiyah*) translated by members of the Muhyiddin Ibn al-'Arabi Society is the translation we cite.

37. Quoted in Reynold A. Nicholson, *The Mystics of Islam*, (Routledge, 1914) 105. Miguel Asin Palacios' study of Sufist influence upon the Spanish Christian mystics such as St. Teresa of Avila (1515-1582) and St. John of the Cross (1542-1591) led him to say that the mystical writings of the latter parallel those of the Shazali order of Sufis still widely present and active in North Africa, Syria, and Arabia. In his *The Other Islam: Sufism and the Road to Global Harmony* (Doubleday, 2008) Stephen Suleyman Schwartz, a Sufi convert, offers a worthwhile account of Sufism.

38. Rumi's poem entitled "Spring" helps us experience God's grandeur:
Again the violet bows to the lily. . .
The green ones have come to the other world
Tipsy like the breeze up to some new foolishness. . .
The ringdove comes asking, 'Where is the Friend?'
With one note the nightingale indicates the rose.
Again the season of Spring has come
and a spring-source rises under everything
a moon sliding from the shadows.
Many things need to be left unsaid, because it's late,
But whatever conversation we haven't had tonight, we'll have tomorrow.

See *The Essential Rumi*, translated by Coleman Barks. (Harper One, 2004) 33-34. Rumi recounts his encounter in 1244 with Shams—a wandering dervish--as the major mystical experience of his life. Shams asked such a profound question that Rumi fell to the ground at his presence. Rumi and Shams became inseparable friends. This caused consternation among Rumi's entourage and may explain why Shams left Rumi's household.

39. Patrick Kirkwood has noted privately that Patanjali's *Yoga Sutras* (4th century B.C.) "sound like pure Lonergan in the perceptive analyses of consciousness, e.g. *pratyaksa* (evidence, immediate perception) *anumana* (argument, inference) *agama* (tradition, scripture), *pramana* (right knowing)." Kirkwood concludes that "GEM exists in all of us. It remains to be discovered and described by seers in different cultures and contexts and practiced by all of us. "In my own (Australian) culture I am intrigued by the indigenous/aboriginal culture and its "dreamtime" which contains history, religion, stories, rituals and all manner of wisdom which we later settlers are still unpacking." Bruce R. Arnold, http://jnanayoga.org/JnanaEssay.htm considers the similarities in practice in Eastern religions. "If you look at Hindu *yoga*, Buddhist meditation, Zen koans, Chinese systems such as *chi qong* and *t'ai chi*, and western systems such as *Qabala* and alchemy, there are remarkable similarities among them." But how are they to agree?

40. Mike King, *Network, the Scientific and Medical Network Journal*,71, Dec., 1999 explores the intersections of and parallels between art, science and the spiritual as related to the deep structure of human experience. A better framework for science-religion debates arises

when we consider the mystical core of religion "and contrast its goals and methods" with those of science. This requires recourse to the 'social', the 'occult', and the 'transcendent'.

41. "Shiva Nataraja. The Lord of the Dance" http://www.lotussculpture.com/nataraja1.html

42. See Andre van der Braak, *Zen Spirituality in a Secular Age: Charles Taylor and Zen Buddhism in the West.* Zen first entered Western culture the 1920's, in the writings of D.T. Suzuki (1870-1966). Some have hailed Zen as a possible universal method of meditation—an apophatic, wordless glimpse into cosmic reality. William Johnston, in "Has Mysticism a Future," *Japan Mission Journal*, Summer, 2006, 82 and in his *Mystical Journey, an Autobiography* (NY: Orbis: 2006), writes that his being in Japan and practicing Zen helped him rediscover Christianity's mystical traditions. Paul Knitter, *Without Buddha I Could Not Be a Christian* (Oneworld, 2009) on how transcultural Christians can strengthen their own faith so as to overcome doubt by examining the larger realities confronting us.

43. Taylor, *Secular Age*, 711, identifies questionable trends in current approaches to spirituality, such as a neglect of ordinary life, "excarnation" ("the steady disembodying of spiritual life"), and the therapeutization of religion. For Taylor, any idea that meaning can be affirmed in a general way, devoid of specific content, is foolish. One might die for God, or the Revolution, or the classless society, but not for meaning (679). When one asks what is worth living and dying for, we are back to notions of spirituality (…not always) associated with transcendence. For Taylor, there is a place for transcendence today; he challenges alleged restrictive, closed world structures' which make disbelief in God appear more incontrovertible than it really is. He identifies "transcendence" with religion, but also identifies a 'nova effect' which has given rise to an 'ever widening variety of moral/ spiritual options' (299). See Christopher Cook, "Spirituality and religion in psychiatric practice" http://pb.rcpsych.org/content/pbrcpsych/34/5/193.full.pdf

44. Mfundishi Obuabasa Serikali, *Tai Chi Chaun*: *An Afriasian Resource for Health and Longevity* (Universe, 2006).

45. www.theguardian.com/politics/2015/aug/02/maajid-nawaz-how-a-former-islamist-became-david-camerons-anti-extremism-adviser David Shariatmadari, Aug. 2, 2015 on the "controversial" advisor to David Cameron.

46. See Sarah Terreault, www.google.de/?gfe_rd=cr&ei=0T0GV-_TB6uK8Qf0rbKoBA&gws_rd=ssl#q=lonergan_l. Both the data of sense (recognized in the scientific method) and those of consciousness affect how we evaluate cultures. Both help mediate human encounters. They play a crucial ethical role in deciding whether persons or communities can be instruments of change. In mediating the past and present or one culture's values with those of another, both types of date are needed to enable us to make valid judgments and take adequate actions.

47. Talal Asad, *Formations of the Secular: Christianity, Islam, Modernity* (Stanford U, 2003). For human rights scholar Louis Henkin, "Human Rights: Ideology and Aspiration, Reality and Prospect," in S. Power and G. Allison, eds., *Realizing Human Rights: Moving from Inspiration to Impact*, (NY: St. Martin's, 2000), 29, the world of religion and the world of human rights often diverge. Religionists are uncomfortable with human rights not rooted in religion. Some religions invoke dogma to justify distinctions based on religion, gender, or sexual orientations, distinctions that may be contrary to the human rights idea." Riffat Hassan www.religious consultation.org/hassan2.htm, "Are Human Rights Compatible with Islam? The Issue of the Rights of Women in Muslim Communities" argues that "Although the Universal declaration of Human Rights is called "Universal", it relies on Western assumptions of individualism. Muslims claim "that it is not meaningful to talk about human rights in Islam because as a religious tradition, Islam has supported values and structures" incompatible with Western assumptions as to human rights.

48. The seeming lack of a method for interdisciplinary cooperation has exacerbated misunderstandings. Such a fact calls for the Church to adapt her traditional role in bridging cultural values and philosophical standpoints.

49. Yves Raguin, *La Profondeur de Dieu* (Descle de Brouwer, 1973). Jacques Dupuis, *Toward a Christian Theology of Religious Pluralism* (New York: Orbis, 1997). Dupuis spent much of his life working on a hermeneutic that could justify valid forms of interreligious dialogue. Today, the data of religious pluralism must be addressed in theologies. Otto Heejung Cho, "Receptive Pluralism in Asian Theology as a New Horizon" on the receptive pluralism

that has emerged through the efforts of Asian Catholic bishops and theologians to understand their situation of religious diversity. Cho argues that this notion constitutes a new theological horizon arising out of a communal conversation about the relationships between culture and religion in Asia. See www.lonerganresearch.org/events/lri-graduate-seminar-heejung-adele-cho-receptive-pluralism-in-asian-theology-as-a-new-horizon/ retrieved May 14, 2016.

50. American Zen scholar Robert Sharf, "Buddhist modernism and the rhetoric of meditative experience", *Numen* 42 (1995) no. 3, 228-283, points out, investigators of religious or mystical experience usually focus on the qualifiers 'religious' or 'mystical', whereas the term 'experience' is taken as self-evident. 'The notion that the referent of the term 'experience' is self-evident is Cartesian--as if experience were immediately present to one's consciousness.

51. There are commonalities in how various mystical traditions have tried to find bridges to other traditions--bridges which respect others' beliefs. Grudzen and Raymaker, *Steps toward Vatican iii: Catholics Pathfinding a Global Spirituality with Islam and Buddhism* (UPA, 2008) suggest spirituality's potential role in underpinning a global ethics whereby religious groups can cooperate with secularists or atheists. Mahayana Buddhism and Zen developed differently in China and Japan. Some Zen schools use koans, others do not. Westerners tend objectify, but Zen Buddhists seek enlightenment. As with the oxherd, once enlightened, one returns to the world to serve others.

52. A derogatory way to refer to ISIL is "DAESH" from the Arabic verb دعس, meaning "to thread underfoot".

53. When Obama decided to support the armed opposition to the Damascus regime in 2011 he, in effect took the side of radical Islamists. The M198 howitzers supplied to the tiny, pathetic, largely imaginary "Free Syrian Army" wound up in the hands of ISIL, along with Humvees wrested from the collapsing Iraqi Army. ISIL also seized U.S.-produced hand grenades, ammunition and rocket-propelled grenade launchers intended for Kurdish forces in Syria.

6. SIXTH FUNCTIONAL SPECIALTY

1. Johannes Metz, *Theology of the World* (New York: Seabury, 1973), 16.

2. Rudolf Otto, T*he Idea of the Holy: An Inquiry into the Non-rational Factor in the Idea of the Divine and its Relation to the Rationa*l (Oxford, 1923) analyzed the holy as what underlies all religion. The holy is "numinous," wholly other-- entirely different from anything we experience in ordinary life." It evokes silence.

3. The influx of millions of Muslims--first Turkish "guest workers" and now refugees from Syria and other Muslim nations--has led to many cultural conflicts in Germany. Muslims tend to honor their own customs and the Quran over German customs and laws. Some praise the Canadian way of attributing points in integrating immigrants as a model to be followed. www.youtube.com/watch?v=KVWAIKoatWM&feature=em-share_video_user

4. See "Islam and Secularization," www.centerforinquiry.net/isis/islamic_viewpoints/islam_and_secularization/ and www.scupe.org/special-event-highlights-a-faith-based-alternative-to-divisive-politics/

5. Cf Francis Schüssler Fiorenza, "Prospects for Political Theology in the Face of Contemporary Challenges" in *Political Theology: Contemporary Challenges and Future Directions* (Westminster: John Knox, 2013, 37-38). Mike Grimshaw, June, 2015, www.palgrave-journals.com/articles/palcomms201525 notes that Gabriel Vahanian in his *Death of God* (1961) asked "What if secularity is a theological condition...the theological and societal experience of both biblical religion and the death of God?" Vahanian wrote of secularity as a distinctly theological *saeculum*: the shared world of human experience that took aim at an "idolatrous concern about secular matters" (196), and resulting in "the idolization of religion" expressed in technological religiosity representing "an unmistakable abdication of faith to reason—or unreason" (197). His *No Other God* (1966) goes into atheistic theologies that treat of the death of God but, in his view, denied it "by sublimating it into a newfangled soeteriological concept" (4).

6. Review of Erdag Gökhnar's *Secularism and Blasphemy: The Politics of the Turkish Novel* (Routledge, 2013). Most educated Turks disdain Pamuk, believing he has betrayed Kemalism (Turkey's combination of French secularism and nationalism) in order to curry favor with foreign readers. "This is the "blasphemy" to which the book's title refers. Foreign readers "have generally misunderstood Pamuk's work because they are unfamiliar with Turkish literary and political" contexts. After decades of criticism for wielding a depoliticized pen, Pamuk has been cast as a dissident. See www.insightturkey.com/orhan-pamuk-secularism-and-blasphemy-the-politics-of-the-turkish-novel/book-reviews/1435 and Jörg Lau, "The Turkish Trauma," *Die Zeit,* 14 April, 2005; translated and reposted.

7. Orhan Pamuk, *Snow: A Novel*, trans., Maureen Freely, (New York: Alfred A. Knopf, 2004). Pamuk, in 2005, was charged with "insulting Turkishness" but in 2006 he was awarded the Nobel Prize for Literature.

8. See review, *Time*, April 18, 2005, 88. John von Heyking, "Mysticism in contemporary Islamic political thought: Orhan Pamuk and Abdolkarim Soroush" in *Humanitas*, March, 2006.Heyking examines Abdolkarim Soroush, *Reason, Freedom, and Democracy in Islam: Essential Writings of Abdolkarim Soroush*, 2002, tr., Mahmoud Sadri.

9. "Irrepressible" at http://www.economist.com/news/books-and-arts/21638092-book-started-it-all-irrepressible

10. With Paulo Freire, we view the word of God as having to be reflected on so as to transform the world. Reflecting on God's Word can help foster needed transformational bridges that mediate between traditional interpretations of Church structures, small communities that pursue spirituality focused on a global ethic and interfaith endeavors.

11. William Sullivan and John Heng in Gerard Whelan, ed. *Revisiting Lonergan's Anthropology*, Rome: G&B Press, 2015 retrieved May 21, 2015 at http://iacbsite.org/FunctionalSpecialties.pdf

12. Tad Dunne http://www.iep.utm.edu/lonergan/ notes that when we try to reconcile opposing moral opinions, we appeal to shared ethical principles which in fact are in themselves opposed. We may then try to reconcile opposing principles "by clarifying how we arrived at them." Because our principles are culturally inherited, "discussions halt at a tolerant mutual respect. . .What is needed is a method in ethics that can uncover the sources of error." There is considerable merit to investigating the innate methods of our minds and hearts that arrive at ethical principles.

13. The examples meet GEM-FS's sufficiently broad and open-minded see-judge-act criteria. These include liberation theologians and some broad-ranging Christian or Muslim initiatives, including an experiment in Kenya where Muslim terrorists have also been active such as in their killing Christians in such cities as Nairobi and Garissa. They also point to other examples motivated by a spirit of community and a logic of the heart's value judgments.

14. Frederick Augustus Voigt (1892–1957) rejected his scientific materialism and returned to Anglicanism. Paul Tillich, *Christianity and the Encounter of the World Religions* (Columbia U., 1963) defined religion as a person's ultimate concern which suggests that everyone has some religious (quasi-religious) commitments. He applied the term pseudo-religious to such extreme movements as Fascism and Communism in the 20th century.

15. Pope John Paul II's charismatic personality and mystical tendencies allowed him to adopt a more tolerant approach to Buddhism and Islam than his successor, Benedict XVI. Yet, John Paul II relied on Cardinal Ratzinger's expertise in Western theology to guide him through the shoals of guiding the Church amidst much pluralism.

16. J. Raymaker, "Challenges to a Religious Global Ethics in an Increasingly Secularized World" www.globethics.net/documents/4289936/13403236/GlobalSeries_4_SharingValues_text.pdf/6162b4a5-5cd2-4af6-bdc5-70699b69d923

17. Denys Turner in *The Cambridge Companion to Liberation Theology*, edited by Christopher Rowland, 212. https://books.google.de/books?id=OBRQmL8z064C&pg=PA212&lpg=PA212&dq=liberation+theology+apophatic&source=bl&ots=PmvsGq0zaA&sig=tY8Jcj XLD6DoaKdJpFuiI0TK0JI&hl=en&sa=X&ved=0CC8Q6AEwA2oVChMIkqf036WCxwIV gwosCh23HwNP#v=onepage&q=liberation%20theology%20apophatic&f=false

18. Richard Shaull and Waldo Cesar, *Pentecostalism and the Future of the Christian Churches* (Eerdmans, 2000) argue that traditional forms of Christianity have not properly

addressed the needs of the poor. In the face of this, fast-growing Pentecostal movements have sprung up in the Third World to address marginalization and injustice. Relying partly on liberation theology, this book examines marginalization among Muslim immigrants in Europe. We regard Shaull and Cesar's approach as an appropriate see-judge-act response to pressing issues. Our view is that all too often religion seems to offer pie-in-the sky promises which fail to address the root causes of poverty.

19. Christa Pongratz-Lippitt, review of Kasper's *Pope Francis' Revolution of Tenderness and Love* (Paulist, 2015). See http://ncronline.org/news/people/francis-theological-spokesman-walter-kasper-publishes-new-book-pope

20. Christopher Shannon, "Romano Guardini: Father of the New Evangelization, in *Crisis Magazine*, Feb. 17, 2014 at http://www.crisismagazine.com/2014/romano-guardini-father-of-the-new-evangelization

21. Gulen has found a way to combine Islamic commitments with tolerance. See Lester Kurtz, "Gulen's Paradox" at http://onlinelibrary.wiley.com/doi/10.1111/j.1478-1913.2005 .00100.x/abstract;jsessionid=0F2589B3FF45827CABC 92433C1BAA050.f01t04?userIsAuthenticated=false&deniedAccessCustomisedMessage= retrieved Dec. 24, 2015.

22. Muslims converting to Christianity face "reprisals" based on a hadith attributed to Muhammad: "Whoever changed his Islamic religion, kill him" (Bukhari 9.84.57). This is recognized by four schools of Islamic jurisprudence. see www.jihadwatch.org/2016/02/even-in-italy-christian-converts-from-islam-live-in-fear-of-reprisals. Umdat al-Salik (9.13) allows captured women to be used as sex slaves, their previous marriage being "immediately annulled." The Spanish word "*macho*" makes it clear that we are not singling out Muslims but a traditional cultural mindset.

23. Edward Said, *Orientalism* (Penguin, 1978) reviewed at http://www.renaissance.com.pk/febbore2y6.htm

24. Dorothy C. Buck, "Louis Massignon: A Tribute to a Pioneer in Interfaith Relations" See http://www.fountainmagazine.com/Issue/detail/louis-massignon-a-tribute-to-november-december-2012

25. Said rebutted, August 12, 1982 Bernard Lewis' unfavorable review of *Orientalism* in the *New York Review*'s June 24, 1982 issue. Lewis had characterized *Orientalism* as "false, absurd, astonishing, reckless." Said countered: "The sheer length of his diatribe and the four years of gestation he needed to produce it suggest that he takes what I say quite seriously…. (His) verbosity scarcely conceals both the ideological underpinnings of his position and his extraordinary capacity for getting everything wrong. Of course, these are familiar attributes of the Orientalists' breed, some of whom have at least had the courage to be honest in their active denigration of Islamic, as well as other non-European peoples. Not Lewis. He proceeds in his usual mode by suppressing or distorting the truth . . . The fact is that the present political moment allows him to deliver ahistorical and willful political assertions in the form of scholarly argument, a practice thoroughly in keeping with the least creditable aspects of old-fashioned colonialist Orientalism. To imply as he does that the branch of Orientalism dealing with Islam and the Arabs is a learned discipline that can be compared with classical philology is" inappropriate. "On the one hand Lewis wishes to reduce Islamic Orientalism to the status of an innocent and enthusiastic department of scholarship; on the other he wishes to pretend that Orientalism is too complex" For Said, Lewis suppresses "a significant amount of history. European interest in Islam derived from fear of a monotheistic, culturally and militarily formidable competitor to Christianity. The earliest scholars of Islam . . . were medieval polemicists writing to ward off the threat of Muslim hordes and of apostasy…. Fear and hostility has persisted to the present day both in scholarly and non-scholarly attention to an Islam which is viewed as belonging to a part of the world, the Orient, counter-posed . . .historically against Europe and the West." See www.nybooks.com/articles/archives/1982/aug/12/orientalism-an-exchange/

26. Fabio Petito writes of Massignon's "divergent agreement" with Said, arguing "that Massignon's work and life stand as a very concrete proof of the possibility of a 'dialogue of civilizations' that escapes the yoke of the Orientalist accusations. See https://millenniumjournal.files.wordpress.com/2010/09/petito-civilization-dialogue-and-orientalism.pdf. For Fabio,

the idea of civilizational dialogue necessitates a multicultural and peaceful world order that can entertain an ambiguous relationship with Orientalism that includes Said's main insight "but acknowledges the risk of an intellectual/ political construction of the Self through the opposition to a negative-valued, dangerous or threatening Other." Massignon points to the possibilities of an "idea(l) of dialogue."

27. http://www.bbc.com/news/world-13503361 The article notes that critics question Hizmet's motives.

28. For Derrida, the West should not restrict itself to Greco-Christian mysticism, but also study Islam's traditional mystic teachings. https://books.google.de/books?id=OM-NEG23goC&pg=PA3&lpg=PA3&dq=sufism+apophatic&source=bl&ots=sqK_YsM5RN&sig=EL7MRDMLwEx3PnUP1W2lRY89l5s&hl=en&sa=X&ved=0CDEQ6AEwBGoVChMIpp2o5YyBxwIVAskUCh2bBwPq#v=onepage&q=sufism%20apophatic&f=false

29. In *The Emerald Hills of the Heart*, titled "*Seyr-u Süluk*" (Wayfaring), vol. 2. Gülen describes Sufi stages of mystical journey such as *seyr ilallah* (journeying to God), *seyr fillah* (journeying in God), *seyr maallah* (journeying with God), *seyr anillah* (journeying from God) in the classical Sufi understanding (Gulen, 2001, 255-73). While all true ways are taken from the Quran, such ways as impotence, poverty, compassion are shorter, safer than others. See http://fethullahgulenforum.org/questions_answers/16/is-fethullah-gulen-sufi? *Tasawwuf* is an orthodox science of Islam. In his Al-Risala al-safadiyya, Ibn Taymiyya describes the Sufis as those who belong to the path of the Sunna. Mustafa Gokcek examines the extent of Sufism's impact on Gulen. Gulen does not want to establish a Sufi order; he aims to revive the activism of the Prophet and his companions "and the consciousness of Sufi scholars." There are strong parallels between Gulen's approach and the views of many leading scholars such as Qushayri and Tusi who strive to bring together Sufism and sharia. They criticize the out-of-sharia practices that emerged within Sufi circles. In his study of Sufi concepts, Gulen lists the relevant Quranic verses and sayings of the Prophet along with various interpretations of a concept by Sufi scholars. A concept should be understood and practiced in daily life. One issue dividing Sufi scholars regards the roles of *sekr* (mystical intoxication) and *sahv* (mystical sobriety). Gulen states that for Sufis intoxication is when "the wayfarer loses himself in ecstasy upon experiencing Divine rays …Sobriety is the wayfarer's coming back to his/her senses. For Gulen, intoxication is a 'station' that cannot be reached by the will of wayfarer, but is only a bounty of God." Sobriety should be preferred to intoxication." Bayezid Bistami favored intoxication. (Annemarie Shimmel, *Mystical Dimensions of Islam*, Univ. of North Carolina, 1975, 58).

30. Gulen had kept Hizmet from political involvements, but Erdogan closed its Turkish newspapers. Hizmet has been engaged in a variety of educational, media, and social service projects that have now expanded into over 100 countries, including the USA. The schools have become models for student excellence in science and math as well as in ethical training. For other views: www.englisc-gateway.com/bbs/topic/24551-militant-islam-on-the-march/

31. See http://scholars.wlu.ca/cgi/viewcontent.cgi?article=2726&context=etd which features Faruk Arslan's PhD Thesis at Wilfrid Laurier University (2014). See also Raymaker, Grudzen and Holland, *Spiritual Paths*, 105-14.

32. See M.F. Gulen, *Toward a Global Civilization of Love & Tolerance* (New Jersey: The Light 2006), 63. We would add that since secularity does not exclude interiority, it can help bridge the secular, Christianity and Islam. But in view of Islamic intolerance on many fronts (such as refugees in Germany attacking one another for perceived violations of their religion), it is well to invoke the history of Sufi tolerance which functions as a bridge of mercy.

33. Claims of "absoluteness" has led to Muslim crimes against Christians in many areas--in refugee camps or in Beirut where a priest was mercilessly persecuted by ISIS affiliates (2014) which ended his good will toward them. ncronline.org/news/global/two-religions-tension-wars-extremism-fray-christian-muslim-relations-middle-east

34. Osman Bakar in The *Muslim World*, 95 (3), July, 1995, "Gulen on Religion and Science", 362.

35. Robert Spencer, www.jihadwatch.org/2016/02/islam-cant-be-modernized-says-worlds-greatest-arabic-poet

36. Arcamone, Dominic, *Religion and Violence: A Dialectical Engagement through the Insights of Bernard Lonergan*. (Pickwick, 2015) explores key symbols of religiously-motivated violence from a GEM-FS perspective. Many have linked religion to violence--religion being viewed as part of the problem. Arcamone replies that genuine religion differs from distorted versions. Distorted religion shapes traditions in ways that would "justify" violence. Genuine religion heals persons, helps them make sound moral decisions in the face of conflict. It explores ways for persons to understand themselves and to shape history toward progress. Arcamone suggests that Lonergan provides categories that can speak to people from other traditions including Islam in today's all-too secularized societies.

37. For another, GEM-FS inspired project in Kenya, based on Brian Cronin's *Foundations of Philosophy: Lonergan's Cognitional Theory and Epistemology* (Langata, Nairobi: Consolata Institute of Philosophy, 2006), see www.shu.edu/catholic-mission/lonergan/upload/ADVANCED-SEMINAR-ON-MISSION-PRAXIS-PROGRAM.pdf

38. Siddhartha Mitter, "Linda Sarsour, Black Lives Matter" at http://america.aljazeera.com/articles/2015/5/9/linda-sarsours-rising-profile-reflects-new-generation-of-muslim-activists.html. While fielding phone calls and tweeting, Sarsour described cases that come in daily — evictions, economic hardship, medical crises, domestic violence, etc. "With her family roots, her self-presentation and her fluent Arabic, Sarsour is able to confront older, conservative immigrants as to e. g. racial issues. Her strong Palestinian identity and her wearing her Muslimness on her sleeve helps her "converse with the aunties and uncles," said one ACLU observer. She seems very traditional, but "her activism is very progressive." For a reference to one of Sarsour's more questionable judgments www.jihadwatch.org/2015/12/some-muslims-in-u-s-irritated-by-obamas-call-for-them-to-root-out-extremism

39. North Korea uses gruesome methods against its 100,000 political prisoners holding them in stress positions, forcing them to eat snakes and mice, rape, forced abortion, and starvation. Some escapees have testified before a UN commission of inquiry, March 2013 that the country targets those who try to flee the country, Christians, those promoting other "subversive" beliefs. See www.economist.com/news/ asia/21596999-un-report-accuses-north-korea-unspeakable-human-rights-abuses-and-hints-chi. China is complicit in its abuse of North Korean escapees.

40. ISIL's leader, Abu Bakr Baghdadi, is reported to have repeatedly raped Kayla Mueller, a captured peace activist. See http://www.theguardian.com/world/2015/aug/14/islamic-state-leader-raped-kayla-muller-abu-bakr-baghdadi When told that Baghdadi claimed to have married her, her parents replied "we all understand what that means… Kayla did not marry this man. He took her to his room and abused her. She would come back crying." Murderous sociopaths can invoke religious doctrine without understanding its meaning. GEM-FS is premised on authenticity.

41. Johanna Markind, "Why Are So Many Muslims in Prison?" Aug 30, 2015 www.meforum.org/blog/2015/08/islam-prison. They make up around 9% of U. S. prisoners. Of France's 64,000 prisoners, up to 60% are Muslim although they compose only 8% of the population. Said prisoners are often radicalized. See also Farhad Khosrokhavar http://cadis.ehess.fr/index.php?/membres-du-centre/membres-permanents/1142-farhad-khosrokhavar

42. http://www.summit.org/resources/essays/the-worldviews-of-destruction-in-the-20th-century/. Noebel has denounced Wellhausen, the pioneer in biblical studies who contributed to scholarly understanding of the origin of the Pentateuch/Torah. Claiming that "higher criticism" is as dangerous as "moral relativism" is unfounded.

43. http://www.aljazeera.com/news/2015/08/trained-syrian-fighters-refusing-fight-150807114420346.html posted on Aug. 8, 2015. Charles Marsh, "Wayward Christian Soldiers," (*NY Times*, Jan. 20, 2006) noted: "White evangelical Christian faith leaders preached 'war sermons' with the theme that our president, "a brother in Christ had discerned "that God's will is for our nation to be at war against Iraq, we shall gloriously comply." Those possessed with the God complex, or an ethnocentric disease of American exceptionalism have no idea what the US did to Iraq.

44. https://wikiislam.net/wiki/The_Meaning_of_Islam; originally, a Muslim was someone who surrendered in warfare. "Islam did not stand for the absence of war, but for one of its

intended outcomes: surrender leading to the "safety" of captivity. Muhammad advocated *aslim taslam*: "surrender (i.e. convert to Islam) and you will be safe."

45. The religion of peace slogan has been rejected by many Muslims, but is now promoted by Western leaders in response to terrorism: George W. Bush and Jacques Chirac after 9/11, David Cameron and François Hollande. After the beheading of 21 Copts on a Libyan beach Barack Obama called upon the world to "continue to lift up the voices of Muslim clerics and scholars who teach the true peaceful nature of Islam." Sadullah Khan calls for peace and moderation; http://islam.ru/en/content/story/call-islam-peace-moderation-not-intolerance-and-extremism. Philip Carl Salzman *Independent Journal Review* March 25, 2016 argues that tribalism still drives the Arabs—in cities.

46. While Islamophobia "is toxic to everyone," one must find ways to deal with Muslim intolerance where it still exists. See http://www.reuters.com/article/2015/10/27/us-turkey-politics-gulen-idUSKCN0SL23Q20151027 As to Muslim intolerance in Germany, www.youtube.com/watch?v=KVWAIKoatWM&feature=em-share_video_user

47. This has to be qualified inasmuch as blasphemy convictions have intensified under Sisi. Raymond Ibrahim, www.meforum.org/5945/blasphemy-convictions-egypt, on how Egyptian poet Fatma Naoot was sentenced to three years in prison in 2016 for criticizing the slaughter of animals during the Islamic festival of Eid al-Adha.

48. Aydoğan Vatandaş, *Today's Zaman* "The Gülen movement as the victim of an orchestrated smear campaign," January 2016 http://fgulen.com/en/press/columns/50178-the-gulen-movement-as-the-victim-of-an-orchestrated-smear-campaign on how Turkish Islamists want to stifle interfaith dialogue—effectively rejecting Gulen's vision.

49. Fearing the development of parallel societies in Europe, Austria passed on Feb. 25, 2016 controversial reforms to the country's century-old Law on the status of Muslims. The new law, aims to integrate Muslims with an "Islam with an Austrian character." It seeks to reduce outside meddling by prohibiting foreign funding for mosques, imams and Muslim organizations in Austria. It stresses that Austrian law must take precedence over Islamic Sharia law for Muslims living in the country. The Austrian government says the new law is a milestone and could serve as a model for the rest of Europe. But Muslim groups say it is discriminatory and have vowed to challenge it in court.

50. Burak Bekdil, January 12, 2016, www.meforum.org/5796/turkey-father-daughter- and Robert Spencer, Jan. 17, 2016 www.jihadwatch.org/2016/01/female-al-azhar-prof-allah-allows-muslims-to-rape-non-muslim-women

51. Germany's Pegida, "Patriotic Europeans Against the Islamization of the West" wants to curb immigration. It accuses the authorities of failing to enforce existing laws. It challenges what it sees as liberal political correctness. Launched as a Facebook group by a graphic designer with a criminal record, Pegida, using social media, attracts right-wingers from some of the established political parties. See www.bbc.com/news/world-europe-30776182

52. "The Legacy of Pim Fortuyn", www.amren.com/features/2014/09/the-legacy-of-pim-fortuyn. Fortuyn favored the introduction of secularist notions. His 1997 book, *Against the Islamization of our Culture* shocked Hollanders. Critics of multiculturalism charge that Europe has "allowed excessive immigration without demanding enough integration." This has eroded social cohesion and trust. Its proponents reply that the problem is not that of diversity but of racism. See Kenan Malike, "The Failure of Multiculturalism," *Foreign Affairs*, March-April, 2015.

53. Wilders, "I don't hate Muslims. I hate Islam," www.theguardian.com/world/2008/feb/17/netherlands.islam

54. See G. Michael Leffel, "The Relational Spirituality Paradigm," www.thedivineconspiracy.org/Z5213B.pdf. Freud insisted that there are "deep currents of meaning, often cross-currents, running through the human soul which can at best be glimpsed through a glass darkly. This if anything, is the Western tradition: not a specific set of values, but a belief that the human soul is too deep for there to be any easy answer to the question of how to live." (263).

7. SEVENTH FUNCTIONAL SPECIALTY

1. Lonergan, "The Functional Specialty 'Systematics', *CWL* 10, *Philosophical and Theological Papers*, 186. Adrial Fitzgerald http://lonerganphilosophycompendium.blogspot.de/ helps students build their own mental scaffolding rather than rely on rote memory. Mark Markuly, "Building Bridges across Meaning Systems: Creating Democracy with Christianity and Islam in a Post-Darwinian World" on achieving comity and democracy in today's world. See http://forumonpublicpolicy.com/summer09/archivesummer09/markuly.pdf for constructive conversations.
2. Bruce Grelle, "Culture and Moral Pluralism," *The Blackwell Companion to Religious Ethics* (Blackwell, 2005) 129.
3. See *Overcoming Fundamentalism: Ethical Responses from Five Continents*, ed H. Hadsell, C. Stückelberger, 2009.
4. F. Heiler, 'The History of Religions as a Preparation for the Cooperation of Religions,"*History of Religions: Essays in Methodology*, ed. M. Eliade & J.M. Kitagawa (Univ. of Chicago, 1959) 160. James Fredericks, *Horizons*, 22/1 1995, "A Universal Religious Experience? Comparative Theology as an Alternative to a Theology of Religions," 67-87.
 D.K. Swearer, "History of Religions," *The Blackwell Companion to Religious Ethics* (Oxford: Blackwell, 2005) 144, notes "Historians of religion bring to the discussion of a global ethic a respect for historical and cultural pluralism both within and among traditions, while …rejecting a skeptical moral relativism. We are not positivists; our maps of religion depict generalizable contours and patterns, not simply discrete particulars." An "inductive method does not preclude the possibility of normative claims regarding moral competence and moral responsibility, but disagrees with the position that the idea of human rights requires a neutrally formulated normative regimen."
5. Lonergan's account of group bias and the dialectic of community (*Insight*, 242-50) is relevant to group dynamics.
6. Emile Durkheim, *Les Formes élémentaires de la vie religieuse* (Presses Universitaires de France, 2003), 65. For Edward Zehr, "A political system nominally controlled by an irresponsible, dumbed down electorate who are manipulated by dishonest, cynical, controlled mass media that dispense the propaganda of a corrupt political establishment can hardly be described as democracy." See http://strike-the-root.com/node/57139
7. Tarde foreshadowed postmodernist thinkers such as Deleuze and Latour. See David Toews, *The New Sociology after the End of the Social* at http://tcs.sagepub.com/content/20/5/81.short He drew heavily from Leibniz's theory of the quantitative continuity of qualitative singulars so as to critique Durkheim's statistics-based social realism.
8. Our GEM-FS bridge focuses first on person-to-person relations. Relations between collectivities are more difficult to bridge because collectivities can only act through their representatives and agents (individual persons empowered to speak and act in the name of the larger collectivity). This requires a degree of political organization of the collectivity as has been argued by Voegelin. Richard Moodey, following Robert Swanson, notes in a personal message that "every organized collectivity, large or small, has a constitution which in many cases is not formally articulated in documents." The constitution of a collectivity should specify who can represent it with what degree of jurisdiction; mutual trust is essential when trying to bridge (overcome) our time age-old differences. For Moodey, science can't save the world! https://groups.google.com/forum/#!topic/lonergan_l/hKDunkR8FYU Science's proper goal is knowing the world better. The more we know, the more effective our actions are likely to be, but there is a big gap between what we know and power-holders' decisions. To the extent that their decisions promote their personal or factional interests, scientific knowledge as such will make no difference. Lonergan knew that powerful decision-makers worldwide are biased. Sociologists have no special knowledge about how to counteract individual, group, or general biases that corrupt our decision-makers' consciences. Still, their input is helpful in an interdisciplinary effort such as this book's.

8. EIGHTH FUNCTIONAL SPECIALTY

1. Lonergan, "Religious Experience," *A Third Collection*, 120-21. *MiT*, 80.
2. Herve Verhoosel pleads: "Choose Humanity: Make the Impossible Choice Possible! We have arrived at the point of no return. . .The world is now witnessing the highest level of humanitarian needs since World War II. We are experiencing a human catastrophe." 125 million persons in dire need of assistance, over 60 million forcibly displaced, and 218 million affected by disasters. See www.ipsnews.net/author/herve-verhoosel/
3. ISIS calls its progaganda Magazine *Inspire*; may moderate Muslims be inspired by GEM-FS-like radical proposals.
4. For Tad Dunne, Lonergan envisioned an emergent reality of actual, historical communities. One's participation in community is the fuller context of one's individual consciousness which is both confirmed and sublated by a "we-consciousness" establishing one as part of a community in love with God. http://users.wowway.com/~tdunne5273/
5. GEM-FS transformative ways are partly made possible by its reduplicative fourfold process. This process enables various human disciplines to engage in FS transcultural bridges but it also urges all persons to start anew.

CONCLUSION

1. Lonergan writes of our collective failure to find an adequate expression of all the dimensions in an economy, i.e. "the totality of activities bridging the gap between the potentialities of nature, whether physical, chemical, vegetable, animal, or human nature, and, on the other hand, the actuality of a standard of living." (*CWL* 21, 232). A possible IGEMA, which would study and disseminate Lonergan's two books on economics, *CWL* 15 and *CWL* 21 as part of its task, is broadly outlined in John Raymaker, *Empowering Bernard Lonergan's Legacy* (UPA, 2012).

SHORT GLOSSARY OF ISLAMIC TERMS IN RELATION TO THIS BOOK'S GEM-FS PROCESS

1. Raymond Ibrahim, "Are Judaism and Christianity as Violent as Islam?" *Middle East Quarterly*, Summer, 2009, 3-12, writes that "Muhammad's pattern of behavior—his sunna for example—is an extremely important source of legislation in Islam. Muslims are exhorted to emulate Muhammad in all walks of life: You have had a good example in God's Messenger." (Qur. 33:21). Muhammad's pattern of conduct toward non-Muslims is quite explicit. Based on both the Qur'an and Muhammad's sunna, pillaging and plundering infidels, enslaving their children, and placing their women in concubinage is well founded. (Qur. 4:24, 4:92, 8:69, 24:33, 33:50.) The concept of sunna—which is what 90 percent of the billion-plus Muslims, the Sunnis, are named after—essentially asserts that anything performed or approved by Muhammad, humanity's most perfect example, is applicable for Muslims today no less than yesterday. This, of course, does not mean that Muslims in mass live only to plunder and rape. But it does mean that persons naturally inclined to such activities, and who also happen to be Muslim, can—and do—quite easily justify their actions by referring to the "Sunna of the Prophet"—the way Al-Qaeda, for example, justified its attacks on 9/11 where innocents including women and children were killed: Muhammad authorized his followers to use catapults during their siege of the town of Ta'if in 630 C.E.—townspeople had refused to submit—though he was aware that women and children were sheltered there. Also, when asked if it was permissible to launch

night raids or set fire to the fortifications of the infidels if women and children were among them, the Prophet is said to have responded, "They [women and children] are among them [infidels]." Sahih Muslim, B19N4321.

Index

Abbasid Caliphate-dynasty, 41
Abd-Allah, Umar, 44
Abu Bakr, 45
Al-Ghazali, 84, 86, 88
algorithms (in computers and in GEM-FS), 6
Ali, cousin of Muhammad and fourth Caliph, 46
Ali, Hirsi, 60
Al Qaeda, 123n16
anatman (non-self), 40
apophatic, v, 1, 2, 9, 12, 15, 22, 66, 72
apophatic universalism, 79
Aquinas, St. Thomas, 13–14, 17, 23, 64
Arab Spring, 58–59
Aristotle, vi, 17, 23
Ash'arites, 45
atheism, 51, 52, 53
Augustine, Saint, 64
authenticity, 11, 52, 53
Avicenna, 17

Beards, Andrew, 125n31
Berger, Peter, 27–28
Bilgrami Akeel, 22
Bin Laden, 68
Boko Haram, 8, 95
Brague, Remi, 78
bridge-building between humans, 8, 9, 11, 13, 14, 15, 34, 64, 67
Buddhism, 11, 13, 29, 36, 67–68, 81

Cardijn, Pierre Cardinal, 15, 103
Chomsky, Noam, 125n36
Community, 115
Complementarity in GEM-FS, 127n51
conversion as developed by Lonergan, 4, 26, 27
cooperation among the world religions, 9, 14
cosmopolis, 66
critical GEM-FS realism, 23
Cusanus, 84

data of consciousness, 7–8, 8, 21
Dawkins, Richard, 52
De Foucauld, Charles, 8
Derrida, Jacques, 7
deconstructionism, 7
Doorley, Mark, 60
Dunne, Tad, 129n70
Dupre, Louis, 78
Dupuis, Jacques, 90

Eckhart, Meister, 94
ethical integrity, 5
ethical secularity, 70

faith-belief distinction, 2, 51
Fatah, Tarek, 60
Feuerbach, Ludwig, 70
Francis, Pope, 4, 99
Francis, Saint, 4

Freud, Sigmund, 72
fundamentalism, religious, 5, 31, 44, 49, 63
functional specialties, radical difference between, 12

Gandhi, Mahatma, 38
GEM-FS subtemplate, 6
GEM-FS template, 6, 7, 9, 11, 13, 36
GEM-FS third way, vi, 11, 24
Generalized Empirical Method (GEM), vi
Giddens, Anthony, 72
Girard, Rene, 55
global secular ethics, 2
Gogarten, Friedrich, 94
Gormez, Mehmet, 107
Griffiths, Bede, 9, 54
Guardini, Romano, 98–99

Harris, Sam, 31
healing-creating vectors in Lonergan's view of history, 25
Hegel, vi
Heidegger, Martin, 150n13
Heiler, Friedrich, 109, 110
Hornung, Maria, 64
Houellebecq, Michel, 96
human good, the, 9
Huntington, Samuel, 55
Husserl, Edmund, 17, 18, 23

interiority, 14, 47, 70, 71, 75
ISIS (ISIL), 4
Islam, 4, 32, 33, 36, 45, 47, 49
Islamophobia, 14

John Paul II, Pope, 97
Johnston, William, 97

Kalam (Islamic theology), 84
Kanaris, Jim, 8
Kant, Immanuel, 7, 23
Kasper, Walter Cardinal, 98
kataphatic, v, 1, 9, 12, 64
Kingdom of God, 40
Knitter, Paul, 126n41
Kung, Hans, 47, 97

Lamb, Matthew, 64
Legg, David, 122n7

Le Pen, Marine, 96
liberation theologies, 6
logic of the heart, vi, 63

Mahayana Buddhism, 40, 79, 88
Malala 104
Marcel, Gabriel, 80
Marsh, James, 128n59
Massignon, Louis, 46, 55, 100
McShane, Phil, 124n20
meaning as mediated, 10
mediating-mediated phases in MiT, 12, 36
Medina Charter, 61
mercy, 4, 13–14, 31, 63
Merton, Thomas, 9, 54, 55
metaphysics as transposed by Lonergan, 22
Metz, Johannes, 94
middle way between Islamophobia and secularism, 14
Moltmann, Jürgen, 94
Moodey, Richard, 146n46
Mouzelis, Nicos, 72
Muhammad, Prophet, 32–33, 41, 44, 45
Murray, John Courtney, 123n9

Nagarjuna, 40
natural law, 47, 48–49
Nietzsche, Friedrich, 27, 50, 59

O'Connor, Flannery, 68, 69
operational range (of GEM), 11, 36
operations, operator role of in GEM-FS, 18, 20, 21, 22, 24
Ottoman Empire, 56

Pamuk, Orhan, 95
phenomenology, 17
Plato, 16
postmodernism, 45, 47, 50, 51
prayer, importance of, 8
Proudfoot, Wayne, 153n23

Quran, 2, 33, 59, 81

radical, three meanings of, 12
Rashed, Sheik Mustapha, 63
Reilly, Robert, 45
Rorty, Richard, 51
Rumi, 64, 87–88, 95

Salafism, 120
Salafists, 49, 63
schemes of recurrence in GEM, 24–25
secular humanism, 2
secularism, 2, 9, 31
secularity, 9, 31, 33, 41, 58, 68, 69, 72
see-judge-act subtemplate, 6, 12, 13, 15, 68
self-transcendence, 6, 24
sharia, 43
Smith, William Cantwell, 80
Spencer, Robert, 164n35
Suad Saleh, 107
Sufism, 57, 64, 85
Sunni-Shiites, 45, 46
Sykes-Picot Agreement, 59
symbols, role of in GEM-FS, 22

Tackney, Charles, 126n43
Tai Chi, 89
Tarde, Gabriel, 110
tawid (oneness of God), 44, 57

Taylor, Charles, 9, 27, 28–29, 29, 31, 66, 69
Terreault, Sara, 155n11
theism, 9
Theravada Buddhism, 40
theory-praxis revolution, 8
third way of mind and heart, 9
Toffler, Alvin, 127n47
transformative prayer, 8, 14
Turner, Denys, 98

Umayyad Caliphate-Dynasty, 41, 45

values, distortions of, 23

Wahab, Muhammad al-Abd, 57
Wahhabism, 120
Whalon, Pierre, 65
Wilkins, Jeremy, 151n5
Williams, Fritz, 79

www.ingramcontent.com/pod-product-compliance
Lightning Source LLC
Chambersburg PA
CBHW021850300426
44115CB00005B/102